PROCESSING POLITICS

STUDIES IN COMMUNICATION,
MEDIA, AND PUBLIC OPINION

―――――――

A series edited by Susan Herbst and Benjamin I. Page

PROCESSING POLITICS

Learning from Television in the Internet Age

DORIS A. GRABER

THE UNIVERSITY OF CHICAGO PRESS

CHICAGO AND LONDON

DORIS A. GRABER is professor of political science at the University of Illinois at Chicago. She is author or editor of thirteen books, most recently *Media Power in Politics* (4th edition, CQ Press, 2000).

The University of Chicago Press, Chicago 60637
The University of Chicago Press, Ltd., London
© 2001 by The University of Chicago
All rights reserved. Published 2001
Printed in the United States of America

10 09 08 07 06 05 04 03 02 01   1 2 3 4 5
ISBN: 0-226-30575-9 (cloth)
ISBN: 0-226-30576-7 (paper)

Library of Congress Cataloging-in-Publication Data

Graber, Doris A.
   Processing politics : learning from television in the Internet age / Doris A. Graber.
      p.   cm. — (Studies in communication, media, and public opinion)
Includes bibliographical references and index.
   ISBN 0-226-30575-9 (cloth : alk. paper) — ISBN 0-226-30576-7 (paper : alk. paper)
   1. Television broadcasting of news—United States. 2. Communication in politics.
3. Human information processing. I. Title. II. Series.
PN4888.T4 G73 2001
070.1'95—dc21

                                                                    00-011810

To Leona Boone with thanks for the priceless gifts of time and inspiration

———————

CONTENTS

ILLUSTRATIONS

Tables

Boxes

PREFACE

How do people learn about politics, and what do they learn? How well do their main news sources serve their needs for current political information? The search for answers to these questions, which are so crucial in making democracies viable, lured me into studying mass-media content and opinion formation at mass and elite levels some three decades ago. Initially, I used public opinion polling data for gauging what various publics had learned. When that wide-angle measure proved too barren of detail, I switched to a closer focus, studying opinion formation and opinion substance at small-group levels, over prolonged time spans, using content analysis of news stories and multiple interviews with news consumers.

In *Processing Politics: Learning from Television in the Internet Age,* I have moved even closer to the target by zooming in on the proverbial black box, the human brain, to fathom what goes on when it processes political information. My rationale for this micro-focus is that scholars must study the stimulus-response relationship at close range in order to understand political learning. They must be at least minimally cognizant of the brain hardware with which human beings are endowed before they can understand how people use their information-processing software to learn about politics and retrieve their knowledge from memory. This is why this book features a very brief overview of the basic brain functions that come into play when mass media stimulate average citizens to absorb, or discourage them from absorbing, civic knowledge.

The opening chapter highlights the major puzzles and problems in the stimulus-response relationship between political news and media audiences. It foreshadows the finding that the nature of audiovisual storytelling is the clue to comprehending these puzzles about political learning, while the need for major changes in story sources, substance, and formats is the key to easing major current problems. I have researched this complex, fascinating story because I firmly believe that political news disseminated by the mass media is the basis for public opinion formation, which undergirds U.S. democracy. This is why social scientists must never stop exploring how it can best serve as a source of essential public political enlightenment. *Processing Politics: Learning from Television in the Internet Age* does just that.

The book is dedicated to Leona Boone and her cohorts everywhere—dedicated women who tend to the needs of the households they serve. Without them, young mothers earning a livelihood in the marketplace often lack the time and energy to pursue their professions to the fullest. Leona Boone worked for my large family and me for more than forty years.

More important than the physical tasks she performed, Leona Boone was a pillar of moral strength and an inspiration to all who knew her. She was a black woman, born on a farm in the rural South, where she helped raise her younger siblings. She had little formal education but more mother wit than most people. She married, moved north, and raised her own family, plus a few "extras," while working five or six days a week as a "cleaning lady." Her family life was an unending stream of adversity, which she faced with quiet courage, self-sacrifice, and unfailing optimism. She never grumbled, never lost faith, and always kept her word because "it was the right thing to do."

I needed such inspiration to overcome the many hurdles that blocked the writing of this book. It saved me from quitting when "all hell broke loose," ranging from family illness, home invasions, and fires, to manuscript reviewers unsympathetic to cohabitation between political science and brain physiology. Compared to Leona Boone's trials, my problems were tiny. So how could I quit when she never did? Leona Boone, and the many faithful souls like her, deserve to be recognized for their contributions to scholarship, though they usually do not even rate a footnote in books and articles.

A book is, indeed, a collective effort. Besides kudos or condemnation for the author, it warrants thanks to the entire supportive cast. In a more traditional vein, I would like to thank my many colleagues who contributed to this book through critiques of and suggestions for various parts of the manuscript. Their insights sharpened my knowledge and rescued me from errors. Their names are too numerous to mention here, but they appear repeatedly throughout the chapters and in the references and notes. However, I would like to name and praise three young scholars who helped with various research tasks while they were students at the University of Illinois at Chicago. They are Geralyn

Miller, Adam Stretz, and especially Brian White. Thanks are also due to John Tryneski and his team at the University of Chicago Press who are masters of the art of transforming raw typescripts into polished books. Freelance editor Sherry Goldbecker provided the careful checking of countless details that authors tend to neglect. I am grateful to her for an excellent job. Last, but by no means least, I want to thank my family for their love and support. It is the bedrock on which all of my work has rested.

1

POLITICAL TELEVISION: PUZZLES AND PROBLEMS

It is as American as apple pie to regard the press as the chief tool of public political enlightenment. The belief that the press is the bedrock of democracy in the United States started with the founders of the nation and has continued through the centuries. As Thomas Jefferson put it, if it were left up to him "to decide whether we should have a government without newspapers or newspapers without a government, I should not hesitate a moment to prefer the latter. . . ." The press, he believed, was the basis for public opinion formation, which "is the basis of our government . . ." (Ford 1894, 253). The press has been transformed in many ways since Jefferson's days, but the significance of its role in democratic governance has not declined. If anything, its potency as information provider, public-sphere agenda setter, and interpreter of the political scene has grown. This is why the debate has never stopped about how it can best serve as a source of essential public political enlightenment.

Processing Politics is part of that debate in its twenty-first-century incarnation. This book raises and answers questions about the role of the press as civic informant in an age when citizens are flooded by information and torn by a multitude of conflicting claims for their attention and consideration. Where can average citizens turn for political news? How well do their preferred news sources serve their political needs as they see them and as sophisticated political observers see them? How well is American democracy served? Is there realistic hope for improvement in whatever problem areas exist at the present time? What guidelines for progress are there? These are the key questions of our age for which we need answers.

At first glance, answers may seem easy. The answer to the first question, "Where do citizens turn for political news?" obviously is television. But the inquiry comes to a rapid halt with the second and third questions. If television is the main source of political information for average citizens, how good is the match between the type of political information presented by television and the public's ability to use this information to attain sufficient political savvy to perform the functions that are essential in a democracy? The quest for answers puts the limelight on a series of intriguing puzzles and problems. Obviously, we need to explore much new intellectual terrain to explain why television is so popular, how it is shaping the nation's civic IQ presently, and what changes are likely to occur as we march, in tune with technology, into the future.

THE PUZZLE BOX

Puzzle #1

The first puzzle facing us has a dual focus. Why does the public prefer television for gathering political information? And why do most political scientists, including many television scholars, claim that print media are far better sources? Why is there such a disparity in evaluations?

First, what do the data show about the public's preference for various news media? The evidence about the public's choices of information sources comes from a long series of public opinion polls. These polls consistently show that television is the preferred political news medium for average Americans. Over the decades since the advent of television as a household fixture in American homes, it has become increasingly dominant, thanks to technological advances and to generational turnover. The newspaper-reliant pre-baby-boomer public is dying, and its replacements grew up with television as beloved nursemaid and prized teacher. When the Henry J. Kaiser Family Foundation surveyed a national random sample of children between the ages of two and eighteen in December 1999, it found that children between the ages of two and seven spent roughly two (1:59) hours a day watching television, while the eight-to-eighteen age group averaged three (3:16) hours (McClain 1999). Although some scholars still contend that the print media are the chief sources for political information because they cover more political stories at greater length (e.g., Robinson and Levy 1986; Robinson and Davis 1990), survey after survey in the waning years of the twentieth century showed that most adult Americans think otherwise. Table 1.1 is a representative example.

Less than a quarter (24 percent) name newspapers as prime information sources, and a mere 14 percent list radio. Instead, a substantial

Table 1.1   Primary News Sources for Various Demographic Groups (%)

Question (asked June–July 1996 of national random sample): Where do you get most of your news about what is important to you—from television, radio, newspapers, magazines, computer on-line sources, or somewhere else?

Demographics	Television	Newspapers	Radio	Magazines	On-Line	Other[a]
General public	56	24	14	1	1	4
Age						
Men < 30	53	22	12	3	3	7
Women < 30	65	16	14	1	< 0.5	4
Men > 30	47	32	16	1	1	3
Women > 30	61	21	13	1	1	3
Education						
Up to high						
school graduate	61	21	14	< 0.5	1	3
Some college	57	23	12	1	1	6
College graduate	43	31	19	3	1	3
Race						
White	52	26	16	1	1	4
Nonwhite	72	12	10	1	1	4

SOURCE: Adapted from News in the Next Century 1996, 24.

NOTE: The data in the table are based on a nationally representative sample of adults eighteen years of age or older, living in television households in the continental United States. Television interviewing was conducted between 17 June and 2 July 1996 by Survey Sampling, Inc., of Westport, Connecticut. The data presented here are a condensation of the information in the original. $N = 1,062$.

[a] Includes other media, people, and respondents naming more than one source or none.

majority (56 percent) claim to get the bulk of their information about current political events from telecasts (Stanley and Niemi 1998; Pew 1998a, 1998d). Table 1.1 shows that this is especially true for nonwhites, women, and the vast majority of Americans who have not graduated from college. Their respective television reliances rank at 72 percent for nonwhites, 63 percent for women, and 61 percent for people without any college education. Politicians and other political activists value television highly as a way to reach large audiences of average Americans. Therefore, they devote the lion's share of their communication budgets to transmitting commercials and other political messages via television. That enhances the appeal of the medium as a political information source.

What explains television's popularity? In a nutshell, most people find that it is the easiest, quickest, most pleasant way for them to keep abreast of current political information. Determining why this is the case requires a careful look at the large body of knowledge about the mechanics of human information-processing that has become available in recent years, thanks to new brain research techniques. These important findings will be explained fully in chapter 2, where I will elucidate the biological basis for liking television.

To summarize the argument briefly for now, citizens like political information that is audiovisually presented because the human brain is exceptionally well suited for processing the rich array of stimuli encased in audiovisuals. Viewing a television news broadcast is the most user-friendly way to get a representative taste of current happenings and keep in tune with the information that friends and associates are also currently receiving. It allows viewers to keep up with the proverbial Joneses when it comes to current news and to soothe a nagging civic conscience that tells them that it is their duty to be politically informed. Audiovisuals broadcast over the air, on cable, or on the Internet, at their best, convey the reality of politics more completely than other modalities, and average viewers find them especially engaging, interesting, and emotionally involving. Since they do not find politics intrinsically interesting, they are grateful for journalists' efforts to create gripping political spectacles that emphasize the human drama of politics, rather than its more abstruse features. Much of chapter 2 dwells on these key pieces of the learning puzzle.

But why are average people concerned about making learning about politics quick and easy? The main reason is that learning about the complexities of politics is difficult for ordinary citizens, whose intrinsic interest in the world of politics ranks relatively low compared to interest and concern for other matters, such as their families, their jobs, and the quality of their daily lives. Although these other matters keep most citizens very busy, many nonetheless turn to television news expressly to learn about politics (Gunter 1991). They feel that they need political information for social or job-related purposes and that they have a civic obligation to keep themselves informed, especially during election periods. Given low interest and many other competing pressures for their attention, people prefer information presentations that are relatively interesting and easy to comprehend with a minimal expenditure of time. Currently, they believe that audiovisual presentations like television best meet these requirements.

Many pundits and social scientists condemn the news medium that the public prefers because they view it from a different perspective that entails different evaluation scales. Political scientists generally prefer to keep the debates about political learning within the confines of the currently dominant political theories, particularly those falling under the fashionable "rational choice" label (Somit and Peterson 1999). They measure actual learning achievements by ideal standards derived from democratic theories and bemoan the public's abject failure to reach these ideal standards. According to rational choice theories, ordinary citizens should be able to base their political choices on careful assessments of a broad array of political data, which they must judge in light of their own political preferences. Neither television nor, for that matter, most other news media supply ample amounts of the kinds of facts and figures that rational choice theorists expect the public to know.

Critics of television base their judgments about the merits of the medium primarily on the substance of factual political information that people can recall when pollsters question them. Then they blame shortcomings in learning on the deficiencies of the television medium, largely ignoring issues related to the information-processing tasks facing citizens as well as the inherent limitations in people's learning capacities. Considering information-processing issues requires crossing disciplinary boundaries into unfamiliar terrain in psychology, communication, biology, and even neuroscience. Most political scientists are loath to do that.

Unfortunately, failure to broaden the research approach beyond traditional political science domains has seriously harmed and impoverished the intellectual debate about political learning (Gazzaniga 1992). Current social science is full of misconceptions about political learning that could be cleared up by closer scrutiny of what happens when stimuli are processed inside the human brain—that proverbial black box of social science (Reeves and Anderson 1991; Blank 1999). Misunderstanding the advantages inherent in processing audiovisual messages is just one of many examples. Without a grounding in biological realities, judgments about the public's political acumen float in the never-never land of unrealizable wishes, rather than in the far earthier reality of flesh-and-blood twenty-first-century citizens struggling with the complexities of all aspects of life, including knowledge about politics.

Puzzle #2

The second puzzle is why television-reliant people claim to be well informed enough to carry out their civic functions, while political scientists claim that the public is woefully ignorant about matters that it ought to know. In response to public opinion pollsters' questions, most citizens say that television news provides them with sufficient information to carry out their civic functions. A typical survey of a

Table 1.2 Adequacy of Media Coverage

Question: Do the media currently put too much, too little, or the right amount of emphasis on this . . . ?

Type of Political Information	Too Little	Too Much	Just Right	Don't Know
Information needed for voting	29	35	33	3
Problems needing solutions	36	18	43	3
Important news about America and the world	24	14	59	3
Important state and local news	29	12	55	4

SOURCE: Adapted from Smith et al. 1997, 60.

NOTE: The data in the table are based on a nationally representative sample of adults eighteen years of age or older living in telephone households in the continental United States. Telephone interviewing was conducted between 8 and 30 November 1996 by Louis Harris and Associates. The data presented here are a condensation of the information in the original. $N = 3,004$.

random national sample of adult Americans reveals that two-thirds to three-quarters of Americans are satisfied that they receive enough or even more than enough information about their political world (see table 1.2).

Despite these high rates of satisfaction, academic critics and pundits excoriate television, complaining that television political fare is intellectual junk food that provides inadequate amounts of information and unduly shuns complex information. They also accuse television of distorting demographic realities, of personalizing the news excessively, and of overemphasizing its dramatic aspects. They claim that such presentations make politics into a spectacle that encourages citizens to become passive observers who watch the political scene with a mixture of amusement and titillation tinged with boredom and disdain for most of the principals in the drama. Worst of all, television fare creates an uninformed, disinterested citizenry that neglects its civic duties. Television discourages viewers from logical thinking about politics, while encouraging them to make political decisions based on emotional reactions to irrelevant personality characteristics of political leaders.

What explains the wide divergence between the critics' harshly negative judgments and appraisals and the much more positive judgments and appraisals of average citizens? The answer requires scrutinizing their respective expectations. For now, it suffices to point out that the critics of the civic IQ base their expectations about what citizens ought to know about politics on a traditional academic approach grounded in democratic theory. Rather than considering what knowledge is essential to performing ordinary civic tasks, this approach focuses on precisely remembered factual knowledge about historically important past and current events. The critics analyze television news content and structure questions used to test civic intelligence to detect this type of information. If it is low or absent in either the media or the public or both, the critics assign low scores of civic merit.

By contrast to the standards used by the critics, most average people focus their learning more narrowly on a limited number of political areas that seem to them salient for their own lives and social relationships. They are more interested in knowing the significance of political events, broadly defined, than in dwelling on factual details. They want to know the impact of particular situations on the people who form their personal environments and on the country in general. In short, average Americans and the critics who deem them pygmies when it comes to political knowledge disagree about the substance, scope, and detail of political information that need to be mastered to qualify as a well-informed citizen. They also disagree about the quantity and quality of political news coverage that would warrant calling political television news an information-rich source.

The respective merits of these judgments will be closely scrutinized in the third chapter. Besides discussing the divergent explanations, we will wrestle in chapter 3 with the problem of determining what standards are appropriate for judging the civic IQ of average Americans. We will gauge the extent of citizens' civic knowledge and the information base on which the public relies and assess how the civic IQ of ordinary Americans relates to the overall health of American democracy.

Puzzle #3

A third major puzzle surrounding the merits and impact of television casts the net more widely beyond the medium's role in informing citizens about politics. Why does television earn the plaudits of many observers as one of the most fruitful inventions of the twentieth century and the condemnation of others as a despoiler of democracy and a danger to the civic health of the nation, especially its children? Political scientist Robert Putnam sparked a nationwide debate in 1995 over whether television was the root cause of vanishing social capital that left television-drenched citizens diminished in their feelings of social and civic responsibility (Putnam 1995; Norris 1996, 2000). Putnam and his followers blamed the medium, while Pippa Norris and other political scientists exonerated it, documenting the many ways in which television enhances social capital. Such debates raise the question whether television has a primarily positive or negative impact on American democracy or whether it is a Jekyll and Hyde force, so that both assessments are correct.

THE TASK AT HAND

Why has television become so widely denigrated and so widely praised? What are the facts and what are the fictions? What blame or praise belongs to the medium or to its messages or both? The resolution of puzzle #3—the impact of television on the quality of American democracy—requires an analysis of many aspects and problems surrounding the current and future role of political television.

Problem #1

Political television suffers from, among other ills, an image problem. Many of the preconceptions and myths that surround it are based on a deeply ingrained veneration of printed messages and resulting disdain of other modes of information transmission. Most critics of television are steeped in the lore of the superiority of print as the medium for carrying serious information about all human pursuits, including politics. The defenders of our print culture have tagged audiovisual messages with a litany of major flaws, as is quite typical for any entrenched establishment. According to the critics, most of these flaws are endemic to audiovisual transmissions. Therefore, they cannot be remedied. The validity of these charges is systematically appraised in chapter 4. There we will clarify which flaws are, indeed, inherent in audiovisual technology and which represent inept or improper uses of audiovisuals, so that their full information-transmission potential is impaired.

Most critics fail to distinguish audiovisual technology as such from the messages that it carries. Contrast this with the criteria they use when they appraise messages delivered via print media. The critics do not routinely condemn print technology because it has been used to propagate hate literature, pornography, and colossal lies and falsehoods. Rather, they praise it for the good it has done and try to minimize the abuses. Similarly, I shall argue, audiovisual technologies should not be berated as a means for carrying political information simply because they have transmitted flawed political messages along with the sound ones. It is not the tool but how it is used that counts.

The critics' low opinion of audiovisuals in general and television in particular is buttressed by the fact that much current political television fare is, indeed, flawed and amply deserves the lengthy slate of criticisms leveled against it. This leads us to the second problem faced by political television.

Problem #2

Even though the opening chapters of *Processing Politics* demonstrate that audiovisual technology can transmit political information effectively, it remains a widely acknowledged fact that the substance of many political television newscasts is poor. America, along with many other democratic societies, therefore faces the problem of finding ways to make sure that news offerings contain what citizens need to know to carry out their civic responsibilities. To move beyond impressionistic assessments of needed reforms to a factual basis, chapter 5 examines to what extent essential political information, as previously defined, forms a part of current news offerings readily available to average Americans. The chapter dissects typical news programs to expose their major weaknesses along with their strengths. When the myths are swept away by examination of actual data, it becomes clear that there is much to criticize and much to praise. Examination of realistic reform proposals follows, keeping in mind how people actually process information, how journalists choose and frame stories, and how the American television news business is financed and operates.

Problem #3

Chapter 5 will show that the supply of political news has grown geometrically, so that the quantity is excellent; in fact, it is overwhelming. Sadly, the same cannot be said about the presentational quality of many of the political news programs. While advertisers have learned to tailor their audiovisual messages to facilitate information-processing, this has not happened on a large scale in news broadcasts. This is why chapter 6 continues the dissection of the news supply, putting the spotlight on problems of framing and formatting that have received little attention in current television critiques. The analysis in chapter 6 will show that there are many simple, inexpensive steps that can be taken to make the framing and formatting of news offerings more user-friendly, thereby taking full advantage of the benefits of audiovisual message transmission.

Problem #4

The fourth problem rounds the circle. If political health requires that the political information needs of average Americans be met, and if television is the medium of choice but has thus far failed to do the job adequately, what policy issues must be addressed to change the situation? Obviously, pious prayer and exhortations will not achieve the goal. A realistic examination of the interests of the various stakeholders is needed to determine what contribution each can and must make. Chapter 7 focuses on the role that private and public policies can play to assure that the public's political information supply is truly tailored to the needs of average citizens and the needs of the country. The chapter ends on a note of guarded optimism, buoyed by the fact that new knowledge about information-processing, fresh assessments of the essential tasks of citizenship, and rapidly improving technologies have moved the goal within our reach. The appendix briefly summarizes various studies drawn from my prior research that are mentioned in the text.

2

POLITICAL LEARNING: HOW OUR BRAINS PROCESS COMPLEX INFORMATION

How do the physiological and psychological characteristics of normal human beings affect what they can learn and recall from the wealth of readily available political information? As mentioned in chapter 1, most social scientists have paid scant attention to this question in the past. Yet the answer is crucial for determining what kind of and how much political information one can realistically expect average citizens to learn in modern democracies. In the absence of precise knowledge about the limits of human information-processing capacities, scholars have postulated ideal citizens who are interested in all major aspects of politics and capable of acquiring and retaining detailed knowledge about them.

Recent research on actual human capabilities paints a far different picture. It suggests that the social science community has expected levels of political learning and recall of factual details that exceed the brain's physical capacity to process information. Many of the failures to learn political information that social scientists bemoan should be viewed as normal occurrences, rather than changeable malfunctions. Problems of overestimation of human thinking capabilities have been confounded by problems of underestimation. For example, studies of brain functions suggest that the contributions of audiovisual messages to human thinking in general, and to memory capabilities in particular, have been vastly underrated.

At the start of this chapter, I explain briefly how the characteristics of the human body influence how information is gathered, processed, and stored, with an emphasis on the problems of learning and recall that social scientists have wrongly blamed on television. This discussion will show that many of the flaws in human perception and recall are due to the nature of human thinking processes. They should not be attributed to the inherent characteristics of the audiovisual modality through which these stimuli were transmitted, as political scientists have been wont to do. After exonerating audiovisual transmissions from much unjust blame heaped on them by television detractors, I will show that audiovisuals actually enhance political learning. The general public's fondness for this medium as carrier of political information is fully justified.

In this as well as subsequent chapters, I highlight the characteristics of information-processing that make it easier to learn from audiovisual media like television than from purely verbal stimuli, whether written or spoken. While this book features televised political messages because they are currently the most widely used sources of political information in the United States, the arguments about learning from audiovisual messages encompass all media that use these technologies. It does not matter whether the message carrier is over-the-air television, cable television, the Internet, or some new carrier yet to be invented.

Advances in brain research since the 1990s have greatly enhanced the opportunities for examining the impact of the brain's hardware and software on political information-processing. Various types of medical specialists have been able to map many areas of the brain. They have discovered where and how numerous conscious and subconscious activities, such as reasoning, feeling, evaluating, and remembering, take place.

Computer-enhanced functional magnetic resonance imaging (FMRI), done at fast speeds, has become an exceedingly helpful tool. It can make movies of the brain's circuitry in action by recording changes in the brain that occur during specific mental processes. The technique is based on the fact that brain cells use more oxygen when they are activated than when they are at rest. When humans process information, their brain cells release chemicals that increase blood flow to the active portion of the brain. Neuroscientists can then gauge the extent of brain activity by measuring how much oxygenated blood is entering specific brain cells and how much deoxygenated blood is leaving (Shulman 1993; National Institutes of Health 1999). The understanding of brain functions has also benefited greatly from studying the physical and mental performance of people who have suffered injuries to certain parts of their previously normal brains. The location and nature of various disabilities related to the brain injury and the recovery that occurs if the damage has been repaired provide clues to the functions normally performed by that part of the brain.

When considering findings from recent research on human brain functions, several caveats should be kept in mind. The research on how the human brain functions on which the discussion that follows is based is ongoing. The tops of the icebergs have been charted, but much of the underside remains unexplored. Some of the interpretations of research findings remain in dispute. Hence some of the inferences drawn from these findings may require revision or refinement in the future. While caution is always required when considering scientific findings, this is especially true in emerging, newly active research areas.

Second, as should become clear, the inferences concerning political information-processing that one can draw based exclusively on brain functions are rarely complete. Information-processing does not depend solely on basic brain structures and functions, shaped by each individual's idiosyncrasies and experiences. It also depends on the external environment and culture in which human beings operate, including the format and content of messages reaching them. In later chapters, we will devote a lot of attention to many of these important contextual conditions that come into play in the United States today. The effects of some contextual conditions are widely shared, while others are idiosyncratic. For example, knowledge about how a normal person's brain functions in ordinary situations may have to be supplemented by information about patterns exhibited when an individual is in an unfamiliar environment or is experiencing unusual positive or negative stresses.

Finally, scientists now know that the brain communication system and its functions are malleable within the boundaries set by the human body. Changes in usage, such as intellectually enhanced early childhood education or enriching educational experiences in adulthood, for example, can markedly increase an individual's brain information-processing capacities. When people are exposed to new stimuli, the physical network of brain connections changes, as do the person's thinking capacities and propensities.

BASIC LEARNING CAPACITIES

Our sketch of brain activities involved in political information-processing begins with a very brief discussion of some of the limitations that brain structures and functions impose on learning about complex knowledge domains, such as politics. It is important to stress these limitations because social scientists have so frequently overestimated what average individuals are apt to learn under normal conditions. An appreciation of general information-processing limitations will highlight the importance of making political learning as easy as possible in order to overcome processing hurdles.

The human brain consists of a network estimated to contain between 10 and 100 billion cells, called neurons (Carter 1998; Blakeslee 2000). Each neuron has highly specialized information-processing capabilities and responds only to the information for which it is programmed. Among the thousands of neurons specializing in vision, for instance, some subspecialize in vertical lines or horizontal lines or a particular color or motion. Neurons are scattered in various brain regions; they become active (fire) only when they encounter their particular trigger phenomena. Neurons thus provide extremely tiny yet distinctive building blocks into which incoming messages are split and from which they can be reconstructed for recall. The high degree of specialization of individual neurons enables the brain to create an unlimited variety of complex mental images in response to external and internal stimuli. But like a cardboard puzzle that has been sliced into tiny fragments, rather than recognizable pieces, the high degree of specialization makes it more difficult to assemble all the pieces of these complex mosaics initially and to reconstruct them accurately when trying to recall them subsequently from memory.

In practical terms, this means that the initial recording of situations is usually defective to varying degrees and is likely to become even more flawed when recalled later. When people are asked to recall very specific situations, such as details from a news story, it becomes apparent that memory is often weak or absent because people have engaged in "on-line processing." They have stored only general meanings. The details have been skipped or merged into the whole, rather than remaining distinct retrievable features (Fiske and Taylor 1991; van den Broek et al. 1999; van Dijk 1999). For example, the question, "Where did march participants sleep during the 1996 Million Man March demonstration in Washington?" is unlikely to evoke a correct answer because most respondents would not store this detail. Inaccurate, incomplete recall of political and other stories therefore should be expected as the norm, rather than considered to be the exception. Nor should it be surprising that there are variations in the specifics that are recalled at different times and that some of the pieces of the reassembled images seem missing, out of place, or even clashing. With so many fragments available for rapid reconstruction, diverse and even wrong choices are par for the course.

The ability to reason effectively depends on the ability to make connections among ideas. In turn, this ability hinges on the presence of electrical connections—called synapses—among the brain's neurons. When neurons are activated, they exchange electrical energy with other neurons, activating them as well. Individual neurons may link to 600 to 1,000 other neurons. This sounds like a lot. But it is only a small proportion of the billions of neurons in the human brain. In fact, most neurons are not connected to each other.

Since responses to a particular stimulus come only from connected neurons, the full range of possible responses is rarely exhausted. When you are watching a Fourth of July parade, for example, your neurons may record particular sights and sounds. But your ability to connect these new impressions to memories of parades in bygone days hinges on the availability of appropriate connections. Absent suitable synapses, there may be no activation of your stored historical knowledge. Failure to think broadly about events, dwelling on most of their significant ramifications, thus is far more likely to have a physiological explanation than a behavioral one. People are unable to make linkages because physical connections between the neurons activated by the current event and the neurons linked to past experiences are absent, rather than because people do not want to consider the full range of implications.

While adult brains are similar in their overall structure and interconnections, the patterns of connections among neurons vary among individuals and even over time. The nature of the variations depends on the particular stimuli to which individuals singly, or within groups, have been exposed and the synapses formed in the past. When faced with previously encountered stimuli, the brain tends to reestablish synapses that were activated earlier. This fact makes it possible to predict individuals' responses with a fair degree of accuracy. It also leads to the canard that you cannot teach old dogs new tricks. Old dogs can and do learn new tricks, but repetition of past patterns is the dominant response. Since synaptic connection patterns differ among individuals drawn from disparate surroundings, the same stimulus may evoke dissimilar responses, particularly when the stimulus is complex, so that it activates many neurons. That makes it irrelevant to speculate about modal responses and to set them up as the gold standard by which all respondents should be judged.

How do people reassemble the tiny fragments into which incoming information is split in order to restore recognizable mental patterns? The answer is that people create and store mental maps, which serve as the general guidelines for reconstructing specific types of events. Various terms have been used for these templates, such as stereotypes or associational networks or concept nodes, or schemas (Lodge and Stroh 1993). In my previous longitudinal studies of information-processing (see the appendix), I have used the term "schema" because it encompasses broader concepts than some of the other terms; I have defined it as

a cognitive structure consisting of organized knowledge about situations and individuals that has been abstracted from prior experiences. . . . [M]ost schemata contain conceptions of general patterns along with a limited repertoire of examples to illustrate these patterns. The general patterns usually are commonsense models of life situations that individuals have experienced personally or encountered vicariously. These models may be embedded in an overarching ideological conception that helps to structure the subordinate levels of the schema, or schemata may exist, side by side, with only tenuous connections. Schemata include information about the main features of situations or individuals and about the relationships among these features. They also include information about the expected sequences of occurrences or behaviors under various contingencies. . . . [People] may have ready-made evaluations and feelings about all aspects of these scenarios, and they make inferences based on these scenarios. (Graber 1993, 28–29)

People attach feelings and evaluations, such as liking and disliking, to objects and situations at the moment of perception as part of on-line processing—the mental strategy whereby incoming stimuli are condensed so that only their essential features and reactions to these features are stored for future retrieval (Graber 1993; Bargh 1995). When a similar stimulus appears later, the prior evaluations can be transferred to it without further effort. People embed a multitude of such mental maps in their various sensory systems, such as seeing, hearing, or touching (Blakeslee 1994a; Carter 1998). As guides to recall, one might liken these mental maps to computer function keys or icons, with the brain remembering which keys or icons need to be activated to make sense of stimuli. Schemas are activated when stimuli are first perceived and are used to first categorize and then store them (Calvin 1997). They may be revised when that seems necessary to adjust to the external world. However, people usually retain these gut reactions intact because they value first impressions highly and because reevaluation requires added mental efforts (van Oostendorp and Bonebakker 1999). Schemas that represent stereotypes are particularly resistant to change even when audiences receive incongruent information.

When new experiences resonate with schemas in memory, and are appraised accordingly, communication experts refer to "top-down" processing. Such processing begins with categorizing the information and appraising it subsequently in terms of the assigned schema category. Top-down processing, which saves the effort of making a fresh analysis, is also an efficient way of coping with a steady deluge of information that might otherwise swamp information-processing capacities. It takes advantage of stored experiences, linking the present with the past (Nørretranders 1998). But, as mentioned, because new situations often are poor matches for the experiences around which the schema was originally formed, top-down processing also produces many glaring inaccuracies.

"Bottom-up" processing reduces such inaccuracies because it involves forming new impressions based on fresh appraisals of the actual stimulus, rather than reasoning by analogy to past experiences. But it requires greater mental effort, and there is no guarantee that the new appraisal will be correct. People are most likely to use bottom-up processing when they are faced with unfamiliar situations that attract their attention or when familiar happenings occur in unfamiliar or anxiety-producing situations (Marcus et al. 2000). This is why political practitioners often use fear messages to stir people into bypassing their repertoires of established beliefs and opinions and going to the trouble of considering fresh alternatives.

The mental effort required for bottom-up processing can be reduced when the new information is presented audiovisually, rather than purely verbally—another reason for advocating audiovisual presentations. Processing speed increases because humans can interpret multiple visual stimuli simultaneously while spoken or written stimuli must be interpreted serially (Paivio 1979; Van Der Molen and Van Der Voort 2000). One quick glance at a complex visual scene may suffice to identify and interpret hundreds of visual cues that would require lengthy verbal descriptions if they were not actually observed. When images are purely verbal, the listener has to construct a mental vision of the situation, which is usually far less accurate than a visually observed image (Burgoon 1980; Gyselinck and Tardieu 1999).

ENHANCING PROCESSING EFFICIENCY

Thus far we have discussed how people record and store complex information that reaches them and how they reassemble information bits from memory albeit with some degree of inaccuracy. Although human brains handle these tasks with awesome speed, it is difficult for modern citizens to keep up with the flood tides of information that surround them. Coping strategies are needed to reduce processing burdens. Accordingly, people have developed numerous strategies that reduce the number of messages that are actually processed.

First of all, they fail to pay conscious attention to most of the information within their reach. The bulk of sensory stimulation remains below the conscious level (Marcus et al. 2000). This explains why so much information to which people are exposed fails to make an impact. For example, immediately following exposure to the average thirty-minute newscast of eighteen to twenty-two stories, most viewers recall fewer than 10 percent of the stories. Another effort-saving device involves keeping the vast majority of sensory stimuli only briefly in temporary memory without ever fully processing them. The brain's temporary memory is similar to random access memory (RAM) in a computer chip. It retains data only as long as needed and readily switches from one set of data to another. Most data in temporary memory are quickly discarded, and only a few are switched to long-term memory. This assures that people do not become overwhelmed with more stimuli than they are equipped to handle. Most political information is sloughed off in this way because average Americans usually find it neither useful nor enjoyable. This explains why the majority of stimuli that people actually notice, including political messages, leave no long-term traces in memory and cannot be recalled even after a brief time lapse (Graber 1993; Glynn 1999).

In fact, temporary and long-term memory are located in different parts of the brain, almost as if to emphasize that totally separate functions are involved. A structure within the brain screens incoming messages, dispatching them into either short- or long-term memory. Fleeting attention in short-term memory may be almost automatic, while long-term retention usually requires deliberate effort (Goleman 1995).

Because it saves time and effort, people are most likely to take note of familiar stimuli for which they already have well-developed schemas that can be used with or without minor adaptations (Rahn, Aldrich, et al. 1994; Granberg and Brown 1989; Marcus 1988). As mentioned, this may have unfortunate consequences. People often interpret the new information within the general framework of previous interpretations, feelings, and evaluations even when this framework may be quite inappropriate under the current circumstances (Graber 1993; Minton 1988; van Oostendorp and Goldman 1999). Rigidity in schema use is particularly dangerous when it characterizes journalists' political messages. For instance, typecasting prevails on television, particularly during elections. Once presidential candidate Jimmy Carter had been tagged as "fuzzy" during the 1976 presidential campaign, there was, according to his press secretary, "[n]o way on God's earth" to shake the image. No matter what Carter did or said, including spending "the whole campaign doing nothing but reading substantive speeches," the image of fuzziness would remain (Arterton 1978, 36). It was indelibly embedded in the images created by journalists' culture and transmitted into the memories of the public.

Efforts to save mental energy in learning about politics and other complex matters mean that most people create fresh images of their world primarily during their formative years and retain most of them throughout life, with only moderate amplifications and revisions in light of new experiences. Human brains privilege childhood learning. Children between the ages of four and ten have a much richer web of neural information receptors, transmitters, and connections than adults. This explains children's superior potential for learning new information. By age sixteen, nerve cell connections that have not been used disappear, and the brain stabilizes at the adult size level. This age-linked disappearance of unused brain capacity underlines the importance of maximum learning in childhood. It also makes it clear that brain capacity is not genetically fixed at birth. Infants' experiences determine which brain capacities develop and which potential capacities disappear when they are not used. Just as people's efforts can affect the development of their muscle powers, so can their mental activities shape their brain circuitry and capacity. While childhood tends to set the basic patterns, substantial changes are possible throughout the life cycle.

Audiovisuals are particularly useful as shortcuts for forming accurate impressions of the many unfamiliar people and events that are so common in political messages and that often evoke bottom-up processing. In fact, viewers can quickly learn many things from audiovisuals that are never mentioned in purely verbal comments. Some of this information may be much more politically relevant to them than the message that the broadcaster intended to convey. Here, for example, are the insights a young Russian gained about the American economy through watching typical scenes from American homes that appeared in a story focusing on other matters:

> The telephone rings and somebody runs over and there is a telephone in the middle of the living room. And then you cut and the kid is

talking on the telephone in his bedroom. In the hall you see . . . [another] telephone, and there is one in the kitchen. In Russia if you have a telephone it is in the closet so you can go in and close the door so nobody can hear you. Then you open a refrigerator in a film and it is stocked full of food and people are taking things out, spilling things. They are treating food as if it was nothing. My God. That is propaganda. I'll bet that many of the people around the world are looking at that and not even seeing the picture. They are watching the food in the refrigerator . . . cars are smashed up . . . we wait five years to get a car . . . here you have kids driving huge cars. And we say to ourselves, "How much gasoline does that car take to go a mile?" *This is political.* (Quoted in Litwak 1986, 105–6; emphasis added.)

Experimental studies substantiate that schemas generated from audiovisual information tend to be more accurate than those generated from purely verbal messages. In one particular study, my assistants and I exposed a panel of adult viewers to twelve television news stories. We found that an average of one-third (32 percent) of the subjects who had listened to the stories without watching the visuals made errors when asked to report the gist of each story's themes. For people exposed to both verbal and visual themes, the error rate dropped to 15 percent (Graber 1990). This happens because visuals present more details than words and provide a better grasp of relationships. Viewers can process the actual visual images, rather than deriving sketchy mental pictures from words (Pryluck 1976; Lewis 1984).

Although audiovisual messages are quite similar to real-life experiences, there are important differences in their ability to convey information. An individual, for example, may have experienced a civil rights demonstration while in Washington during the civil rights march led by Martin Luther King Jr. in August 1963. The sights and sounds and feelings absorbed during that experience, melded with other relevant experiences already stored in memory and tempered by the observer's personality characteristics, may form that person's basic schema about the march. By contrast, another person may have learned about that march only indirectly, whether from media accounts or history books or word of mouth. The most important difference between the two modes of learning is that firsthand experiences allow observers to become their own gatekeepers. They decide on what aspect of the event they want to focus and how they will interpret it. Events that are directly observed generally create more vivid and detailed images, activating more visual, sound, touch, and smell neurons in the brain than indirectly experienced events. Because more systems are activated, it becomes easier to recall them later. In vicarious experiences, even when they are audiovisual, someone else selects the limited array of dimensions of the event that will be noted and supplies an interpretation. The preferences of that "someone else"—usually a journalist—may not match the preferences of the information consumer. When journalists focus on aspects of the news that are of little interest to the audience and therefore relatively unmapped in the brain, as often happens, they reduce the chance that their stories will be processed.

Besides the active learning that occurs when individuals strive to extract information from their environment, there can be passive learning. Brain cells can be stimulated mildly even when the person makes no effort to learn. Such learning is fairly common if the same stimuli recur repeatedly and fit into existing schemas (Zukin and Snyder 1984). In fact, because motivation to learn about politics is low for average Americans, much learning about politics is, indeed, unintentional. This is why individuals who claim to totally ignore political messages often turn out to be reasonably familiar with current happenings. They may have gleaned the information by being inadvertently exposed to newscasts or even newspaper headlines or by overhearing political conversations.

DENOTATION VERSUS CONNOTATION: WHAT DOES IT SHOW AND SAY? WHAT DOES IT MEAN?

Information-processing involves multiple complex tasks beyond the initial recording and storing of messages discussed thus far. People generally extract two different types of information from messages. One type is denotative—a simple recording of the information detected by the sensory organs. The other is connotative—the assignment of meanings to the observed events. Connotations are, to a large extent, derived from the meshing of processed information stored in the brain with the fresh information provided by the senses.

Extracting meanings often requires discerning the symbolic implications of situations, in addition to their other meanings (Tuchman 1984; Edelman 1995). An official rebuke of a foreign country may connote that hostilities are imminent. It may also symbolize that the president is a man of action. Knowledge of political symbolism is part of the storehouse of information that people acquire through formal education and experiential learning. But because the meanings embodied in existing schemas generally are carried over to the new information, the same message may carry different connotations for different people, depending on whatever knowledge and interpretations they have stored in the past (Jensen 1986; Langston and Trabasso 1999). This makes it difficult for scholars, as well as for political practitioners who do not know the thinking patterns of their audiences, to predict the reactions that political messages are likely to generate. It also leads to charges that many citizens fail to think rationally about politics. What may seem like a rational response to an investigator proceeding from particular schemas may not seem rational at all to a person whose thinking is based on different schemas.

Connotations can also be provided by the press or other opinion leaders. For example, when a politician announces that the costs of government are increasing, the press is likely to inform the citizenry that this connotes that taxes will shortly be raised. Media audiences may then accept and store this interpretation or disagree with it or develop their own connotations. Assigning appropriate meanings to political information requires a large array of sophisticated political schemas. When people have failed to develop such schemas in their own thinking patterns and when their environments do not provide them with ready-made connotations, the meanings of messages may elude them. Scholars who measure political knowledge routinely ignore the importance of connotative thinking. They prize people's ability to remember facts and denotations, without testing whether they understand the significance of the information. Yet the ability to capture the connotations of situations is one of the hallmarks of political sophistication that differentiates political experts from the politically naïve.

The political world depicted by news media, which are the public's main sources of current information, often lacks sufficient details to allow audiences to capture the messages' connotations. Rather, as journalist Walter Lippmann (1965) said, journalists' stories, like a flashlight in a dark room, pinpoint primarily whatever may be unusual in that room. The more bizarre it is, the better. The darkness of the areas surrounding the flashlight beam blots out much of the context that could put events into clear perspective. For media consumers who cannot draw on their own past experiences to put the targeted situations into context, audiovisual cues can be a particularly helpful source for capturing connotations. For example, a picture may show a leader's physical decline or the primitive condition of a country's roads or the enthusiasm of a crowd greeting an advancing army. The connotations drawn from such pictures may help the audience make sense out of otherwise obscure situations.

Interactions of various message components may change the meaning of each component. For instance, the messages produced when words and pictures are combined often differ from the meanings conveyed by each singly. Words can alter the meanings of pictures; conversely, pictures can alter the meanings of words. Words tell people what the focus of their attention ought to be as they watch the unfolding pictures and how the pictures should be interpreted. The choice of particular pictures to accompany a story determines what aspects of a situation are apt to influence most viewers' assessment of the situation.

The impact of contextual information on the interpretation of pictures has been called the "Kuleshov effect." Film theorist Lev Kuleshov demonstrated that viewers ascribe different emotions to an agitated face depending on whether it is coupled with pictures or words about a funeral or a wedding or the return of a prisoner (1974). Similarly, anthropologist Ray Birdwhistell points out that people construct meanings through assessing the interactions of various factors present in a particular situation. To quote Birdwhistell (1970, 96):

> It is difficult, if not impossible to answer the question: What does this symbol or gesture mean? Meaning is not immanent in particular symbols, words, sentences or acts of whatever duration but in the behavior elicited by the *presence* or *absence* of *such behavior* in particular contexts. The derivation and comprehension of social meaning thus rests equally upon comprehension of the code and of the context which selects from the possibilities provided by the code structure. (Emphasis in original.)

How changes in verbal messages can alter the interpretation of visuals has been repeatedly tested in the laboratory (Zadny and Gerard 1974; Chase 1973; Loftus 1979; Loftus and Ketcham 1994). In one experiment, investigators showed a videotape that pictured two men walking around an apartment to two groups of people. They told one group that the men were burglars and the other group that they were narcotics agents looking for evidence of drug use. Later, all viewers were asked what they had seen in the apartment. People who had been conditioned to think about burglary remembered costly items most. People who had been conditioned to think about a drug raid recalled mostly objects that might be useful as drug paraphernalia. The verbal introduction had conditioned people to look for particular visuals. The reverse happens as well. A story on crime that depicts only poor, inner-city neighborhoods is likely to suggest that crime is worse there than in poor suburban areas even when the words say otherwise.

Frequently, the meanings of media messages become clear only when they are considered as part of a message block. A television story's main thrust may remain obscure until several scenes have been viewed either consecutively or intermittently. Showing the president meeting with heads of other governments, addressing Congress, and dedicating a monument may collectively convey the idea that he performs his ceremonial tasks with dignity. The meaning of each picture may thus become apparent only after various segments have been viewed and their meanings coordinated (Metz 1974). Of course, the same may hold true for purely verbal messages, though it seems to occur less often.

MAJOR INFORMATION-PROCESSING DETERMINANTS

To summarize the information presented thus far about the findings from brain research that shed light on the biological determinants of political learning, we have found that human beings are prone to

1. develop the templates for much of their adult thinking during the early years of life when the capacity for mental development is at a peak;
2. ignore much of the information that they encounter in their environment;
3. concentrate attention and processing on limited aspects of various situations, rather than seeing them in their totality;
4. usually store only the summarized essence of the information, rather than all details;
5. fail to put situations into proper perspective to allow fully informed assessments of meanings;
6. develop mental stereotypes, including feelings and judgments about many situations, and apply them willy-nilly to subsequent experiences;
7. perceive some information incorrectly initially and compound the errors when recalling it from memory;
8. process audiovisual information more quickly, easily, and accurately than information lacking audiovisual data; and
9. absorb some information unintentionally.

In terms of learning about politics, it means that their recallable knowledge is likely to be eclectic and sparse, general rather than detailed, and often error-prone.

MEMORY ISSUES

We now turn to some of the major problems involved in recalling stored political information from memory. Retrieving information from memory is particularly difficult when it has not been kept fresh through frequent repetition. The traces imprinted on the brain by the electrochemical activity involved in processing the information initially tend to fade out quickly, although decay rates are variable. For example, the memory of times and places where information was first obtained tends to decay faster than the memory of the event itself. Older memories are overlaid with newer ones and may be reshuffled. Memories become contaminated by leakage from related bits of information. People often draw inferences from situations and then store them later as actual happenings, confusing reality and unreality.

What happens prior to an individual's efforts to recall information is important, as the "priming" phenomenon shows. Because the brain's memory traces are strongest when they have been recently created or refreshed, individuals find it easier to retrieve more recently encoded or used information than information that has remained dormant for a while (Iyengar and Kinder 1987). Information linked to issues that have been in the news recently therefore is easier to locate because imprints left by the earlier presentation "prime" the retrieval and deflect it from the paths that it might otherwise take (Bargh et al. 1996). The impact of mass media news choices thus is broader than generally realized. What the media feature is important not only for its direct impact on audiences, but also for its conditioning effect on the audience's future information choices and interpretations. As substantiated experimentally, citizens are likely to judge political candidates by their performance in an issue area that has been primed by recent news stories. If stories concern foreign policy, the candidate is apt to be judged by the most recently publicized foreign events. If stories feature welfare policy, that probably will be the measure for judgment (Iyengar and Kinder 1987).

The ease of retrieval of information from memory varies for many reasons, including the emotional elements of the situation (which will be discussed later). The nature of the information is very important. Proper names and numerical data are examples of especially elusive items. If stored at all, they seem to be located in more obscure, less accessible areas of the brain. A phenomenon called "source amnesia" has also been documented. It means that people forget the place and situation in which an activity or encounter occurred, though they remember the activity or encounter (Goleman 1995). Bringing these types of memories into sync is quite difficult for many people. To compensate for poor memory of sources, people often embellish experienced events with facts drawn from unrelated, more easily accessible parts of memory in an attempt to link them to some source.

Retrieval may also hinge on how well the search stimulus is framed to match the framing used by the individual during original processing. For example, a news story about a local teachers' strike may be encoded and stored with a focus on teachers' grievances or school tax rates or childcare facilities. The ability to retrieve such stored information depends on whether the retrieval stimulus is framed so that it becomes a mental key that opens the correct storage drawer. The most common retrieval strategy is "straight matching" (Graber 1993; Morton 1996). This means that people search their memories for information that broadly matches the new stimulus even though the details differ.

If no matches are found, two more elaborate and time-consuming strategies are available, "segmentation" and "checking." But most of the time people fail to undertake these additional steps because they are not profoundly interested in the information. Segmentation involves dividing a message into its component parts and then searching for matches for some or all of these parts, rather than the whole message. For example, if one does not recall a teachers' strike, one could search for memories of strikes in general or memories related to teachers' activities. Checking happens when a respondent reflects on the merits of matches located initially and decides to try additional matches that might be a better fit or might broaden the perspectives from which a particular message is viewed. Segmentation and checking are often combined. The results normally are well-considered judgments, unlike the snap judgments that are so often reflected in mass survey responses.

The ability to locate matching schemas is particularly important in learning new information, which is apt to be rejected if people cannot easily relate it to familiar concepts. In the vast majority of political news stories, framing does not match the manner in which ordinary Americans tend to store such information, making matching difficult or impossible (Graber 1994b). Stories tend to be overloaded with facts and figures and names, which are search cues that most people fail to store (Graber 1996a). For example, journalists often refer to pending congressional legislation only by the name of a particular bill or by its expected price tag. They give little substantive identifying information, such as that it is the bill to remove silt from the St. Lawrence waterway. Audiences then find it difficult to process the information and may therefore abandon the effort—which means that incompatible framing has prevented learning (Cappella and Jamieson 1997). Incompatible framing of questions may prevent retrieval of information that is actually present in memory. This is why people often rephrase the questioner's construction into a format that is more compatible with their thinking patterns.

How do people select a particular memory storage category when they encounter new information? Three factors are important. One is the strength of the sensory evidence, including the verbal commentary, that indicates that a stimulus belongs to a certain category. The second factor is the individual's decision bias. Thus, individuals who are greatly worried about tax increases will route stimuli about a teachers' strike into schemas relating to the tax consequences, rather than those relating to the teachers' grievances. Finally, the pertinence of the stimulus to the individual's prior experiences affects to what it will be linked (Bundesen 1990). For example, the perspectives people used to categorize Gulf War mass media stories hinged on their prior knowledge about the situation, the extent of their media exposure, and their interest in the war (Krosnick and Brannon 1993).

Aside from the impact of message factors on processing, demographic factors play a role as well. Men and women, for example, differ somewhat in the areas of the brain they use to perform certain tasks and in the patterns of their synapses (Carter 1998). Women have greater brain density—and hence ability—in areas related to language, while men are slightly better in spatial tasks. Women and men therefore tend to learn and recall political information somewhat differently. Men are also more likely to be in situations where politics, including the daily news, is discussed. This increases their motivation to process political information and their opportunities for rehearsing it. It allows them to develop richer schemas that are more deeply etched into their brains. This is one reason why men do far better than women in general in remembering names of political actors and factual details. When knowledge scores are based on such factual data, as is common in tests of political knowledge, men excel. To what extent such data are a valid measure of political knowledge is discussed in the next chapter.

Table 2.1 Large (15-point) Differences in Knowledge of Politics (%)

Survey Item	Men	Women	Men Advantaged	High SES[a]	Low SES	High SES Advantaged
What is a veto?				96	81	15
Does the U.S. have a trade deficit?	91	73	18	95	68	27
Can a veto be overridden?	90	75	15			
Does the U.S. have a budget deficit?				88	66	22
What is the name of your state's governor?	81	66	15	82	67	15
Did the U.S. support the Contras in Nicaragua?	76	57	19	88	59	29
What is the name of the vice-president?				91	58	33
Must students pledge allegiance?				84	69	15
Can states prohibit abortion?				84	69	15
Which party controls the House of Representatives?				85	63	18
Who reviews the constitutionality of laws?				85	55	30
Are the Contras rebels?	68	42	26	79	47	32
What was Franklin Roosevelt's party?				72	56	17
Define "recession."	65	50	15	72	44	28
What was Harry Truman's party?				65	50	15
Who appoints judges?				72	46	26
Name one of your U.S. senators.				75	49	26
Can a communist run for the presidency?	59	41	18	63	38	25
Which party controls the Senate?				77	46	33
Describe a recent arms agreement.	57	39	18	65	34	29
Define the effects of a tariff.				60	42	18
Define one Fifth Amendment right.				61	40	21
What is the size of the federal budget?				57	41	16
What are the first ten amendments called?				66	37	29

Table 2.1   (continued)

Survey Item	Men	Women	Men Advan-taged	High SES[a]	Low SES	High SES Ad-vantaged
What vote percentage overturns a veto?				54	26	28
Describe one First Amendment right.				46	31	15
What percentage of Americans are jobless?	41	14	27	46	22	24
Who declares war?				48	25	23
What is the ideology of Justice Rehnquist?				44	26	18
Name both of your U.S. senators.				44	13	31
What is the Superfund?	24	5	19	34	9	25
What percentage of Americans are poor?				29	8	21
Define the New Deal.				29	13	16
What percentage of Americans are black?				26	5	21

SOURCES: Abbreviated from Delli Carpini and Keeter 1996, 158–59.

NOTE: Scores are listed as percentages of correct answers. Data are based on the 1989 National Election Studies survey.

[a] SES = socioeconomic status.

Table 2.1, based on a fifty-item survey of political knowledge, shows the ten items where men's scores exceeded women's by fifteen percentage points or more. Overall, the median score of correct answers was 56.5 percent for men and 42 percent for women. However, polls conducted at regular intervals by the Pew Research Center for the People and the Press show that the knowledge gaps are narrowing. In fact, on issues in which women are especially interested, women are just as knowledgeable as men and often more so (Pew 1999). For example, women and men were equally aware of the fact that President Clinton had defined education as his top priority in his second term, and more women than men knew that the U.S. Supreme Court had ruled on parental notification about abortion in 1990. Even when knowledge levels are similar, the genders may differ substantially about their policy preferences based on dissimilar perspectives on the news. Accordingly, there was a twenty-one-point differential between men and women in May 2000 when they were asked whether gun-owners' rights or gun control was more important. Forty-nine percent of males ranked gun-owners' rights as more important, compared to 28 percent of women, while 67 percent of women privileged gun control, compared to 46 percent of men. Overall, the top three news interests of women are health, crime, and community news. Men are most interested in sports, crime, and science and technology (Pew 2000b).

Factual knowledge tests routinely show a strong association between education and high recall scores and between education and the individual's potential for knowledge growth. This has become known as the "knowledge-gap" phenomenon (Tichenor et al. 1980). It springs from the fact that formal education, travel, and ample contacts with well-educated people stimulate schema growth and refreshment in intellectual areas that are deemed the hallmark of the well-informed American. These repeatedly refreshed schemas provide a multiplicity of access points for incorporating other socially prized information. People deprived of the learning and refresher opportunities that are readily available at higher socioeconomic levels lack the chance to command these schema resources. Consequently, new learning of socially prized information is more difficult. Knowledge growth flourishes for the knowledge rich and privileged, while it remains stunted for the knowledge poor.

Table 2.1 also shows the thirty-three items for which the scores of people of high socioeconomic status exceeded the scores of their low-status counterparts by fifteen percentage points or more. Overall, the median score for correct answers was 65 percent for high-status respondents and 41 percent for low-status respondents.

The knowledge gap between the privileged and the deprived continues to grow throughout life, increasingly disadvantaging the poor. This tragic phenomenon makes it clear why it is so important for all human beings, especially children, to partake of education and experiences that allow them to develop ample schemas in areas of knowledge deemed important in their societies (Grabe et al. 2000). There may be areas of knowledge where the poor, trained in the school of hard knocks, may excel. But scores of streetwise knowledge are not usually gathered and reported.

HOW AUDIOVISUALS SHAPE POLITICAL LEARNING

As noted repeatedly, audiovisual message transmission facilitates learning. This is particularly important during infancy. During infancy and early childhood, prior to extensive verbal learning in aural and written form, audiovisual learning is the richest source of schema development. Audiovisual learning thus becomes the foundation for all future learning. Even young children are able to process visual information with a great deal of sophistication without formal training (Greenfield 1984). For example, they can make adjustments for the many distortions of vision that constantly face people who observe the same phenomena from different angles and distances, in varying shades of light, and full of obstructions that blot out portions of the picture (Messaris 1994).

Somewhat later in life, following repeated exposures, most people master the standardized picture codes through which television tells its stories. For example, they learn that the wide-angle shots of the opening scene show where the action is taking place. When the camera then moves in for a close-up, the object that seems to be growing larger—though it is not—is the center of the story until the camera focus changes once more. By contrast to the seemingly instinctive comprehension of the meaning of visual images, the ability to process verbal information, particularly when it is in written form and deals with complex matters, usually requires formal schooling. Many people are never able to master verbally complex messages and reading.

Given that schema formation is most prolific during the early years and therefore provides templates in which future learning can be readily embedded, heavy reliance on audiovisual information continues throughout life. This lifetime reliance on audiovisual learning holds true for people irrespective of age, culture, socioeconomic level, or level of education. Systematic comparisons of learning about important political issues in national and international politics show that television coverage yields significantly more information gain than newspaper reading for unfamiliar issues that may be difficult to imagine (Neuman et al. 1992). For many adults who are deficient in verbal comprehension and reading skills, audiovisual learning is by far the most significant source of knowledge acquisition throughout life. That includes most of the world's people because functional illiteracy remains a major problem even in the developed world, as shown in a 1999 report of the United Nations Human Development Program. In the United States, for example, 21 percent of adults are functionally illiterate; in Poland, the rate peaks at 42 percent (Clarity 1999).

Visual experiences are not limited to seeing or recalling vistas appearing in each person's external environment. Because the visual building blocks drawn from actual perceptions are stored in the brain and can be combined in novel ways, people can and do construct visual scenes they have never actually seen. This ability to imagine what has never existed greatly stimulates creativity. Albert Einstein, venerated for his ability for abstract thinking, for example, explained, "If I can't picture it, I can't understand it" (quoted in Blakeslee 1993). He attributed his first insights into relativity to concocting a vision of chasing after a beam of light at the same speed as the beam. While the ability to see images in your mind's eye is extraordinarily useful, it, too, can have troublesome consequences. People can imagine things that never happened and mistake these visions for reality. Studies of eyewitness reports about crimes, accidents, or even ordinary incidents reveal that such reports can be readily tainted when people construct highly realistic, yet deeply flawed visual images from available information fragments (Loftus 1979).

Seeing with the mind's eye differs from direct perception. When people imagine visual scenes evoked by verbal stimuli or by other visual scenes or through contemplation or even in dreams, processing occurs in reverse (Kosslyn 1994). Previously encoded images—whether directly perceived initially or imagined—travel from memory to the visual buffer where they are perceived albeit less distinctly. Considering how frequently average people draw on visual memories in addition to processing actual scenes directly or vicariously from television, there is much more use—and much more impact—of visual images than is commonly considered. Einstein's comment aptly illustrates this.

Many social scientists believe that the quality of thinking elicited by audiovisual messages is shallow and short on rationality (Robinson and Levy 1986; Robinson and Davis 1990). That view is entirely unwarranted. Brain research clearly shows that stimulation of visual neurons activates a great deal of higher-order reasoning. At the most elementary level, the brain routinely corrects flaws in visual perception springing from shortcomings in the visual apparatus or in the stimuli presented to viewers. For example, our eyes see the world upside down, but our brains put things into proper positions without our conscious awareness. When a bush hides three-fourths of a dog's body, human observers, including small children, still know that they are seeing an entire dog. Even a young child's reasoning powers allow her to equate the stick figure of a human with a real person, often even with a specific familiar individual. Infants learn quickly to interpret perspectives, so that a stranger appears threatening only when the image is close rather than at some distance.

When televised stories do not hold a mirror to the world that presents statistical reality, media audiences easily correct the distortion mentally by appraising the visuals in light of other prior cognitions (Gregory 1997). Most adults are not misled when television—or a stroll on city streets—routinely shows more men than women or depicts only the trail of wreckage left by a tornado, without showing the intact portions of the town. However, when unfamiliar situations are involved, so that no corrective cognitions exist, visuals can become more deceptive.

How are visual stimuli linked to reasoning? When human eyes receive a visual stimulus, such as a police officer walking his beat, the brain identifies characteristics of the observed object as well as its spatial location (Kosslyn 1994). These stimuli, which have not yet been identified as a police officer, are then passed on to the portion of the brain where schemas containing prior memories (associative memories) are stored. If a relevant schema is found, which is likely to contain a lot of information associated with the image, such as the jobs police officers do or the viewer's past experiences with police officers and feelings about them, the identification process is at an end. The riddle of the meaning of the audiovisual message has been solved. If no match is found in memory, the information moves to those parts of the brain where more active, fresh reasoning takes place, such as deciding that the picture must represent a police officer because the person is wearing a nonmilitary uniform. Signals are then sent back to the visual buffer where recognition takes place. All these operations take place with lightning speed.

Audiovisuals ease two major information-processing problems: failure to embed information in long-term memory and inability to retrieve it when needed (Woodall 1986; Crigler et al. 1994; Berry and Brosius 1991; Brosius 1993). It is true, as Crigler and her associates (1994, 134) warn, that "[v]isuals do not uniformly or automatically enhance the learning, recall, or comprehension of news stories." But they also point out that "[p]articularly vivid or concrete visuals have been associated with increased recall of the specific information contained in the visuals and, in some circumstances, have been associated with greater retention of the story as a whole" (p. 135). Whether the recall overrepresents the visual elements of the story or extends to all its elements varies from case to case (Brosius 1993). All else being equal, when messages include visuals rich in relevant information, memory is enhanced. As noted earlier, its accuracy improves as well. Good visuals make a situation more graphic and vivid. They come closer to reality than purely verbal descriptions. Therefore, they are etched more deeply into memory initially than nonvisual messages. In turn, because they are more easily recalled, they are frequently refreshed, which then prevents fading.

Since audiovisuals are richer in storable details than purely verbal descriptions, they leave a larger array of traces. This makes it easier to find a match for an audiovisual stimulus than for a purely verbal one. Retrieval from memory may also be easier because audiovisuals are encoded "in terms of both their picture content and their verbal content. . . . The presence of an additional memory code for picture items would enhance their probability of being recalled because if one code was forgotten or simply unavailable for retrieval, the other could be used instead" (Paivio 1979, 387). This dual-coding hypothesis has been repeatedly validated experimentally (Van Der Molen and Van Der Voort 2000).

Supporting evidence for the strength of visual memory, especially when it arouses emotions, comes from numerous studies. Communications scholars Annie Lang and Marian Friestad (1993) have demonstrated experimentally that information processed in the right side of the brain, which is the primary site for visual-spatial processing as well as for negative information, tends to be remembered better than information processed in the left brain. The left side of the brain is the primary location for verbal information-processing and for positive information (Kinsbourne 1982). Lang and Friestad therefore hypothesized that memory for negative messages is likely to be more visual than verbal and therefore stronger. Experimental tests, using a free-recall measure, confirmed the hypothesis and underscored the strength of visual memory. When purely verbal questions were asked about the negative messages, thereby shifting activity from the right to the left brain, the memorability advantage was lost.

As always, there is also a negative side. Some research findings lend credence to the charge that television pictures may focus the audience's attention on irrelevant visuals at the expense of important substance. Vivid television news presentations may decrease recall of factual details significantly and reduce the cognitive complexity with which viewers think about these stories (Milburn and McGrail 1992; Frey and Eagly 1993). Reduction of "cognitive complexity" means that the viewers considered fewer elements of the problem shown dramatically on television and were less successful in integrating the various elements of the story (Tetlock 1983).

Various factors may make dramatic features a distraction from factual content. Most commonly, disinterest in the factual minutiae of the story is the reason. If the dramatic factors are gratifying to viewers and therefore capture their attention, viewers are less likely to tackle the boring facts. The innate desire of all organisms to avoid life-threatening dangers may provide yet another explanation. Audience members, captured by dramatic visuals, may oversimplify the situation and perceive the story only in stark terms of potential danger or escape from danger. Iyengar and Kinder (1987), for example, have reported that melodramatic presentations make viewers dwell on empathy for the victims—with whom they identify—and less likely to think abstractly in terms of the social and political conditions that caused the unfortunate situation. Politicians, eager to win unquestioning support, may use dramatic visuals to arouse people's fears and then promise to be their saviors.

Unsophisticated television viewers may also find it difficult to cope simultaneously with messages that require complex processing at both the verbal and the audiovisual levels, especially when these modes of transmission are poorly coordinated. Faced with this dilemma, they tend to concentrate on the audiovisual messages (Rahn, Aldrich, et al. 1994). By contrast, sophisticated individuals are stimulated by such complexity and benefit from richer and more diverse messages (Rahn and Cramer 1996). The fact that audiovisuals do not uniformly or automatically enhance learning or recall of news stories has yet another explanation. Many visuals shown in television news are totally uninformative. The verbal texts carry most of the information as well as guiding the interpretation of the visuals. Meaningless pictures and meaningless words, by definition, carry little information either separately or in combination.

THE ROLE OF EMOTION AROUSAL

Visuals excel in emotion arousal compared to most nonvisual stimuli. Audiovisual stories that generate strong emotions, such as vistas of starving children or wartime destruction or reunions of long-separated relatives, are more likely to be embedded in long-term memory and to be retained even when they are infrequently rehearsed. The reasons are largely physiological. Emotional arousal induces human bodies to release stimulants into the bloodstream that sensitize perceptions and speed reactions. Superior alertness enhances chances for survival when humans are faced with danger (Damasio 1994, 1999). The familiar "fight or flight" syndrome is an example of such quick reaction capacities. Experiments have shown that emotion-induced stimulants travel along pathways in the brain that lead to strengthening the memory of emotional events so that the dangerous situations will not be forgotten. Studies of stroke victims demonstrate that emotional event memory weakens when these pathways are blocked, even when memory about non-emotional events remains at the same level (Damasio 1994).

Of course, the term "emotions" encompasses a wide range of phenomena ranging from very basic likes and dislikes to love and hate. Intensities for these emotions can vary from slight feelings of discomfort to paralyzing fears or from mild amusement to ecstatic pleasure. We still know very little about the variations in the body's hormonal system that occur when different types of feelings and different levels of intensity are involved. The current assumption is that low levels of intensity have lesser effects. In fact, there may be thresholds of intensity for triggering the physiological consequences of emotional reactions.

The common belief that emotions, when aroused, ipso facto impair reasoning is among the many false myths that brain research helps to demolish. Neuroscientists have discovered that the connections between emotions and reason are far closer than hitherto imagined (Blakeslee 1994b; Damasio 1994; LeDoux 1996). Emotions are a common trigger for thoughts and vice versa. When an emotionally charged image is processed, the brain simultaneously signals the center where emotions are processed as well as the centers where most reasoning occurs. The body's responses to the emotional arousal are also transmitted to the centers of the brain that alert people to their body's physical responses to the emotional message, such as a pounding heart or a belly laugh. The various messages produced by emotional reactions are then processed cognitively.

In fact, centers of reasoning have an exceptionally large number of connections to other parts of the brain, so that reasoning is constantly evoked. Functions such as decision-making, planning, and executing behavior all involve the primary reasoning centers in addition to those parts of the brain that deal with emotions or spatial relationships or timing. This is why emotional responses are tempered by non-emotional memories. For example, the overwhelming feelings of pride and love one might feel if a family member wins nomination for a coveted public office do not prevent average people from also considering that their financial resources will be depleted by the campaign and that the candidate may lose the election. Emotions thus do not stop reasoning; in fact, the reverse is actually true: emotions are an essential part of the ability to reason (Sniderman et al. 1991; Damasio 1994; Marcus et al. 2000).

When the ability to feel emotions, running the gamut from fear to elation and love to hatred, is lost through injury or disease, decision-making, planning, moral reasoning, and motivations to act or desist are seriously impaired as well. One of the most frequently cited stories to illustrate this phenomenon concerns Phineas Gage, a nineteenth-century railway worker whose brain was accidentally pierced by a large iron rod. The injury destroyed the centers of the brain that record emotions. Gage had been a quite reasonable young man prior to the injury, capable of making decisions that benefited him. The injury did not impair his cognitive capacities, such as speech and memory. However, the loss of emotional capacity produced dramatic changes in his reactions to his environment. He could no longer feel joy or empathy or make sound, self-serving judgments about the present and future. It seems that reasonable decisions and adaptive social behavior spring from the combination of logic with emotion, rather than from logic alone. The patterns seen in Gage's case have been documented in numerous more recent cases where individuals have suffered damage to similar portions of the brain. In each case, the patient's IQ, memory, and speech capacities remained intact, but she or he could no longer experience feelings and could not make decisions that reflected the totality of the situations with which she or he had to cope (Damasio 1994; LeDoux 1996).

Gut feelings and intuitions, which, like emotions, do not meet the standards of strictly logical thinking, are also important for human decision-making because important factual data are often missing, dooming a purely rational approach. Resort to these mental resources seems to be a blessing, rather than a curse, because experimental findings show that decisions based on gut reactions tend to be correct more often than decisions based entirely on abstract reasoning (Wilson et al. 1989). Besides, how people feel about a situation—whether it "feels right" or "feels wrong"—can often be established instantaneously, whereas more deliberative cognitive approaches take much longer. Gut reactions thus have the additional advantage of speed and an extra pinch of accuracy (Sniderman et al. 1991; Brosius 1993; Neuman et al. 1997).

SOUND: THE SIAMESE TWIN

In audiovisual presentations, sound and visuals are inextricably inter-linked. Each affects the other. Yet compared to knowledge about visual processing, we know very little about how auditory processing operates and how variations in aural stimuli affect what and how political in-formation is processed. We begin our brief exploration of the impact of processing the sounds of audiovisuals with a discussion of the com-plexities that explain some of the prevalent information-processing failures. As we did in the discussion of visual processing, we then turn to some of the advantages that aural messages have over their written verbal counterparts.

Sound encompasses a vast variety of aural stimuli, including the tim-ber, cadence, and inflection of human voices; the sounds made by ani-mals, by weather phenomena, and by the motions of physical objects on land, on water, and in the air; and the music of single instruments or orchestrated combinations. Most of these sounds are laden with cues to the interpretation of the meaning of messages. We do know that, like visual processing, auditory processing involves specialized neurons. Some of these neurons are geared to distinguish sound frequencies, while others compute the direction and intensity of the sound. Ul-timately, all the information, including emotional reactions, is inte-grated with other perceptual stimuli through processes that are not en-tirely clear yet (Nelson and Boynton 1997; Blakeslee 1994a).

Among messages carried by sounds, processing of the speech stream is especially complicated. Listeners must identify individual sounds while keeping track of the overall meaning of words and phrases. Com-prehension of speech becomes particularly difficult when it is very fast, so that words blend into each other, as often happens in political broadcasts. This is why substantial portions of televised speech are never processed. Unlike printed texts, the audience cannot readily re-view a message that it failed to fully grasp initially. The difficulty of comprehending rapid speech becomes dramatically apparent when we try to make sense out of unfamiliar foreign languages where we need to recognize individual words quickly. Much of the vocabulary of politics is so dense that the task of deciphering its meaning is as difficult for av-erage people as understanding rapid discourse in a foreign language.

Articulating one's thoughts is a complex process that may prevent lay people as well as experts from clearly expressing their political views. Audiences may fail to fully understand what message a politi-cian is trying to transmit because the message lacks clarity. Inexperienced speakers who participate in discussions or respond to surveys and interviews are apt to encounter difficulties in conveying their thoughts. Psycholinguists believe that three distinct brain networks are involved in handling, respectively, decisions about speech content, word order and syntax selection, and speech sound creation (Carter 1998; Blakeslee 1995b). These networks must be synchronized as one moves from thinking about speech content to searching for words to express thoughts, to selecting particular words from tens of thousands of words encoded in memory. Before the words can be strung together, grammatical rules must come into play so that words appear in the right order, tenses, and forms. Finally, the speaker has to find the right sounds and inflections to pronounce the word. Pronunciation involves mapping syllables onto motor patterns generated in the mouth, lips, larynx, and lungs.

Sound amplifies the emotional impact created by pictures. Written language lacks many emotional qualities that spoken language and especially nonverbal sounds, like music, supply. The tone, pitch, and tempo of speech and nonverbal sounds can produce a broad range of feelings, such as attraction, revulsion, sympathy, or fear. Sounds can make messages persuasive that might otherwise be bland. In campaign advertising, the qualities of sound delivery are crucial in arousing people's attention to messages and in creating moods conducive to accepting the information and feelings that messengers want to transmit (Nelson and Boynton 1997). Nonverbal sounds are a universal language that carries meaning across cultures and across education-level divides.

The brain processes music sounds separately from other sounds. Research indicates that tonal patterns can evoke visual patterns (Blakeslee 1995a). Brain mapping also shows that musical networks extend into the brain's emotional circuits, so that people often experience strong emotional reactions. Patriotic fervor when listening to martial music is an example. The potential for stirring emotions motivates politicians to use music effects in political messages and at political rallies (Budd 1985; Bendavid 2000). The desired effect often comes from the interplay of a variety of stimuli where, for example, the music interacts with the words, the substance of the pictures, the color schemes, and the sequence and pace of scenes. Finally, music, like other perceptions, can also be imagined because people store representations of songs, melodies, and sounds of instruments in memory. When a political advertisement reproduces a small portion of a familiar tune, the entire tune can be mentally relived, along with the situation associated with that tune.

Table 2.2 Orchestration of a Campaign Advertisement

Music	Visuals[a]	Words[b]
Fanfare, cymbals, upbeat and nearly heroic music, with lush strings and a subtle pulsing	Eagle perched on crag springs into the air. Eagle wings in slow motion over wooded mountains. Eagle (toward camera) swoops to catch fish. Eagle starts to rise, turning back to left.	25 years ago, America made a commitment to a healthier environment. And today our air is cleaner, our drinking water is safer, our rivers and streams less polluted. But now,
Horror bass, then horror ting and ring through this part's end	Picture freezes, screen goes gray.	
	Fades diagonally down a gray Capitol dome;	the polluters are back— teamed up with other special interests . . . and a new majority in Congress
Next three horror snicks, one per headline	Three gray news articles with black headlines overlay the Capitol.	
One timpani drumbeat	Screen goes black as bold white letters zoom out to fill screen's center.	to weaken our environmental protection laws. **Don't Let Them Turn Back the Clock.**
Upbeat/heroic music returns and ascends to concluding fanfare	Eagle returns close-up in bust pose, with eye at viewer; centered below its head are the numbers in big gold letters and sponsor's name in small gold letters.	Call 1-800-334-2100 to find out how you can help. *This Message Sponsored by the Sierra Club.*

SOURCE: Nelson and Boynton 1997, 173.

[a] In the Visuals column, each period indicates a visual cut. The words pause while the headlines of the news articles appear: "Congress Moves to Weaken Environmental Protection," "Polluters Help Water Down Bill," and "Sneak Attack on the Environment."

[b] In the Words column, words in boldface were both spoken and printed. The italicized words appeared only in print.

In a fascinating study of the aural portions of political advertisements, political scientists John Nelson and G. Robert Boynton (1997) analyzed how various sound tracks and visuals support, enhance, and even alter the impact conveyed by identical verbal messages. Table 2.2 gives an example from an advertisement in support of environmental legislation sponsored by the Sierra Club. The table describes the interacting messages conveyed through music, visuals, and words.

Analysis of the ad shows that the themes of good and bad happenings presented in three modalities reinforce each other, making it easier to notice and comprehend them. Each set of messages is further enriched by stirring, familiar symbols that carry emotional meanings. The opening musical fanfare heralds the commitment to environmental issues. The music is vibrant and upbeat. The visuals show the national bird, a soaring eagle, which swoops down to a clean river full of fish. A confident male voice announces that Americans are saving their treasured environment. The music and tone then switch suddenly to terror, signifying new environmental dangers. The colors fade; the landscape becomes a grainy, dim gray. Printed messages emphasize the danger themes. The last part of the ad becomes upbeat again in music, visuals, and words as Americans are urged to conquer the dangers by helping the Sierra Club. The tones are reassuring, suggesting that help is possible. Overall, the triple burst of stimuli, appealing to emotions and cognitions, is far more powerful than would be the case for a purely verbal message.

The thirty-second presentation of the relatively simple political message contained in the Sierra Club advertisement is a perfect example of the complexity of mental operations entailed in deciphering such messages. The brain must record, coordinate, and interpret the complex sounds presented by the music and the spoken and written messages. In response to tonal stimuli, it must register joy and fear, often linked to past memories of similar types of musical stimuli. The tone of the voice must be interpreted, including estimates of the degree of confidence or doubt that it expresses. Besides the ordinary meaning of the words, colloquialisms, like "turn back the clock," have to be interpreted. The meanings of the visuals are almost entirely symbolic, from the images of the soaring eagle and the clear stream, which symbolize environmental cleanups, to the gray and then black tones of the screen, which suggest the environment is being destroyed. A great deal of formal and informal learning over long periods of time and the ability to retrieve it nearly instantaneously from memory are required to be able to penetrate such symbolism. It is no wonder that mistakes are common.

REPRISE

To return to the main argument: there are sound reasons grounded in human psychology that privilege audiovisuals as carriers of complex political information. We have probed how well human brains are suited to learning and recalling political information, especially when it is presented in audiovisual modes. The inquiry has shed light on the tremendous potential of human brains to process information if they are properly trained during childhood, adolescence, and early adulthood.

The inquiry has also shown that many of the characteristics of political learning that social scientists have observed and measured in various ways have a physiological basis. Examples include instances of faulty learning or failure to learn at all from political messages, which are byproducts of the brain's need to economize on information intake and information-processing activities. For example, schema formation strategies, which permit construction of well-organized memories and ease selection among incoming messages, also encourage top-down processing, which is a major source of misperception and misinterpretation of political messages.

The insights gained about some of the conditions that make it more difficult to learn even suggest ways for steering around the hurdles and improving learning. For instance, journalists can avoid filling their stories with information unlikely to resonate with their audiences or difficult to retrieve, such as numbers and names. They can supply context that is essential to discovering the implications of stories. And they can stress the emotional angles of stories without worrying that this will short-circuit the audience's reasoning faculties.

How well do average Americans manage to cope with complexities of message transmission so that they can learn what they need to know about politics? In chapter 3, we turn to the political subject matter that average citizens must process to meet the civic obligations that are essential for a functioning democracy.

3

TO KNOW OR NOT TO KNOW: QUESTIONS ABOUT CIVIC WISDOM

Keeping the nature of human learning capacities in mind, how can people best learn what they need to know about politics in twenty-first-century America? The most important message in this chapter is that average Americans are far more correct when they claim to be reasonably well informed than the critics who contend that citizens' political knowledge is woefully inadequate. Average Americans possess a great deal more political insight than the most commonly used indicators show. I will also argue in this chapter that these widely used indicators are seriously flawed because they focus on irrelevant competencies, and I will suggest that civic competence should be appraised in light of the political tasks that average citizens face.

THE CIVIC IQ CONTROVERSY

Most American social scientists contend that the average American's political knowledge is slim and below the standards that should be expected (Delli Carpini and Keeter 1993, 1996; McGraw and Pinney 1990; Smith 1989; Zaller 1992). They cite statistics like the 1991 National Election Studies (NES) surveys, which showed that only 17 percent of the respondents could identify Tom Foley, then Speaker of the House of Representatives, or William Rehnquist, a sitting U.S. Supreme Court justice. A mere 25 percent knew the length of a U.S. senator's term, while a paltry 37 percent could specify what majority was needed in the House and Senate to override a presidential veto (Delli Carpini and Keeter 1993).

A smaller number of social scientists, many relying on information-processing research and intensive methods for studying citizen knowledge, have reached far more positive conclusions about average Americans' knowledge about important public policy issues (Conover and

Feldman 1984; Gamson 1992; Sniderman et al. 1991; Graber 1990, 1993; Neuman et al. 1992). This raises the question, How can one determine what citizens *ought* to know and how much of that they actually do know? Political scientists Michael Delli Carpini and Scott Keeter (1993, 1996) wrestled with that question when they devised a test of basic civic knowledge. Rather than asking average citizens what they deem essential or investigating what types of political knowledge they actually acquire, Delli Carpini and Keeter examined the content of high school and college textbooks and theoretical treatises on citizenship and civic education. They also sampled fellow political scientists for their views about what citizens ought to know, and they scrutinized the accuracy of responses to factual questions in public opinion surveys. Based on this research, they constructed the National Civics Test.

The test contains forced-choice factual questions about the basic structures and values of the American government, the two-party system, the two houses of Congress, the role of the judiciary, and the organization of the cabinet. It covers items of political history and political economy as well as the facts and history of major political issues and the stands of the parties on each. They also constructed a parsimonious five-item knowledge index. The index questions asked (1) which party in the House of Representative controls the most seats (55 percent answered correctly), (2) what kind of majority vote by the House and Senate is required to overturn a presidential veto (37 percent answered correctly), (3) which party is more conservative (57 percent answered correctly), (4) which of the three named branches of government determines whether a law is constitutional (68 percent answered correctly), and (5) the current vice-president's name (84 percent answered correctly). Scores of correct answers are based on 1990 and 1991 NES surveys. Respondents who were knowledgeable in the limited domain covered by the questions were presumed to be well informed about other political domains. However, Delli Carpini and Keeter concede that knowledge of the information domain tapped through their test may be only weakly correlated with knowledge of other issue domains.

Delli Carpini and Keeter justify their testing philosophy by claiming that "factual knowledge is the best single indicator of sophistication and its related concepts of 'expertise,' 'awareness,' 'political engagement,' and even 'media exposure'" (1993, 1180). They argue that citizens "should" be able to answer the factual test questions about the American government and its political and economic history. They also point out that factual civics questions correlate well with various types of active political behavior, such as forming political opinions, feeling politically effective, and participating in political activities. This is not surprising, of course, because the questions are geared to political *sophisticates* who, by definition, are likely to have learned and rehearsed such formal civics knowledge repeatedly and who find it useful professionally and socially (Rahn, Krosnick, et al. 1994).

I contend that the underlying philosophy of the National Civics Test and its counterparts, as well as the methodology, are flawed and that the conclusion that most average citizens are political dunces is wrong. My arguments join a long string of often heated debates about the civic IQ of average citizens. That debate has surged back and forth between positive and negative verdicts, depending on the investigators' yardstick for the appraisal and varying judgments about the types of behaviors to be deemed "rational" (Popkin 1994 summarizes this debate).

My challenges to the Delli Carpini/Keeter approach rest on four main contentions. (1) Current knowledge indexes are methodologically flawed because they set physiologically unrealistic standards about the type of rote memorization of factual details that should be expected from average Americans. (2) The assumptions about the usual steps in political decision-making are also flawed because they ignore the heuristics that most people actually use for making sound political choices. (3) The test questions are ill-designed for maximum information retrieval because they do not match individual memory storage patterns. Besides, they probe for political information that respondents are unlikely to have for various reasons and fail to probe for salient information that respondents are likely to have. (4) The assumptions about the kind of information that is essential for "rational" political choices are flawed because they ignore the main civic functions that citizens perform. In fact, much of the formal political "knowledge" disclosed by factoid civics tests is irrelevant to the political activities of average citizens. When it comes to functionally useful knowledge, average citizens are moderately well informed. Let's examine each of these issues in some detail.

RATIONALES FOR NEWS CHOICES

As pointed out in chapter 2, human information-processing and -storing capacities are limited. Average individuals cannot absorb the massive amounts of political and other information that surround them, nor do they wish to do so. Psychobiological limitations force them to learn selectively and parsimoniously, for the most part. Therefore, they extract only the essence of new information about familiar topics that fits into the many memory schemas they have developed throughout their life span (Krosnick 1990; Ottati and Wyer 1990). Accordingly, average Americans limit their learning about politics to what they consider useful or enjoyable in light of their past experiences (Graber 1993; Rosenberg 1988; Page and Shapiro 1992; Popkin 1994). The type of schoolbook knowledge for which social scientists have tested people is not a high priority. If they learned it at all, it has vanished from retrievable memory by adulthood because information that is neither useful nor gratifying is unlikely to be periodically recalled.

That average Americans are cognitive misers when it comes to absorbing the heavy doses of political news to which they are exposed almost daily throughout much of their adult life is well illustrated by polls that have recorded attentiveness to nationally prominent news. When researchers for the Pew Research Center for the People and the Press asked media audiences in a series of monthly polls how many of 763 major news stories they had watched very closely, they found the respondents had ignored many entirely or paid only slight attention (Pew 2000a). Overall, a majority of the audience had paid close attention to less than 5 percent (4.58 percent) of the stories and exhibited a decided bias against political news. Although nearly two-thirds of the stories in the Pew Research Center news sample were political, less than half of the stories mentioned by a majority of the audience were political. Obviously, average Americans do not think of themselves primarily as political creatures, let alone political junkies. Other interests in their lives are generally far more important to them. No wonder that 96 percent of Pew survey respondents in 1998 knew that high cholesterol is generally deemed a health hazard, whereas only 57 percent could identify much-publicized Newt Gingrich as the Speaker of the U.S. House of Representatives (Pew 1998d).

However, the fact that many political stories are ignored does not mean that average people lack political knowledge. Rather, it means that their active search for news is oriented toward information that seems useful and interesting to them at a particular time. Given that different population groups have different interests and concerns, one should expect their funds of stored knowledge to differ (Delli Carpini and Keeter 1991).* The variations in domains of interest and attention

---

*Since many political stories are perennials that reappear regularly, substantial passive learning adds to the fund of information held by average individuals.

are in line with widely accepted uses and gratification communication theories, which predict that learning is a goal-directed strategy. It allows individuals to cope with the challenges posed by their environment and to gratify their intellectual curiosity about selected aspects of life (Jeffres 1997; Lupia and McCubbins 1998). But these theories are generally ignored in the design of knowledge tests even though they describe entirely rational choice criteria.

Judging from the kinds of information that people do absorb, interest and concern about the subject matter are, indeed, the key motivations. The simplicity or complexity of particular news items is of lesser importance. Average human brains can cope with difficult mental calculations. When people are deeply concerned, they do learn about complex economic issues, and they even commit names and numbers to memory, and retrieve them, albeit for relatively brief periods of time. However, to save time and effort, people engage in on-line processing for most stories, extracting the essence of information and discarding most details, except in areas of special concern to them (Graber 1997). This explains the low scores when people are asked to recall details from news stories. However, it does not mean that their views are ill considered. The discarded details have played a part in an individual's reasoning. Many social scientists ignore this fact, claiming that the opinions of average Americans lack a factual base (Graber 1993; Lupia and McCubbins 1998).

The time- and effort-saving cognitive maneuvers of average people—as well as political elites—are quite in line with Downs's (1957) ideas of what constitutes rational behavior. Resources, including intellectual efforts, should be spent where they have the largest payoff for the individual. Typical cognitive maneuvers also fit Herbert Simon's (1967) argument that resource constraints, including scarce time, force all citizens to "satisfice," rather than "optimize," when processing information and making decisions under conditions of uncertainty. The usual information-processing behavior is well suited to the political functions average citizens commonly perform, such as voting in elections, discussing politics within their social circles, and, on occasion, lobbying.

STEPS IN POLITICAL DECISION-MAKING:
THE LOW-INFORMATION ROUTE

Ideal citizens in an ideal democracy would carefully weigh all important political issues facing the nation and assess the actual and potential performance of every political candidate. Few average Americans satisfy these standards, which are quite unattainable, given time and resource constraints and information-processing capacities. Instead, most Americans have developed a number of sensible shortcuts to minimize information costs when they engage in their normal civic tasks (Popkin 1994; Lupia and McCubbins 1998). Political scientist Samuel Popkin refers to the kind of political reasoning used by most people for political judgments as "low information rationality" (Popkin and Dimock 1999). It means that they have learned a series of judgmental cues that allow them to make decisions quickly and easily (Sniderman et al. 1991; Mondak 1994). Cues may be informational, such as knowing which party is likely to be closest to their own political preferences, so that the party label becomes the cue for voting. They may be values, like a preference for self-reliance, rather than support from others, or beliefs about the goodness or depravity of most members of the human race. Or they may be related to feelings, so that one may feel hostile or friendly toward some groups, depending on their ethnicity or lifestyle. This latter approach has been labeled the "likability heuristic." It allows people to make reasonable choices on the basis of their likes and dislikes, often based on gut reactions (Ottati and Wyer 1993).

Believers in the efficacy of "low information rationality" contend that the vast majority of citizens, for example, have fairly accurate views about the basic orientations of political parties. This enables them to have reasonably good notions about the concordance of their own political views with those of members of the major political parties (Popkin 1994; Conover and Feldman 1984, 1989; Rahn 1993). It also allows them to make reasonable inferences about the likely behavior of candidates whose party identification they know. When party labels are lacking or when there is flagrant evidence that the candidate does not conform to the major features inherent in the party stereotype, people are quite able to examine other available information about the candidate and form opinions to guide their vote choice (Rahn 1993). For instance, they may accept the recommendations of trusted media commentators or of respected political leaders. However, when the party label is available, most voters, including "sophisticates," prefer using it because it is a time-saving shortcut.

For talking about politics, average people who are willing to engage in political discourse usually keep on top of the daily news headlines although they forget them quickly when topics shift. For lobbying, even ordinary Americans need expertise. People who are politically active at that level usually have the necessary savvy because they lobby mostly for matters that interest and concern them greatly. Their relevant schemas are apt to be rich, so that it is easy to absorb additional information.

How sensible are some of the most widely used shortcuts? The ample literature that explores how people actually make electoral choices indicates that the shortcuts work well. During election campaigns, most voters are very concerned about whether candidates are trustworthy, capable, and empathetic. Through practice in daily life, where they assess these qualities in others through facial expressions, body language, and behavioral cues, their abilities to judge the trustworthiness, intelligence, and general competence of political leaders are well honed. They have learned to make realistic choices quickly, based on familiar cues to character traits, in situations that always involve ambiguities and compromises.

Party labels remain a reasonable guide for making sound political decisions for ordinary people who do not want to bother to learn a lot of facts and to analyze political issues on their own during election campaigns. For voters who have generally found themselves in agreement with candidates from one particular party, it makes good sense to vote on that basis. Similarly, if there are trusted political elites or respected friends and co-workers who are known to follow the news and who seem concerned about the country's welfare, it is sensible to follow their advice. In fact, it may be more sensible to adopt the judgments of political elites when complex political issues require evaluations than to attempt one's own judgment (Zaller 1992). It seems naïve to argue that average citizens can become their own experts about a multiplicity of complex issues as a sideline to their other preoccupations.

It is even questionable whether voting choices should be based primarily on the proclaimed issue stands of the candidates, as rational choice advocates recommend. Besides the inherent difficulty of judging the merits of complex policies to be carried out in the future under unknown conditions, it is always uncertain whether the key policies on which voters might peg their choices will ever make it to the legislative or executive docket. It is also unlikely that one candidate embodies all the policy preferences that a voter might have, while alternative candidates embody none. Hence a vote for one preferred policy may mean a vote against others. A candidate's eagerness to see certain policies enacted and carried out does not necessarily mean that the candidate has the needed political skills, control over decision-making, or executive ability to carry out a policy mandate. Therefore, choices based on the candidates' trustworthiness and leadership qualities may be best after all. One identifies the "better" or "worse" individuals based on prior experiences with evaluating people. Similarly, voting on the basis of party is meaningful because it translates reactions to past performance by the party (based on a multitude of specific but forgotten incidents) into a vote for or against "more of the same."

"Potpourri rationality" might be a better term than "low information rationality" for this type of decision-making because the word "low" carries negative connotations when paired with "information." Decision shortcuts rest on a solid information base albeit a different one than recommended by most "rational choice" aficionados among social scientists. The process does not lack an adequate informational base (Mondak 1994; Chong 2000). Even Congress members use simple heuristics, such as party cues and committee votes, when making decisions about complex bills outside their area of expertise (Kingdon 1981). They are rarely condemned for low-information choices because, as Arthur Lupia and Mathew McCubbins put it, "reasoned choice does not require complete information. Instead, it requires *knowledge: the ability to predict the consequences of actions*" (1998, 6; emphasis in original).

FRAMING QUESTIONS TO MATCH MEMORY ENTRY CODES

Scores on political information tests, even for factoid questions, would be far better if the chances for information retrieval had been optimized in line with knowledge about the retrieval of information from memory. As discussed in chapter 2, human brains are filled with stored information about a vast variety of topics. The most recently learned information is easiest to retrieve. Older data, such as lessons from early schooling, are hard to retrieve unless they have been recalled frequently over the years. When it comes to tapping into stored information, even when it was learned fairly recently, access and retrieval are often thwarted because questions do not encompass appropriate search concepts (Feenan and Snodgrass 1990).

In the ordinary interview situation, where closed-ended questions predominate, people's thought processes are guided only in a limited number of directions. The few cues that are provided to assist in memory searches may not resonate at all with the respondents' memory structure. When respondents, for example, are asked whether health insurance companies can or should be allowed to refuse to pay for expensive experimental procedures, most may be unable to give a "yes" or "no" answer because the question does not readily match an established schema. More open-ended approaches may be the solution because they encourage respondents to think about issues from multiple perspectives, which may then trigger appropriate memories. During focus group discussions of experimental medical procedures, for instance, participants may mention numerous experiences with finding money for experimental medical treatments. This dialogue creates alternative keys for each focus group member for tapping into related stored experiences. Stored opinions may then surface, thanks to the additional cues, which are also useful for formulating new opinions on the spot.

Since political situations are rarely clear-cut, it is likely that people have a variety of schemas that relate to particular policies. Their answers to questions posed by researchers hinge on the cues embedded in the question. For instance, questions about public policies may evoke different responses, depending on whether respondents are led to think in terms of a desirable service, like universal health care; the tax consequences of such a service; or the need for such a service compared to other needs. Open-ended methodologies may uncover the contingencies on which these opinions are based, revealing complex thinking. Answers to closed-ended questions rarely indicate the contingencies on which these answers are predicated. Open-ended questions also allow respondents to rephrase the questions into language of their choice with which they are comfortable. This is important because the words used in questions are often unfamiliar to poorly educated people, who then fail to give correct answers even when they know the appropriate information (Lupia and McCubbins 1998).

The customary tests of factual knowledge inquire about many items of information that are rarely mentioned in media stories and that most citizens no longer remember from their early schooling. Political scientist Samuel Popkin said it well when he warned against taking civics test scores at face value in judging citizens' ability to vote intelligently:

> [A]ssessing voters by civics exams misses the many things that voters *do* know, and the many ways in which they can do without the facts that the civics tradition assumes they should know. . . . [T]he focus on voters' lack of information about many political issues underestimates just how much information they pick up. . . . It focuses on what voters don't know instead of on what they do know, who they take their cues from and how they read the candidates. (1994, 20–21)

The fact-based knowledge tests also fail to explore either the comprehension of the story or the information gain attained through reasoning beyond the bounds of the main story line. Genuine political insights come from combining past understandings embedded in memory with a pinch of new factual data and using powers of inference to construct new meanings. For example, most assessments of the capabilities of particular, hitherto unfamiliar, politicians are made through inferences drawn from a small array of biographical data. From information made available about demographics, experiences, and statements of motivation, average citizens know how to extrapolate to unknown qualities. Inference-making skills are not domain specific. The person who can infer the likely development of health care policies from news stories about current happenings probably can do the same with stories about aid to a war-ravaged foreign country or tax relief for military personnel. However, most people limit their interests—and their inferences—to a narrow range of policy domains.

Nonetheless, the ability to draw inferences from new and old knowledge, albeit without detail retention, has remained underrated and largely unexplored in current knowledge tests, while the ability for rote memorization of detail is deemed high-quality learning. This is a serious failure (Lupia and McCubbins 1998). Media researchers have repeatedly shown that skill in inference-making is highly correlated with political learning. By contrast, few political insights spring from rote memorization of the kinds of news story facts that civics tests probe.

Just as questions ignore comprehension and inferences, so they tend to disregard important knowledge gleaned from visual information. Even though people would score well on such questions because they remember visual information better than verbal data, they are seldom asked about the content and meaning of pictures seen on television. In fact, visual learning is largely dismissed as inconsequential by researchers who claim that it cannot be important because it does not surface in routine tests. The reason, of course, is that the test questions focus exclusively on verbal texts and ignore visually conveyed information.

Besides, as already mentioned, it makes little sense to ask all respondents the same sets of questions, based on the researchers' ideas about what constitutes relevant knowledge, when people differ about what is relevant based on their political interests and needs. This is particularly true for political issues. As discourse scholar Teun van Dijk (1988, 106) has remarked: "[U]nderstanding is essentially relative to personal models and goals, on the one hand, and socially shared goals, frames, scripts, attitudes, or ideologies on the other hand." Questions designed to assess a respondent's scope of political knowledge should therefore be tailored to the respondent's knowledge domains, rather than to the investigator's prescriptions about what the respondent ought to know about extraneous issues.

While the totality of publics concerned about specific public policy issues is quite large, it is split among numerous individual "issue publics," which often are quite small, because few issues are highly relevant to large segments of the public (Krosnick 1990; Ottati and Wyer 1990). The likelihood that most individuals will be concerned about a broad array of policy issues is diminished further because issue specialization has a spiral effect, given that learning is incremental. People are more likely to learn additional facts about the limited number of topics that are already familiar to them than to learn about totally new topics that do not appear to be particularly useful or interesting. Similarly, most people do not acquire knowledge for its own sake or because scholars and pundits tell them what they ought to know to be deemed well informed by political elites.

WHAT PEOPLE NEED TO KNOW

Leaving theories behind, how well or ill suited to effective citizenship is Americans' actual knowledge about politics? The question of what constitutes an adequate knowledge base for effective citizenship resolves into many subissues about which there is little agreement. In fact, what is and what is not relevant in making political decisions is largely a subjective judgment. Substantively, how does one decide about what issues people need to be informed? Does everyone need to be informed about the same topics, or can and ought there be some specialization in our complex age? How detailed does knowledge have to be to make it usable for citizenship tasks? Is it enough, for example, to know that people are starving in Somalia before advocating aid, or must average citizens also be fully informed about the precise dollar amounts and about the politics of that troubled country? Or is it enough if they believe that resources should remain in the United States because "charity begins at home" and there are unmet needs among American citizens?

The answers to such difficult questions hinge on the all-important determination of the purposes for acquiring political knowledge (Smiley 1999). As mentioned, for most citizens those purposes are voting and political discussions. The heuristics developed by most Americans to carry out these civic tasks seem quite serviceable although they are remote from the ideal of the fully informed citizen who enjoys in-depth knowledge about all aspects of politics. That ideal, even if it were attainable, would be impractical for most citizens in our complex age, where they must attend to many other pursuits besides politics. However, citizens who want to lobby for specific political actions need more specialized information in the particular areas of their lobbying efforts. In general, judging from testimony offered in formal and informal public hearings, they attain this expertise in those domains in which they have chosen to be active.

Is there empirical evidence that demonstrates that average Americans who perform poorly on standardized knowledge tests have sufficient political knowledge to cope with their civic needs? The answer is "yes." There are data that demonstrate adequate civic competence among the poor performers. The data presented below are examples. They are drawn from focus groups and depth interviews that involved many of the groups of citizens—women, minorities, and people ranking low on socioeconomic criteria—whose scores have been lowest on traditional tests. The focus group and interview protocols covered conversations about political topics.

WHAT ORDINARY PEOPLE KNOW:
CASE STUDY EVIDENCE

Using data from twenty-one focus groups, as well as transcripts from twenty-six individual depth interviews, my assistants and I assessed the scope of knowledge that ordinary citizens brought to bear on the discussion of then current political issues. We recorded demographic information for participants as well as data on group characteristics and interaction patterns within the focus groups. To avoid inflating the level of political acumen recorded for average people, we ignored comments based on specialized information that individual participants had acquired through unique experiences in work or social settings. Examples are police officers' discussions of police procedures and chemists' comments on air quality standards.

Beyond recording participants' areas of political interests and concerns, we assessed the levels of sophistication of their political dialogue. The notion of cognitive complexity used for this coding project is based on integrative complexity theory, which was developed to assess the sophistication with which people use information to make decisions (Tetlock 1993). To detect sophisticated reasoning, analysts focus on two aspects of information-processing: differentiation and integration. Measures of differentiation establish the number of distinct evaluative dimensions that a person uses in judging a situation. Once a problem has been appraised from various perspectives, measures of integration assess the person's ability to establish the connections among the different facets of the situation.

We began by coding five levels of knowledge and sophistication but ultimately collapsed them into two basic categories labeled "simple" and "complex." "Simple" comments in our coding scheme—which does not mean "simplistic"—are statements of facts, descriptions, and reports of what others said, expressed in generalizations. For example, the following statement about education policy was coded as "simple": "We need to create more schools that give children better education because our community has grown and is becoming more diverse. I heard that the mayor is planning a new school bond issue."

"Complex" statements entail reasoning beyond the mere statement of facts. For example, appraising a problem from a variety of distinct dimensions, connecting ideas causally or drawing on valid analogies, making meaningful comparisons, drawing inferences, and discussing consequences would all be considered evidence of complex reasoning. The following statement was coded as "complex": "We need to create more schools that give children better education. If we do that, they'll become professionals who create wealth for our community. That will help everybody, including the elderly who don't want to vote for giving more money for schools. Spending money on education is like putting money in the bank. It's an investment that pays dividends in the future in terms of economic growth, tax revenues and personal satisfaction." Black voters' remarks about economic problems reproduced in the box below illustrate a typical sequence of predominantly complex commentary.

ECONOMIC PROBLEMS AS SEEN BY BLACK VOTERS
Excerpts from Focus Group Dialogue

Voter A: I'd love to hear someone talk about self-employment as a viable option for communities. I would love for a politician to talk to me about how to really sign along to the empowerment zone issues. How can community members be involved in the planning for empowerment zones?

I would love to hear political leaders talk about economic development as a separate entity from community development because a lot of people say you're going to do economic development slash community development. And it's two separate issues.

Voter B: I like to see my politician get involved with, like A said, about self-employment. My interests are companies that are letting people go and how they go about that. My concern with politicians is that somehow we make this fair but you just don't wipe out our jobs for the minorities and then just leave it for non-minorities. And if you choose to let these people go, to provide retraining so that they have choices—not just the choice to take another job but possibly a choice for re-education or for going into business yourself. I believe that this should not be something that corporate America is doing and that nobody is talking about.

Voter C: I would also like to hear a political person say that one of the viable alternatives to crime in our neighborhoods is really lobbying for minimum wage standards . . . not just talking about minimum wage but how do we get people who have smaller stores to expand and employ more people. I mean really identify corporations that have a tendency to lay off people every year around November and pick folks up around February. . . . How do we talk to Sears about having part-time staff with no benefits?

Voter D: I think everyone in my community wants development because on major streets we have vacant buildings. It's supposed to be industrial. . . . In some neighborhoods—like white communities—it's developed. But if you go in the black communities you see abandoned buildings or buildings that have just been standing there for ten years or so or boarded up or just vacant. You would rather for them to be torn down or be utilized for the community . . . more day care for the girls and for some of the people who want to work so that they don't have to worry about their children.

Voter E: You know, the City of Chicago has what they call a head tax. Each employer has to pay a tax on each of their employees. It's about $3 or $5 per person. . . . It seems as though this has created a problem for a lot of employers as far as locating within the city of Chicago. They don't want to pay this head tax. If this is the problem, I believe that they need to get rid of this head tax . . . so that they can bring employment into Chicago. . . . If you have a big factory that employed 1000 people and the real estate tax that you're receiving off the building is more than that $5 you're receiving with a head tax. So why do you want this company to close up and abandon the factory. . . . [N]o taxes are being paid on that property.

Voter F: Let me speak to that. There are several programs—incentive programs—that have been used by the government that would wipe that head tax that they have. . . . There has been enterprise zones that give you tax incentives to companies to stay in a city.

Voter E: Economically, if you're in business and you want to employ 500 people and you're truly an entrepreneur business spirited person, you're going to think of the best way to boost your income. That's not a white, black, or government thing. That's business.

Focus Group Characteristics

The largest and most useful cluster of focus groups in the analysis included ninety-eight people gathered as part of a research project designed to measure the fit between media messages about an election campaign and the concerns of the voters. The researchers engaged nine distinctive focus groups of voting-age citizens from the Chicago area in conversations about concerns that they might express to candidates running for local and statewide office in 1994. The dialogue for each group started with the moderator's query: "What are the issues that are most important to you in your community, however you define that? What would you tell an elected official?" After the focus group members had mentioned a large list of issues, the moderator narrowed the list by asking group members about their priorities. The most important issues were then discussed. Most of the focus group findings presented here highlight this cluster of focus groups.

A cluster of four focus groups conducted with mostly lower-middle-class, older Americans in two medium-sized midwestern communities ranked next in richness of political dialogue.* In each city, members of one group were fifty to sixty-four years old, and those in the second group were sixty-five years of age or older.

Much of the conversation in this cluster was nonpolitical, except for the reactions to the moderator's broad question: "What's going on in

---

*The videotapes for all focus groups, aside from the Illinois cluster, were made available by Professor Cliff Zukin, Rutgers University, from his research collection. I am deeply indebted to him for his unfailing support.

the country's politics at the present time, aside from the 1994 election?" The subsequent discussion focused broadly on the role citizens ought to play in government, on the reasons for their general attitudes toward government and politicians, and on the role that government ought to play to benefit the country and individual citizens. Compared to the Chicago cluster, this group dwelled far less intensively and more superficially on political issues. A significant exception was conversation about the health care issue, which predictably was of major concern for senior citizens.

Finally, a cluster of eight focus groups is important for the nonfindings that it produced. The discussions in these groups illustrated that politics does not pervade the life of ordinary citizens so strongly that it always rises to the fore when they talk about public policies. The issues discussed by these groups of low- and high-skill workers had important economic and political facets, but the political facets surfaced only rarely despite many opportunities for including them. Six of the groups explored how a variety of workplace problems were handled by management as well as the merits of proposals for increasing workers' participation in company management. Two groups assessed the pluses and minuses of television offerings, with a heavy emphasis on negative aspects of television, such as the ample featuring of sex and violence and other issues deemed inappropriate fare for children.

In the sixteen hours of discussion represented by these eight groups, there was so little discussion of current political problems, politics, and politicians that coding of political discourse was not worthwhile. That does not mean that the discussions did not reveal a good deal of knowledge and simple and complex reasoning about worker-management relations and the impact of television on average Americans of all ages. In fact, analysis of political and nonpolitical aspects of the entire set of tapes indicates that sophistication levels are comparable for a broad array of issues. Average people can think effectively and draw sound inferences on many fronts.

The same conclusion emerges from scrutiny of the depth interview transcripts where respondents could air their views at length, undistracted by other respondents.* These interview protocols show variations in sophistication, depending on the nature of the issues under discussion and the background and interests of the interviewees. For example, while one respondent might dismiss the issue of AIDS infection

*I am indebted to Professor W. Russell Neuman, Annenberg Public Policy Center, University of Pennsylvania, for the use of these transcripts from his research.

as a problem to be handled by individual gay men, another respondent might reveal full understanding of the medical and public health aspects of the disease in the United States and abroad. Overall, the findings about political awareness and thinking complexity closely match the focus group data reported for Chicago area citizens.

The Findings

Table 3.1 lists the ratios of "simple" to "complex" statements for the seventeen political issue categories that the Chicago area respondents from the nine-focus-group cluster identified as most important. These issues generated extensive discussions in which everyone participated and no single individual dominated. Entries are in underlined italics when "simple" statements are dominant. For three issue categories, discussion was predominantly complex for all groups: Mass Media, Elections, and Taxes. All other categories elicited a mix of predominantly complex or simple statements.

What kinds of issues do these categories encompass? A small sampling must suffice. Role of Government includes discussions about specific services that government should provide, such as jobs or low-cost housing, or areas that should be beyond government management, such as family relationships. The groups discussed obstacles that make it difficult for government to perform its tasks, such as fierce partisanship, and they talked about the support that citizens ought to give to public officials to make their tasks easier. Complex statements dominated for all groups, except Latino nonvoters.

When Politicians were the center of discussion, negative comments abounded about politicians' low ethical standards, favoritism that benefits wealthy interest groups and hurts average citizens, and failure to carry through on promises. These complaints were balanced by comments about the difficulties politicians face, including their brief terms of office and lack of resources. In addition to discussing politicians in general, focus group members assessed the performance of named individual politicians at the local, state, and national levels. Overall, the three groups of nonvoters showed the least sophistication in their analysis.

Comments about the Bureaucracy were as unfavorable, though sparser than comments about politicians. The groups provided examples of bureaucratic unresponsiveness, senseless rules, and misplaced priorities. But here, too, the discussions revealed integrative complexity, as group members noted the obstacles faced by bureaucrats and the

Table 3.1 Complexity of Issue Discussions: Ratio of Simple to Complex Statements—Chicago Area Cluster

Discussion Issues	City Vote	City No-vote	Sub-urban Vote	Latino Vote	Latino No-vote	Black Vote	Black No-vote	Gen. X	Home-less
Role of government	7:10	6:7		1:4	**5:2**	1:10	0:5	0:11	2:5
Role of president/ vice-president	**1:0**			1:1			**1:0**		
Politicians		**9:4**	2:3	1:4	**4:1**		1:1	2:15	9:16
Bureaucracy	1:4	1:1	1:3		**4:1**	**1:0**	**1:0**	2:3	1:3
Government accountability		**10:9**	2:5		**1:0**	0:1	2:3		
Role of citizens	1:1	**3:2**	1:5	1:2	**4:0**	1:4	4:5	1:2	0:1
Mass media			1:5	0:1			3:4	4:9	
Elections			3:4			0:1		0:4	0:1
Race relations	**1:0**			1:1		0:1	0:1		0:1
Economy	1:1	0:1		1:1		1:2	**4:1**		
Taxes	1:1	1:2		1:3	0:4	1:1			
Education	4:9	**1:0**	1:2	1:2	0:2	1:3	**2:1**	0:1	
Health care	1:4				**1:0**	**1:0**			
Welfare	2:5		1:2		**2:1**		**2:1**	0:1	
Homeless	**1:0**		1:2						0:1
Crime	3:4	2:3	1:2	0:8	**3:1**	0:1	1:3	2:3	**1:0**
Corruption					**4:1**	1:1			

NOTE: Groups (left to right, from Chicago area) with group member sizes in parentheses: City Voters (12); City Nonvoters (11); Suburban Voters (13); Latino Voters (12); Latino Nonvoters (10); Black Voters (12); Black Nonvoters (10); Youth/Generation X (11); Homeless/Streetwise Vendors (7). Entries are boldface when simple statements are dominant.

reasons behind flawed performances. For city and suburban voters, for students and homeless people, complex statements preponderated.

Government Accountability received a good deal of attention from five of the nine groups because group members felt that it was not taken seriously enough. They proposed numerous reforms, such as formal annual reports by public officials about achievements and failures in various policy areas and closer monitoring of expenditures. All groups condemned corruption unequivocally. Every group discussed the Role of Citizens and the shortcomings of most citizens in performing these duties and in keeping adequately informed. A broad range of reasons was cited to explain this state of affairs, including feelings of alienation from an unresponsive government and lack of knowledge about ways to lobby public officials. The groups stressed the importance of voting in elections, despite small payoffs, and they commented on the need for campaign reforms. Complex statements were the mode, except among Latino and city nonvoters.

Issue areas were frequently linked during discussions. For instance, the focus group members felt that weaknesses in the Economy and poor allocation of Taxes were intertwined with the problems discussed under the headings of Education, Health Care, Welfare, Homelessness, Race Relations, and even Crime. Homelessness was linked to Race Relations, Health Care, and Welfare. The Mass Media were blamed for contributing to major societal problems, such as upswings in juvenile crime and poor school performance. Though the focus group participants emphasized problems in all these areas, they also showed sympathy for the human actors whose lagging performance was partly due to circumstances beyond their control. Many specific, quite sophisticated reform proposals surfaced.

If we take table 3.1 as a report card on the civic knowledge of Chicago area citizens from various walks of life, ranging from the inner city's homeless to suburbanites, what do we find? If we discount balanced responses, we find that eight to twelve of the seventeen political issue areas had caught the attention of every group and that complex responses predominated in 82 percent of the categories that group members chose to discuss. There was a preponderance of simple responses in only 18 percent of the categories. Overall, while not ideal, this seems like a reasonably satisfactory level of political knowledge in important political issue areas and an encouragingly high degree of political sophistication for a group dominated by citizens with low incomes and limited formal education.

Overall, voters covered slightly more issue areas and showed somewhat greater sophistication than nonvoters. Table 3.2 highlights the complexity levels of each group. Looking at the voter cluster, it shows that complex commentary predominated among suburban voters, whose discussions ranged over ten topic areas. For city voters, the simple-to-complex ratio, excluding ties, was 1:2; for Latino voters, excluding ties, it was 1:7.

The groups from which one might expect the least interest in politics, and hence the least amount of sophistication—nonvoters, young people, and possibly the homeless—scored higher on cognitive complexity than expected in light of studies that show interest is a key factor in political learning and sophistication. The homeless, who registered

Table 3.2 Complexity Levels by Focus Groups—Chicago Area Cluster

	City Vote	City No-vote	Sub-urban Vote	Latino Vote	Latino No-vote	Black Vote	Black No-vote	Gen. X	Home-less
No. of issue areas	12	9	10	11	10	12	12	9	8
% complex	50	44	100	64	20	58	50	100	88
% tie	25	11	—	27	—	25	8	—	—
% simple	25	44	—	9	80	17	42	—	12

NOTE: Groups (left to right, from Chicago area) with group member sizes in parentheses: City Voters (12); City Nonvoters (11); Suburban Voters (13); Latino Voters (12); Latino Nonvoters (10); Black Voters (12); Black Nonvoters (10); Youth/Generation X (11); Homeless/Streetwise Vendors (7).

comments in a comparatively narrow range of only eight issue categories, had a ratio of 1:7 between commentary that was predominantly simple and commentary that was predominantly complex. It is possible that their educational level was far higher than one might expect from their current socioeconomic misfortune. The Generation X focus group, which was composed entirely of college students, engaged in predominantly complex discussions in all of their nine subject areas, giving rise to some optimism about the political acumen of the nascent leadership pool.

Black nonvoters exhibited a simple-to-complex ratio of 5:6 if one excludes the tie on the topic of Politicians. City nonvoters covered nine topics; excluding the tie on Bureaucrats, their ratio was 1:1 between simple and complex dialogue. Latino nonvoters showed the least complexity overall. Their ratio was 4:1 based on ten topic areas. We do not know to what extent language difficulties and cultural differences played a role in this score. Latino voters, by comparison, ranked above average in cognitive complexity.

To better understand the suitability of the public's knowledge base for performing its civic tasks, it is worthwhile to ascertain in which issue areas the focus group members seemed best and least able to make sense out of relevant information. Table 3.3 therefore ranks the issue areas according to the complexity of discussion noted for the Chicago area cluster.

Discounting the first-ranked item, Mass Media, because there was comparatively little discussion about it, it is comforting to note the high proportions of complex discussion on issues relating to the functioning of the government in general as well as on specific policy issues. In fourteen of the seventeen policy areas, sophisticated responses were

Table 3.3   Complexity Levels by Issue Areas (%)

Rank	Issue Area	Complex	Tie	Simple
1	Mass media	100	—	—
2	Role of government	88	—	12
3	Crime	77	—	22
4	Education	75	—	25
4	Elections	75	25	—
5	Role of citizens	66	12	22
5	Homeless	66	—	34
6	Government accountability	60	—	40
6	Race relations	60	20	20
6	Taxes	60	40	—
6	Welfare	60	—	40
7	Politicians	57	14	29
8	Bureaucracy	50	12	38
9	Economy	40	40	20
10	Health care	33	—	66
11	Role of president/vice-president	—	33	66
11	Corruption	—	50	50

NOTE: The rankings in boldface indicate that the issue that is listed first was discussed by more groups than the issue listed subsequently. The remaining ties are listed in random order because they were discussed by the same number of groups.

dominant. Average people may not know the length of terms of various types of public officials, but they have solid ideas about the roles that they want their governments to perform or shun. They understand many of the political ramifications of electoral politics and see citizenship as a two-way street involving giving as well as receiving. They are familiar with major policy areas, such as the role of government in education, crime control, and coping with problems of homelessness. They are also reasonably well informed about salient aspects of tax and welfare legislation.

The fact that the discussion of health care issues reached a complex level in only one of the three groups that covered the topic was surprising, considering the high levels of complex reasoning in other, less salient areas. The reason why few groups touched on the issue at all, and then only in simple fashion, was that the many different plans presented by politicians and the media coverage of these plans were extraordinarily confusing, a fact also noted by members of the senior citizen clusters. In addition to the inherent difficulty of the issue and the deficiencies in media coverage, citizens' efforts to make sense of it suffered because politicians, in all too typical fashion, deliberately fogged the arguments.

Analysis of the comments of the focus group participants reveals that they possess reasonably sophisticated, politically useful knowledge about current problems that confront them and that the issue areas covered by this knowledge are generally quite well suited to carrying out the actual tasks of citizenship that most Americans perform. Though most group members would probably have scored poorly on the Delli Carpini/Keeter citizenship quiz, they deserve to be called politically informed citizens. Most would rate a passing civic IQ grade for their performance in voting and in discussing a selected array of public policy issues. The passing grade for civic knowledge does not denote an ideally broad and diverse knowledge base. Far from it! It merely means that ordinary citizens know enough about many important political issues to function passably well. Given the complexities of modern life, they cannot be expected to know everything that would be useful. Neither can they be familiar enough with all issues that touch their lives to systematically prioritize them.

That judgment does not ignore the fact that large numbers of citizens, including political sophisticates, lack adequate knowledge about many important policy issues that touch their lives directly or indirectly. For example, surveys have documented that many citizens do not know how to apply for support from public assistance programs designed for them (Donelan et al. 1995). When issues are more remote, few citizens can judge the merits of programs, such as foreign aid, because they grossly misjudge their scope and expense. Such ignorance has political costs, including skewing election results (Bartels 1996; Gilens 1999, 2000).

THE GAMSON FOCUS GROUPS

The quality and breadth of the information levels of our Chicago-area focus group members are not unique (Chubb et al. 1991; McGraw et al. 1991; Lodge and Stroh 1993). For example, portions of transcripts of focus group conversations reported by sociologist William Gamson in his book *Talking Politics* (1992) also reveal substantial political knowledge among average Americans. Gamson selected 188 respondents to represent working-class Americans. Roughly half of the group was Caucasian, and most of the others were African Americans. Their median age was thirty-three. Typical participants were cooks and kitchen workers, bus drivers, medical and laboratory technicians, nurses, firefighters, and auto service workers. Fifty-eight percent of the group had never attended college, and most of those who had attended college did not graduate. In short, this was a group of ordinary people unlikely to be exceptionally well informed and interested in politics.

The discussions, which took place in 1986, centered around four important political issues that had been amply covered by the news media over prolonged periods of time. All of the issues were salient for voting, for political discussions, and even for lobbying. The issues were the pros and cons of affirmative action, government support of financially troubled industries, government regulation of the nuclear power industry, and U.S. involvement in the Arab-Israeli conflict. While affirmative action and the problems of industry breakdowns may have had a personal impact on group members' lives, nuclear power plants and the Arab-Israeli dispute probably were remote issues for most of them.

The focus group protocols reported in the book feature "typical" responses. They clearly show that group members knew about the situations, knew what the chief problems were, and had views about possible solutions. The focus group members, for example, could define the character and intent of affirmative action programs. They were familiar with attacks on affirmative action as reverse discrimination and even mentioned the basic facts involved in the landmark *Bakke* case (*Regents of the University of California v. Bakke,* 438 U.S. 265 [1978]), which had been decided eight years earlier. They also discussed the pros and cons of establishing racial quota systems and of busing school children for integration.

The focus group members commented intelligently on the federal government's loan to financially distressed Chrysler Corporation, drawing parallels to the troubled steel industry. They characterized government subsidies as political rather than primarily economic actions and felt that the big companies always come out ahead, while workers suffer. They also argued that more aid should go to displaced workers. They noted the waning power of big unions and pointed out that companies in areas of labor trouble are likely to relocate to other parts of the United States or abroad. They also talked about the problems of relocating older workers and discussed actions that government should take to help workers in troubled industries.

Turning to matters beyond their own immediate concerns, they saw the Arab-Israeli conflict as an arena of the cold war power struggle between the United States and the Soviet Union, each wanting allies.

They counseled against further U.S. involvement, since past efforts had failed, and warned that intervention would deflect attention from pressing U.S. problems. The group members drew parallels to the conflict between Catholics and Protestants in Northern Ireland, but distinguished the situation in South Africa under apartheid as one in which the government used its authority to victimize its own citizens. They also talked about other foreign trouble spots that had involved the United States in the recent past.

The focus group members framed the nuclear power issue as a struggle between the demands of the public for protection from the industry and the power of the industry to resist government regulation. They talked about priorities and declared that protecting human lives is more important than cheap electric power. They discussed the fact that the Soviet Union's Chernobyl nuclear power plant, site of a nuclear reactor explosion, lacked the kinds of safety devices common in American nuclear power plants and characterized it as forty years behind the latest technology. But they also talked about media sensationalism in reporting about the Chernobyl disaster and pointed out that more people die in car and plane crashes than nuclear mishaps. They argued about whether nuclear power is needed or not.

Obviously, the comments of the focus group participants reveal that they were informed about current problems that confronted them with varying degrees of urgency. They could discuss them and use them in making intelligent voting choices involving these issues. Though most group members would probably have scored poorly on the Delli Carpini/Keeter citizenship quiz, they certainly were politically astute in these four knowledge domains.

SOCIALIZATION EFFECTS

It is one of the axioms of democratic politics that citizens must share basic political values and knowledge so that they can deliberate about public policies. Given that knowledge creation is idiosyncratic, as explained in chapter 2, how is it possible for millions of citizens to share basic political values and an adequate range of political information? The answer is political socialization—the teaching of the basic values and norms of political life to succeeding generations. Through formal and informal education, through a shared mass media environment, and through common direct and vicarious experiences, political socialization creates a scaffold of shared memories that people hold along with unique memories based on their personal life. A person who grew up in the slums of Chicago, for example, will have different experiences and memories about many aspects of life than a person raised in the city's affluent suburbs. But in the age of audiovisual news coverage about the local scene, both are likely to be acquainted with each other's situation and are likely to vicariously share many experiences.

Audiovisuals help in constructing more powerful and accurate collective memories than was possible before pictures of the world's political happenings were routinely displayed in most of America's living rooms. Faced with heterogeneous audiences, television broadcasters try very hard to convey common meanings through word and picture clichés that most audience members have learned to recognize. "Everything the camera sees, it necessarily interprets" for the viewers, telling them what the preferred interpretations are (Tiemens 1978, 363). News comprehension tests following television broadcasts clearly demonstrate that audiences can agree broadly about the messages conveyed, including the verbal and visual symbolism, unless it is exceptionally subtle (Philo 1990). Likewise, when the meanings that the message senders said they intended to transmit through specific cues have been compared with the meanings that audiences assigned to the cues, transmission accuracy has generally proven high (Kraus 1979; Sullivan and Masters 1993). The psychological literature on perception of people and events and the cognitive processing literature support the fact that people who live in the same cultural environment assimilate its values and share many perceptions. Faced with stimuli that relate to shared concerns, they draw on their shared cultural assumptions, knowledge, and experiences to extract shared meanings—though not necessarily shared evaluations (Altheide 1985; Messaris 1994; Goode 2000).

TAKING STOCK

This chapter has addressed the second puzzle—why average Americans consider themselves to be reasonably well informed, while critics charge that most of them, particularly those in the lower socioeconomic groups, are political dunces who lack elementary knowledge about American politics. I have shown that the critics have reached wrong conclusions because they have used faulty knowledge tests that infer learning propensities from imaginary ideals. I have also shown that these ideals ignore human physiology and are unrelated to the civic functions that average Americans actually perform. The focus group evidence presented in the chapter demonstrates that average Americans from all walks of life are capable of familiarizing themselves with basic information about many important political issues and that they can think about these issues in complex ways. While their unique individual needs and interests determine the areas of politics to which they pay attention, there is a common core of knowledge based on shared childhood and adult socialization that makes political dialogue possible.

If average Americans draw most of their political news from television because it is the most congenial source, as shown in chapter 2, and if this source allows them to be reasonably competent citizens, as argued in chapter 3, why are there so many detractors of television news? We will try to resolve puzzle #3 in the next chapter.

4

FREEING AUDIOVISUAL TECHNOLOGIES
FROM THE GUTENBERG LEGACY

Around 1440, Johannes Gutenberg, a goldsmith, hounded by creditors, invented a workable printing press in his shop in Strassburg, Germany, in hopes of paying off his debts. The aim of the new press was to speed book production and decrease costs through mechanization and printing on paper, rather than parchment. The new invention was used first to print bibles, but before long it was also used to reproduce most of the extant literary works. The modest cost of the printed books put the stored wisdom of the past within the reach of thousands at a time when the ranks of eager customers were swelling rapidly. European universities were expanding. Their students and the growing middle class had broken the literacy monopoly formerly held by the clergy.

The book trade in medieval Europe proved to be well organized for marketing the flood of new books produced by a rapidly growing number of presses. By the time the fifteenth century drew to a close, an estimated fifteen to twenty million books, mostly theological and legal works, had been published. The Gutenberg era was well under way. It has been an era of veneration for the written word as the carrier par excellence of human thought. To be literate—to be able to read—has meant that one has access to the stored intellectual treasures of the past as well as to the evolving treasures of the current age.

At the start of the Gutenberg era, while written and printed volumes often contained pictures based on drawings or paintings, the written text generally carried the substance of the messages. Pictures, which in prephotography days often depicted reality poorly, were considered merely supporting illustrations or inconsequential decorations for the text. The view that pictures make only limited contributions to written texts and that texts are best suited for conveying complex ideas has persisted. The tremendous technological advances that make it possible to experience a close semblance of reality through a combination of pictures and sounds have not driven print from its pinnacle.

These technological advances did not go unnoticed. They led to arguments and aphorisms that stressed the equal merits of pictures and words, or even the superiority of pictures. "One picture is worth a thousand words" became a common saying, recognizing that words are symbols that ponderously describe what the eye and brain can comprehend in an instant. In the field of politics, picture language was widely used even before the advent of audiovisuals. It is credited with making powerful political arguments during the birthing of the nation, during its wars, and during other times of upheaval, particularly during elections (Somers 1998).

Benjamin Franklin was the first, in 1747, to publish editorial cartoons in his political pamphlets. Paul Revere's engraving in 1770 picturing "The Boston Massacre" was credited with rallying colonists to oppose Britain's policies. Currier and Ives, a lithography firm founded in 1835, marketed propaganda cartoons pleading the causes of both sides during the Civil War. President Lincoln deemed Thomas Nast's emotionally powerful Civil War illustrations in *Harper's Weekly* "our best recruiting sergeant" (quoted in Somers 1998, 6). Cartoons showing an ape, labeled "Spanish Brute," resting his bloody hands on the tombstone of Americans killed in the explosion of the battleship *Maine,* were used to whip up war fever for fighting Spain at the turn of the twentieth century. Albert Bigelow Paine called the 1872 presidential election campaign "the first great battle of pictures ever known in America" (Paine 1904, 247). By the 1890s, newspaper and magazine publishers had learned to adapt photographs to print media, allowing them to switch from expensive drawings, woodcuts, and engravings to this much cheaper form of pictorial journalism.

But none of these claims about the power of pictures to convey messages proved persuasive to the heirs of the Gutenberg legacy even in the age of television. Television made it possible to produce virtual reality through the combination of multihued motion pictures with vibrant sounds and spoken words that capture nuances of meanings and emotion subtly expressed in tone of voice, emphasis, and speed of delivery. Still, the heirs of Gutenberg argue that the new technological advancements cannot overcome the deficiencies and flaws in visual and audiovisual representations that make audiovisuals inherently unsuitable for accurately conveying important ideas.

In this chapter, I shall address the main arguments that have been made to denigrate the capacity of audiovisuals—on television, on the web, on movie screens, or in whatever form they may take—to communicate complex political ideas to mass audiences. I shall indicate to what degree the contentions about audiovisual transmissions are warranted or unwarranted. In the past, pleadings for the virtues of audiovisuals as a mode of information transmission have been treated as heresies because belief in the supremacy of the spoken and written word has amounted to a religion. Fortunately, the technical advances brought by the twentieth-century communications revolution have produced attitude changes in the generations who grew up in the television age and beyond. These changes herald an opportunity to break the Gutenberg shackles of prejudice that are an unfortunate legacy from the era when print was king.

In the context of the discussion that follows, it is important to reiterate that the claims made about the merits of audiovisual messages are based on the combined use of words and pictures. The combination of these two modes of information transmission takes advantage of the strengths of each. These strengths differ (Messaris 1994). Words are more efficient in delimiting the circumstances when something is true. They can disclose how often and under what circumstances a condition shown on screen occurs, whether it is rarely, three times a month, or never on Sunday. Pictures are better at showing particular conditions, be it a parade, a scientific experiment, or the counting of ballots by hand after an election. While pictures excel in presenting the event, they are somewhat less adept in making propositions about it. It stands to reason that the combination of words with pictures reaps the benefits of the combined strengths of both modalities.

VISUALIZING POLITICS

Images as Cues

One of the main charges made by aficionados of verbal symbols is that audiovisuals are an inadequate language that can convey little beyond the visible. The facts are otherwise, as is clear if one keeps in mind how message meanings are actually constructed. Pictures serve a dual function. Besides their superior ability to depict visible phenomena, pictures serve as cues for retrieving information stored in memory. Neither purely verbal nor purely audiovisual messages, whether conveyed by the mass media or through interpersonal contacts, express all message elements explicitly. Rather, most messages contain symbols that tap into the audience's stored schemas to augment the meanings conveyed explicitly. The full sense of most messages thus depends more on the memories activated by particular cues than on the explicit words and pictures embodied in the message. In the words of Michael Griffin (1992, 125): "The question then becomes not, what is the relationship of news to reality, but what is the form and structure of the image/text that is created for us daily, what are the recurrent patterns of its own system and how do they relate to other systems in what Gerbner has called our 'symbolic environment?'"*

If one envisages two situations where the words are the same, but they are accompanied by relevant pictures in one case and no pictures in the other, obviously the audiovisual message adds explicit content, thereby making it possible to access a broader array of memories. Even as simple a visual as a picture of a ballot box, used to symbolize the fact that elections are taking place in a hitherto undemocratic country, serves as a powerful cue for television audiences that major changes may be afoot. They are apt to equate elections with democracy and democracy with a broad array of governmental features. Absent the visual, these images might not pop up from memory.

"The facts, names, and details" of news stories "change almost daily; but the framework into which they fit—the symbolic system—is more enduring. And it could be argued that the totality of news as an enduring symbolic system 'teaches' audiences more than any of its component parts" (Bird and Dardenne 1988, 69). People learn which larger scenarios certain visuals suggest regardless of whether these scenarios are even related to these visuals during a particular news presentation. Through well-chosen and widely familiar cues, pictures can illustrate, as well as evoke, rich images of what it means that a dictator is ruthless, that a health care system is equipped to handle major emergencies, or that pollutants are poisoning the environment. We have already discussed how the availability of visual cues and the ability to visualize situations make recall easier and enhance accuracy in recall. Table 4.1 provides a list of typical visual cues drawn from a random sample of visual scenes in 150 local and national newscasts (Graber 1991; see appendix).

Audiovisuals have been widely praised, even by many of their detractors, for illuminating some of the most crucial social and political events of the twentieth century, giving viewers a clearer, more lasting picture of what actually occurred than words alone could have done. The pictures of President Nixon's first trip to China or the launching of space missions, including the *Challenger* space shuttle disaster, are

---

*The reference is to George Gerbner, then dean of the Annenberg School for Communication at the University of Pennsylvania.

Table 4.1 Sample Visual Cues for Common Themes

Theme	Visuals
Controversial issue, e.g., abortion	Close-up of audience with sharply mixed reactions watching antiabortion film
Civil disturbance is serious	Riot scenes; government leader reviews police or military forces
Public official is physically fit	Official walking firmly or engaged in vigorous physical exercise
Public official has wide support	Large rally of ordinary people cheering for official; other officials in poses suggesting agreement
Public policy causes harm	Evidence of damage; parade of experts or ordinary citizens alleging damage
"Live" reports are authentic	Scene of location of event (establishing shot) with or without reporter
Diplomats are negotiating	Negotiators shaking hands with flags identifying nations involved
Refugees' lives are precarious	Crowded refugee camps; close-ups of children, mothers, frail old people
Government budgets shrink	Graphic of programs to be ended; government check cut apart; bar graphs of fiscal data
Civil rights anniversary	Scenes of past segregation in South; scenes of integration in same location at later date

examples of significant audiovisual rhetoric that helped viewers to create new schemas and enrich existing ones. Audiovisual images presenting candidates during election campaigns and the riveting images of democratic revolutions in progress in China, the Soviet Union, and Indonesia carry rich visual and symbolic meanings. A video made by the Central Intelligence Agency (CIA) to support the Federal Bureau of Investigation's (FBI) conclusions about the causes of the crash of TWA flight 800 crystallized the event for the public far more instructively and convincingly than purely verbal narratives (Gyselinck and Tardieu 1999).

Television's ability to provide viewers with a ringside seat during major national and international events, such as presidential inaugurations, major floods, or summits of the world's leaders, has often been described. But the political consequences of watching these events have rarely been teased out and documented. The Kennedy assassination is among the few exceptions. It shows that witnessing the orderly succession of government can generate a sense of reassurance and calm in the public when a president has been assassinated and rumors of political conspiracy abound (Mindak and Hursh 1965). "At these times, for these matters . . . television reports penetrate viewers' minds to affect their perceptions and judgments, to trigger the processes of public opinion and mobilization that eventually produce resolution. These are the stories that refused to go away until surveillance can finally lead to reassurance" (Fowles 1992, 198).

Another example is the acceleration of disaster relief in the wake of graphic visual evidence that lends reality to the tragedy and puts human faces on tales of suffering. Pictures of famine in Africa or flood damage in the United States are likely to increase relief offerings and hasten their dispatch by government or private organizations. While disasters are in progress, visual demonstrations of rescue procedures and relief measures can be crucial in preventing loss of life and property.

Pictures are especially useful for providing tangible evidence to citizens about major problems and possible solutions. How can one fully and convincingly describe the deterioration of America's roads and bridges without showing rusty girders, pothole-marred streets, and warped railroad tracks? There is no better way to bring to life the contrast between inner-city and suburban schools than by contrasting pictures of spacious and crowded classrooms, rich and sparse libraries, and well- and poorly equipped laboratories. Even more important, for events that are remote from the ordinary citizen's experiences, pictures can provide insights that otherwise could not be correctly imagined.

Table 4.2 shows the type of information that information-rich visuals contribute to foreign affairs stories, and it indicates the percentage of stories featuring particular visuals. It is based on my content analysis of all (1,147) foreign affairs stories shown on nightly news broadcasts by ABC national news between March 1993 and February 1994. Nearly all of these stories (97 percent) contained helpful visual information, including pictures of foreign heads of state and political elites in action and scenes of normal political and economic activities in foreign settings as well as scenes of political violence and disaster and maps and close-ups of locations that served to orient viewers.*

Barbie Zelizer in her book *Remembering to Forget: Holocaust Memory through the Camera's Eye* (1998) discusses the use of pictures in print press stories of the liberation of German death camps such as Buchenwald and Bergen-Belsen. Journalists who covered these stories told how

---

*Routine visuals that added little important information to the textual messages were excluded from the table. A comparison of ABC news broadcasts with CBS and NBC broadcasts during this time period revealed no major differences in the nature and significance of their visual rhetoric.

Table 4.2   Visual Information in Foreign Affairs News

% Stories	Information Content
15	Views of top government leaders in action, revealing facial and body language cues; types of people that surround them; nature of official sites
8	Scenes of everyday life in foreign countries, including pictures of people, living conditions, and natural environments
8	Views of political elites in action, including opposition figures and major private-sector figures, revealing facial and body language cues, environments
7	War damage to people, structures, the environment; close-ups and panoramas
7	Scenes of ongoing protests, riots, civil disobedience showing the people involved and their behaviors; close-ups show facial and body language
6	Close-ups of locations where events are taking place; includes interiors and exteriors of buildings
6	Close-ups of crime scenes and surrounding areas
5	Close-ups of citizens commenting about the events reported in the news
5	Close-ups of prisoners, refugees, homeless, showing their living conditions
4	Scenes of fighting by military and paramilitary forces
4	Scenes of activities by UN forces
4	Close-ups of natural and manmade disaster sites providing insight about the magnitude, consequences, and chances for recovery
3	Pictures related to a foreign country's art, entertainment, religion, and history
3	Vistas of economic conditions, trade practices; many graphics and charts
3	Views of public meetings, hearings showing participants and their interactions
2	Views of negotiation sessions showing participants and their interactions
2	Maps displaying precise locations of events and showing relations to other sites
2	Close-ups of weapons used by military and paramilitary forces and civilians
2	Pictures of elections abroad, from campaigning to voting to ballot counts
1	Views of scientific experiments and achievements; interviews with scientists

NOTE: $N = 1,147$ stories on ABC national news, March 1993–February 1994. Of these, 198 stories (1.7 percent) contained no visuals.

impossible it was to describe in words the scenes that they had witnessed. In a bow to the power of visuals as compared to words, the most horrible aspects of the story were deliberately concealed. For example, emaciated nude bodies were rarely shown in their entirety; gruesome injuries were blanked out. Similarly, during the Gulf and other wars, the military banned pictures—though not printed accounts—of body bags arriving at Dover Air Force Base to avoid inflaming the public. The pictures as such were innocuous because the content of the bags was invisible, but the schemas linked to the pictures were inflammatory. During the Vietnam War, public support for American involvement plummeted after nightly network newscasts began to feature bloody scenes of injuries, deaths, and destruction.

If the face is, indeed, the mirror of the soul, television viewers get an excellent chance to look into this mirror, often even better than people who witness situations in real time. Television magnifies a political candidate's facial expressions to the point where nuances that are not ordinarily noticed become prominent. Since people are trained to observe facial expressions for cues to a person's character and motivations, television provides them with an extraordinarily large audiovisual data base. Similarly, audiovisuals provide a chance to observe body language more accurately.

Some critics object to giving voters such cues, claiming that they are not the bases on which political leaders should be judged. They forget that body language reflects physical and mental states. Despite their rich meanings, facial and body views are not, and should not be, the sole basis for most judgments. Sound political appraisals require combinations of various types of evidence. However, as just discussed, visuals are particularly well suited for evoking related visual and nonvisual cues from memory so that they become available for decision-making. The schemas held in memory are linked in various clusters. Activation of one cluster then spreads to associated clusters within the schema network (Anderson 1983).

Picturing Abstract Concepts

Pictures can convey many of the abstract ideas like "power" or "democracy" or "change," which their detractors claim to be beyond their reach. Pictures can even convey nonexistence even though something that is absent, by definition, cannot be seen. Twinned with words, as is the case for audiovisuals, visuals can express the full range of human knowledge, experience, and emotion.

There are multiple techniques through which the picture aspects of audiovisuals can convey abstractions. The concept of change can be communicated through successive views of a scene or person, each noticeably different. For instance, showing a president's face at the start and finish of his term usually is graphic evidence that several years have passed and the strains of office have taken their toll. Flashbacks can reveal a person's likely ongoing thoughts while current action is shown on screen. A politician's facial expressions and body language can tell about her feelings, values, and reactions to situations. For greater clarity, facial expressions can be intercut with shots of events. Appropriate music can underscore the mood surrounding the event. The power of the pope can be conveyed audiovisually by showing that thousands of cheering people line the route of his motorcade or flock to his huge outdoor masses.

Intimacy or distance can be shown through variations in camera position that mirror the signification of closeness and distance in real life. Close-ups convey intimacy; wide-angle views convey distance. Moving toward a target indicates an increase in intimacy; moving away suggests distancing. Audiences are prone to like politicians better after a close-up view (Biocca 1991). When the eye of the camera looks up to a person, the picture suggests that the subject is a person of authority. Politicians' public relations staffs are fully aware of these nuances and stage visually covered events accordingly.

Nonhappenings can also be pictured. For example, to illustrate that a governor is absent from his job, one can show his empty desk chair in his office—or an empty chair at a meeting or the official residence without the pennant that indicates that the governor is there. An empty granary or an empty store shelf can depict the absence of food. Aided by pictures, the brain can interpret what is missing and observe or project the consequences. Computers can alter pictures so that one can show what might have happened under circumstances that never came to pass. For instance, computers can simulate how a plane should have landed; they can visually conjecture about how a crime might have been committed. They can even create unlikely scenarios, such as showing two politicians wrestling physically over a bill, rather than merely arguing verbally. Simulations are very useful in clarifying complex situations, but they should be clearly identified as composites or simulations. This does not always happen.

Symbolic artifacts are useful for conveying abstract concepts. Democracy, for example, can be symbolized by ballot boxes and visual evidence that there are choices among candidates and parties. Expensive housing, furnishings, and clothing, on one hand, and living conditions bereft of amenities, on the other, can symbolize wealth and poverty. Presenting these conditions next to each other highlights and dramatizes the contrasts. Scenes from a familiar past event, such as Martin Luther King Jr.'s "I Have a Dream" speech, resonate with civil rights efforts by American blacks in America's collective memory. A backdrop of international flags signifies that a situation has international importance.

PICTURES AS LANGUAGE

What about the argument that pictures do not carry commonly recognized explicit meanings? They are polyseminal, carrying diverse meanings for different audience members and under different conditions, so that accurate communication between message senders and receivers is never assured. As media scholar Joanne Morreale (1991, 191) points out, when discussing political films: "Pictures do not assert so much as suggest and their meaning remains ambiguous on some level. In the film there is more freedom to mislead than there is in the speech."

Nonetheless, the argument that pictures may derail communication accuracy is largely—though not entirely—spurious on two grounds.* First, as the Kuleshov effect predicts, the verbal text in audiovisuals, along with other context elements, sets limits to interpretation. Second, picture language deals in stereotypes that have become part of specific cultures and subcultures. Because the time available for individual stories is brief, television news producers must tell them with a limited vocabulary of familiar audiovisual clichés that the audience can process quickly. Given the rapid pace of words and pictures, the audience has no time for reflection, for careful searches for alternative meanings, or for close scrutiny of pictures to detect hidden cues. Assuming a modicum of attention by viewers, misinterpretation of the visuals should be a minor problem.

Videographers share ideas about the appropriate vocabulary and grammar for televised mass communication. They "decode, either intuitively or intellectually, the messages to be relayed . . . before producing them . . . knowing what a given spectator might conclude from a series of shots . . ." (Salvaggio 1980, 132). As discussed in chapter 2, the psychological literature on human perception and the cognitive processing literature confirm that most viewers readily understand the audiovisual language of television and extract shared meanings along with personalized interpretations. Even inexperienced viewers usually have adequate cultural stocks of assumptions, knowledge, and experiences to comprehend what most television news stories are trying to convey (Altheide 1985; Messaris 1994; Graber 1994b).

---

*Presentations like Oliver Stone's controversial film *JFK* and the *X-Files* are likely to become somewhat more believable when people "see" the evidence of conspiracies or government deception or when they "see" aliens. Naïve viewers who know little about history and fear unfamiliar situations may be particularly susceptible to the deceptive power of such films.

The fact that audiovisual language is stereotypical does not mean that similar stories convey completely identical information. Audiovisuals of presidential inauguration ceremonies, for example, while sharing major features, still provide unique information about the particular event. Scenes of student demonstrations, satellite launchings, and election campaigns have appeared thousands of times. Yet television viewers still notice new elements in successive televised versions of such events. When I content-analyzed 135 typical audiovisually conveyed themes from television news stories, more than half (59 percent) contained information that was new to some degree, rather than redundant with what had been presented previously. Viewers noticed this new information. Recall tests showed that 81 percent of the audiovisual scenes that contained new materials (compared to 35 percent that were redundant) were recalled by the majority of the audience (Graber 1991).

AROUSING EMOTIONS

False beliefs about the capacity of audiovisuals to carry serious information and to convey it clearly are not the only obstacles to giving them their due. There are also charges that audiovisuals jeopardize rational decision-making because of their greater propensity to arouse emotions. Rational choice modelers, who have become powerful voices in the social science community, argue that sound choices require using rational self-interest criteria. Choice elements that might interfere with these criteria are undesirable distractions. We have discussed the evidence that contravenes this argument in chapter 2 as well as pointing out that all modalities of message transmission, including purely verbal messages, also frequently arouse emotional reactions as well and tap into stored visual memories.

To recapitulate: there is a symbiotic relationship between feelings and cognitions. Emotional involvement therefore is essential to sound decision-making.* Furthermore, gut feelings are often crucial in decision-making because they compensate for insufficient objective data. This finding has been frequently misused to belittle the strengths of audiovisuals. Gut feelings—"intuitions" might be a better word—are

---

*In fact, it is quite difficult to determine the respective roles of cognitions and emotions in specific decisions because people often rationalize their emotions even as their reasoning often evokes emotional reactions (Eagly and Chaiken 1993).

labeled as inferior default options used only when cognition fails, and only when people lack the motivation or ability to assess messages cognitively (Petty and Cacioppo 1986a, 1986b). The same critics who condemn televised political messages for introducing emotional elements into judgments often blame the medium for turning viewers into passive, uncaring couch potatoes. Can passions be simultaneously aroused and suppressed? This apparent inconsistency raises further questions about the soundness of the critics' judgments.

Many questions about the arousal potential of audiovisuals remain unanswered. It is still unclear whether emotional pictures are universally arousing, whether arousal is issue specific and which issues are most incendiary, and how the intensity of the arousal may vary, depending on the perceiver and even the circumstances when perception takes place. Not all content that most observers might label as emotion-arousing is, indeed, arousing for everyone in the audience or even for the majority of viewers. For example, in experiments testing the impact of attractive, emotion-arousing versus unattractive animal pictures on people's reactions to a fund-raising appeal for an animal welfare agency, the impact depended on the context. Responses were not automatically positive when the picture was emotionally appealing (Gunnthorsdottir 1995). Such pictures had the most impact on people already disposed toward protecting animals and knowledgeable about them. People who cared little about environmental issues were more likely to judge the request for funds based on cost-benefit calculations.

There has been much speculation about the impact that emotional footage actually has on public opinions and the spur that these opinions may provide for public policies. Audiovisuals have been accused of generating emotionally fueled public opinion pressures that push the government into unwise policies. The facts remain unclear because we still do not know whether there is, indeed, a "CNN effect." When CNN and other television news providers show emotional scenes of human suffering, the CNN effect reputedly leads to irresistible public demands for official relief missions. Some foreign policy scholars have argued that humanitarian interventions, such as troops sent to Somalia in the 1990s, were spurred by picture-driven public opinion pressures. Others contend that they were prompted by strategic considerations that had been set in motion prior to the public release of the pictures (Livingston and Eachus 1995).

While critics of television have stressed the likely negative consequences of an emotionally aroused public opinion, substantial positive effects of emotional footage have been slighted. Television broadcasts that arouse the audience's emotions tend to increase citizen interest in government and may spur increased participation in civic pursuits. Both are considered positive developments (Graber 1990; Sniderman et al. 1991). One may also wonder whether it is really bad to make decisions guided by emotions, rather than rationality, when the concept of rationality is generally depicted as taking a self-interested stance based on maximizing one's own material welfare. Would this really be a better political world without a sense of love, caring, fear, shame, and all the other qualities that temper cold-blooded calculations?

Numerous researchers (e.g., Sears 1993) have pointed to occasions when emotion-driven altruistic predispositions have overridden self-interest in the decision calculus. For example, images of disasters bring outpourings of donations from the public. Americans routinely respond to pictures of starving people in all parts of the world, the brutality of civil and international wars, and damage caused by natural disasters. Responses come in the form of money, supplies, and donated time. They skyrocket when a disaster story is featured on the front pages of newspapers and is pictured on television. Some of these actions may turn out to be ill considered. But in the words of television critic Walter Goodman (1992): "Can anyone help wishing that cameras had brought pictures of German concentration camps into American homes 50 years ago?"

Nonetheless, if citizens know that their material stakes are very high in a particular decision, it is not likely that emotions will short-circuit self-centered, dispassionate calculations unless there are powerful rationalizations or religious commands that overcome the materialistic considerations. Similarly, when politicians attempt to tug at the audience's heartstrings by stressing their caring, particularly for children and the elderly, this does not automatically supplant the language of public policy with the language of relationships (Jamieson and Campbell 1988). Even when assessments based on human relationships become powerful, judging politicians by their display of qualities of human caring is a worthy criterion that traditionally has played an important part in American politics.

There is a more serious problem, however. Research by Shanto Iyengar and Donald Kinder (1987) shows that when journalists frame news stories around emotion-arousing experiences of particular individuals or groups, the stories create the impression that individual rather than societal concerns are at stake. The public is then likely to assess the plight of the single small farmer shown on television who has been displaced by agro-business as a personal tragedy, rather than considering the larger issue of small-scale versus corporate farming and its implications for public policy. Such episodic judgments are, indeed, common and may deflect public attention from major societal problems. The root of the problem, however, does not lie in the audiovisual footage. Rather, it lies in journalists' failure to embed their stories into appropriate contexts.

LYING WITH PICTURES

Among the charges leveled against audiovisuals, none is more serious than the claim that they lend themselves readily to unintended or deliberate deception and that this has been a major danger and abuse in politics, especially during election campaigns. Audiovisual presentations of politics therefore stand accused of debasing it.

Critics charge that audiovisuals lend themselves readily to skewing reality through their content and structure or through the juxtaposition of unrelated pictures, often from diverse times and places, to create a false sense that the concepts that they present are linked (Jamieson and Campbell 1992; Jamieson 1992; Morreale 1991). While we are focusing here on charges leveled against audiovisual message transmissions, it should be kept in mind that speeches and print news, unaccompanied by pictures, are equally and possibly better suited for creating false associations. Politicians and journalists can and have used a multiplicity of communication modalities to concoct deceptive narratives that suit their political purposes. But even when the verbal or written message expresses the same or similar ideas, critics condemn the audiovisuals more harshly, claiming that they heighten and prolong the impact and are apt to raise the emotional pitch. This is probably correct but counterbalanced by the fact that lying with words is more common than lying with audiovisuals because it is more difficult to produce deceptive visuals than to lie with words.

Among common deceptions attributed to television's picture language is the claim that it deliberately or unintentionally creates a false sense of empowerment. Roderick Hart, in *Seducing America* (1994), contends that enabling average Americans to bring images of the world into their living rooms misleads them into believing that they are powerful when, in reality, they are powerless. The illusion of power lures them into becoming merely passive observers. Ultimately, such illusory beliefs about the public's power lead to disenchantment and cynicism

(Hart 1994). Similarly, Neil Postman (1984) charges that television makes viewers overconfident about their ability to judge political events. When they see situations unfolding on television, they are tempted to feel that they have "seen for themselves" what is happening, so that they can judge the merits. Unfortunately, like the prisoners in Plato's cave, they may have seen only the shadows of events, and distorted shadows at that (Dayan and Katz 1992; Larson and Park 1993). Undetected distortions can become dangerous when they lead to wrong collective opinions and actions.

What Hart and Postman deem negative Joshua Meyrowitz (1985) views in a more positive light. He argues that television blurs the private and public spheres and breaks down social barriers—at least in the mind's eye—by allowing everyone into the inner temple. There is something very leveling about watching Dan Rather or Ted Koppel interrogating a major political leader as if he or she were a truant child. Meyrowitz (1985, 1994) believes this is good because world leaders, seen close up, warts and all, become, as was said of President Harry Truman, the "average man, writ large." The focus on personal appearances, body language, and indices of emotions demystifies leaders and empowers their followers to view them more critically and to form their own opinions about public policies, rather than relying on the guidance of "experts." Television thus becomes a great equalizer. It permits ordinary people to not only know about places and events beyond direct observation, but also to vicariously experience these places and events. Public spaces are transported into their living rooms, obliterating barriers of distance, time, and social standing.

Hart (1987), on the other hand, finds it objectionable that close-up views of leaders' behavior may produce an ideology of equality and a disappearance of social distance because they destroy the majesty and mystery of government. Banal people and banal actions cannot inspire people. In a world of personal politics, personal foibles become unduly important, especially when they are dramatized by the media. It is an anti-utopian world without heroes. The public knows enough to become disillusioned but not enough to empathize and understand. Similar arguments, pro and con, blossomed forth in abundance during the microscopic media analysis of President Clinton's conduct in the Lewinsky sex scandal, which culminated in a vote to impeach the president in the House of Representatives in 1998.

Critics also complain that the use of audiovisuals in news stories is apt to turn them into melodramas that obscure the story's significance. In hijackings and hostage crises, for example, the visual focus is always on the human tragedy, including the direct victims themselves, as well as members of their families and even their friends and neighbors, rather than on the politics of the situation (Hallin 1986). When the camera zooms in on a small group of protesters in a large, supportive crowd, the extent of protest often becomes vastly exaggerated. Campaign hoopla stories tend to distort the size of crowds and misrepresent their mood by selectively focusing on the most enthusiastic or the most hostile groups without adequate explanatory comments. The use of audiovisuals to generate drama seems to be generic to the modality. Obviously, it is not an exclusively American phenomenon. In a book that analyzes media coverage of the assassination of Italian Prime Minister Aldo Moro in 1978, Erica Wagner-Pacifici (1986), for example, notes that most of the news stories she followed used melodramatic techniques.

The fact that dramatic pictures are likely to be repeated over and over again enhances their potency because repetition deepens the memory traces. Most Americans remember the haunting pictures of black motorist Rodney King's beating by white police or murder suspect O. J. Simpson's legal triumph when courtroom scenes showed that the alleged killer's glove did not fit his hand. When dramatic footage, like urban riot scenes, is shown over and over again, it enters collective memory much faster and more indelibly than most verbal accounts. If the scenes are distorted through overemphasis or lack of appropriate contextual information, events can become permanently misconstrued in the minds of many citizens.

The fact that audiovisuals excel in creating a sense of reality obviously has enticed expert communicators to use them to make distorted realities believable. Again, it is a case of unfairly blaming the messenger when the message and its sender are the problem. Politicians often misuse pictures to provide "visual proof" for claims that might be difficult to substantiate. Through montage rather than logical arguments, candidates link themselves to cherished American values, such as work, family, the flag, and patriotism. Old footage of war scenes abroad with voice-over by the politician may be used to "prove" that he or she was brave and patriotic by serving in a foreign war when, in fact, service was at home behind a desk. Conversely, negative associations have often been designed to harm political enemies. Featuring a politician's image or policies against the background of decaying neighborhoods or desolate farmlands presumably ties the negative emotions connected to these scenes to the politician's persona and policies. New digital videotape technology now enables journalists to entirely fabricate events or present them in versions that diverge widely from the actual happening (Tomlinson 1993; Kaid 1998).

Senator Paul Wellstone (D–Minn.) was particularly adept in winning support for his 1990 congressional campaign through clever pictorial symbols. For example, Wellstone suggested through story formats, pacing, and pictures in his commercials that he was a plain man who would respond quickly and efficiently to challenges (Nelson and Boynton 1997). One commercial showed him racing from one campaign event to another at a ridiculous pace, with the scene shifting with every spoken phrase. His mouth moved even faster than the sound track. The visuals also implied that most politicians use ads to mislead the public but that Wellstone can be trusted because he ridicules conventional behavior. Old-style film clips, like the Keystone Cops, were shown in order to associate Wellstone with tried and true values. Since such claims were not made explicitly, it was difficult to refute them. Wellstone also used color symbolism. One of his icons was a green and white bus, evoking ties to the environmental movement through a shared color scheme. The bus as such linked the candidate to children, to teaching, and to the future. Repeated use of such visual symbolism, the campaign designers hoped, would link the candidate with the audience's positively evaluated schemas.

As discussed in chapter 2, music unobtrusively heightens the effects of other audiovisual elements. Just as people may be unaware of many of the visual symbols that arouse their feelings and thoughts, so they are often unaware of background music and how it taps into their memories and evokes images and emotions. Sometimes the music or other background sounds become the main message, conveying feelings of horror or peacefulness or joy or sadness (Perris 1986). The sounds of country and western music may suggest old-fashioned small-town values, while the national anthem and other patriotic songs may stir strong feelings of patriotism. Sacred music may suggest religious ties.

Even the overall style of a message can influence how it is perceived. In the process, it may lead viewers to the wrong conclusions. If a televised scenario is structured like a news item or an investigative report, viewers may assume that it meets journalistic standards of accuracy. If it is structured like a fairytale, they will discount accuracy and expect some fanciful message that deserves to be discounted. If black-and-white film is interspersed with natural colors, the black-and-white scenes are often grainy or blurred. This may denote negative situations, like bankrupt factories or farms, or old-fashioned events, like barbershop quartets or country fairs. Inside a documentary, the use of black-and-white still photographs suggests authenticity and dipping into a historical past. Camera positions or the positions of the photographed subjects carry widely shared connotations that can be abused. For example, pictures of children gazing upward can conjure up visions of innocence and a promising future when the purposes of the message are sinister.

THE INHERENT DISTORTIONS OF NEWS PRODUCTION

Many of the message distortions blamed on the audiovisual modality spring from the characteristics of news production—print as well as audiovisual—rather than from deliberate manipulation by message framers. Even when journalists strive to be accurate and truthful, the use of visual imagery "unavoidably alters the spatial and temporal dimensions of reality, creating mediated versions of people, places and events that are fundamentally different from unmediated experience" (Griffin 1992, 127; see also Philo 1990; Donsbach et al. 1993). The classic study to demonstrate the distortions that come from normal television news-editing practices was carried out by Gladys Lang and Kurt Lang (1953). They stationed observers along the parade route traveled by General Douglas MacArthur in 1951 during ceremonies honoring him in Chicago. The observers noted fairly small crowds and limited enthusiasm for the general, who had recently been relieved of his duties by President Truman. By contrast, the television version, relying on selected visuals and supporting commentary, suggested that the event was a triumphal march. Each of the pictures was accurate; yet the story as a whole was not. The distortion was not testimony to the flaws of the medium. Rather, it was due to the necessity of condensing events for news coverage coupled with journalism norms that mandate making news stories as engaging as possible. Other distortions spring from people's posing for the camera when they become aware of being filmed. That almost invariably changes their body language and often their entire behavior (Kepplinger 1991).

If "telling the truth" means that television messages should be exact replicas of the reality that surrounds humans, then television, even if it is three-dimensional and filmed live, can never fully tell the truth. Watching two-dimensional pictures, or even seemingly three-dimensional pictures, on a screen is not identical to the visual experiences of real life (Messaris 1994). Virtual experiences, no matter how realistic, remain vicarious. Despite the best efforts of journalists, they can never produce totally neutral and "truthful" visuals.

Pictures concentrate on a limited array of perspectives. Camera operators choose angles and distances that may be quite different from the angles and distances that viewers might select if they were at the scene. When close-ups depict people outside the closest family circles, they convey a sense of intimacy with strangers that is lacking in real life. Voice-overs, which permit running commentary, are deceptive because they suggest that the voice is occurring simultaneously with the event on the screen—which it is not. Overall, broadcasts are a seamless depiction of reporters, their subjects, voice-overs, and real talk that seems realistic though it is entirely constructed and therefore quite unnatural. At times, reporters deliberately abandon efforts to be neutral so that they can reflect a viewpoint that indicates how something looks from a particular person's perspective. Reporters may think that these types of slants are obvious even when this is not the case.

It must also be remembered that news stories are not intended to be full accounts of all of the details of the situations they describe. Rather, reporters try to capture the essence of events, or of some of their aspects, and report the story in comprehensible language that relates to the experiences of their audiences. Replicating the exact scene in all its details is less important than conveying what the reporter perceives to be its meaning. Building "brief, exciting, unified, and complete" news narratives from bits and pieces of sound and picture may represent a form of cultural production whose relationship to the "reality of everyday events is, at best, far removed" (Griffin 1992, 124–25). This is why mediated versions of an event so often have a different flavor than the original. As is done in caricatures, they try to highlight a limited number of characteristic features of the person or situation—which unavoidably exaggerates whatever is chosen.

Reality is also skewed because most news stories are constructed by stringing together nonsequential vignettes. Selecting the scenes to be used for a television story, for example, and the sequence in which they will be shown—the framing of the story—is always a deliberate choice. Whatever activity or situation is depicted or verbally discussed immediately before or after a politician is shown is apt to become linked with her or him in the minds of the audience regardless of the motifs of the journalists. New technologies are making it easier for irresponsible television journalists to deceive their audiences.

In television stories, the attractiveness of pictures becomes a major factor in deciding which aspects should be featured. To capture audience attention, reporters focus on eye-catching aspects and shun tedious details. Again, it must be emphasized that shaping stories to rivet attention on their most interesting aspects is also an ever-present feature of print news stories. In fact, this impossibility to reflect everything is not even limited to reproductions of reality—it also plagues unmediated perceptions. Human information-processing limitations forever condemn humans to a limited view of their universe.

Nonetheless, if journalism norms required that accuracy take precedence over considerations of story appeal, many distortions could be avoided or minimized. It often is entirely possible to produce attractive stories that create accurate impressions and avoid melodrama and excessive attention to eye-catching sex and violence. Journalists have moved in the direction of quality programming on numerous occasions. But there are also many instances where strictly conveying reality would produce dull news that most audiences would ignore. Presented with the choice of more Puritan standards versus greater story mass appeal, mass appeal usually wins out.

The strong worries voiced by critics that misleading audiovisuals will distort the public's knowledge about policies run counter to most of the evidence about long-term media effects. As discussed in chapter 2, most viewers correct many of the deficiencies of visual images almost automatically. When sketches omit details of persons and objects or when sizes do not correspond to their real-world counterparts, whether vastly enlarged or miniaturized, even inexperienced viewers can readily compensate for such discrepancies. Picture perception resembles real-life visual processing. The brain first assembles an overview of a scene, identifies its general category, and then fills in details of color, shadings, and the like. It is a short step from this natural procedure to drawing on memory to supply missing details of a picture or correct flawed perceptions (Messaris 1994).

Similarly, viewers generally reject pictures as accurate representations of reality if their memories tell them otherwise. A politician shown in front of his humble childhood home is not automatically regarded as a man of the people, and a leader accused of acting like Adolf Hitler is not automatically seen as evil when the image activates a host of other schemas associated with that politician. Conversely, it is unlikely that a hated politician will become beloved merely because he is shown against the backdrop of a simple farmhouse, the state capitol, or the flag or with pictures of his attractive grandchildren on a side table. Given the realities of schematic information-processing, it is preposterous to claim that people's perceptions are readily swayed by exposure to symbolism that contradicts their views. Most people, for most political stories, draw on a broad array of facts and long-standing feelings. They are not naïve and are generally quite skeptical, testing news stories against their own experiences and beliefs and rejecting them if they have doubts about them (Lupia and McCubbins 1998).

The idea that people automatically respond to a media stimulus in predetermined fashion goes back to the discredited early stimulus response theories based on a hypodermic model (Bineham 1988). This model is based on the assumption that the meaning of a message is clearly imprinted in it, exactly as intended by the creator, and that the imprint will be incorporated into the receiver's memory. The model ignores the fact that message meaning also depends on how the receiver interprets the message. If audiences have stored negative attitudes about a political figure, these are apt to prevail even when broadcasts link the individual to positive symbols.

People who rely heavily on television for learning political information are more likely to reflect television portrayals in their schemas about social and political relationships than is the case for light viewers. Scholars at the Annenberg School for Communication have monitored the impact of television violence in entertainment programming on adult viewers for several decades, starting in 1967. They found that heavy television viewers—defined as viewing for four or more hours daily—tended to judge the incidence of crime and other real-world social and political phenomena based on the reality created by entertainment television, rather than on actual data (Gerbner et al. 1986). These findings are somewhat problematic because heavy television viewers may differ from the general public in a variety of ways. Their heightened fear of crime, for example, may be attributable, at least in part, to their social status. The heavy-viewer group included a preponderance of women, elderly people, and poor people, whose chance of victimization was greater than average (Fowles 1992).*

---

*Other scholars have claimed that the results reported by the Annenberg scholars spring from flaws in the research design or are side effects of priming that leads people to recall their most recent experiences first when questioned (Shrum and O'Guinn 1993).

If the subject of a news story is unfamiliar, there may be no counter-vailing stored schemas. In that case, misleading symbolisms or juxta-positions can be persuasive. The case of Ruby Clark, an African-American housewife, is in point (*Clark v. ABC,* 684 F.2d 1208 [6th Cir. 1982]). A jury awarded damages to Mrs. Clark because a picture show-ing her walking along a Detroit street was used in an *ABC News Close-Up* on prostitution. Shortly before her picture appeared, the narrator stated that most of the prostitutes in this area were black and that black women walking at night in this area were assumed by others to be pros-titutes. The narrator did not identify Mrs. Clark as a prostitute, but the jury believed that the juxtaposition of the video of an unfamiliar per-son and the text was likely to suggest to many viewers that she was a prostitute (Grimes 1990).

Although established cognitions neutralize many deceptions, studies of viewer reactions confirm that viewers are at times uncritical when viewing news broadcasts if they are not specifically alerted to watch for biases (Hacker et al. 1991). These problems can be lessened by teaching naïve audiences, especially children, the tricks of the trade of audio-visual persuasion. Besides learning how images can be cropped and framed and angled to produce certain effects, adult and preadult view-ers can learn how sequencing, contrasts, and symbols can be employed to manipulate their perceptions. Advocates of training in visual literacy have long made that point. Regrettably, their efforts to make visual lit-eracy training mandatory in schools have borne little fruit. However, program guides that help viewers interpret controversial broadcasts have become more common. On the Internet, access to diverse per-spectives on controversial issues is made easy through cross-reference links listed within programs or through regular Internet search engines (Barry 1997; Messaris 1998).

Aside from concerns about the deception potential of misleading broadcasts, especially during election campaigns, one must acknowl-edge that the vast majority of television messages, even during cam-paigns, are accurate and offer important substantive content. When films clips that show the beauty of life in the United States are inter-spersed with scenes of a current political event, fashionably cynical journalists often deride them as intentionally misleading cover-ups of the negative aspects of political life. That charge ignores the fact that public life in the United States, besides its regrettable aspects, has many positive aspects as well. Showing these aspects may serve as a healthy antidote to the prevalent journalistic caricatures of politics that depict it as a totally sordid, venal enterprise conducted by politicians to enrich themselves at the public's expense (Patterson 1993).

IMITATION EFFECTS

Because most people lack direct experiences with many of the social and political happenings in the larger society, serious concerns have arisen about the impact of socially undesirable information on young children and impressionable adolescents. When the story is told in audiovisuals, rather than only in words and print, youngsters can extract meaning from it long before their reasoning powers are mature. We know that young people are apt to accept the television messages—as they comprehend them—at face value whenever they lack established countervailing schemas (Flavell et al. 1990). Television's ability to guide youngsters' thinking has been demonstrated repeatedly in the laboratory, most often in experiments involving asocial behaviors. The results have led to worries about the consequences for children's socialization because television provides an ample audiovisual repertoire of misbehaviors that children might undertake when seemingly suitable opportunities arise and the youngsters are predisposed to the behavior (Huesmann and Eron 1986; Condry 1989).

Concern about adverse effects of audiovisuals on the public's thinking often obscures the fact that positive consequences are more likely. Television may rob some children of their innocence by revealing too much of the seamy side of life, and it may stifle their curiosity, so that their educational achievement scores plunge (Fowles 1992). Yet it is also a major source of learning, from *Sesame Street* nursery school lessons to space walks, scenes from foreign lands, and attendance at the most important public functions of their age presented on adult television programs. That story is told more fully in the next chapter.

Adults may also be tempted to copy behaviors they see on television. There is some evidence that viewing violence triggers violent thoughts already stored in memory. These may then trigger violent actions without much conscious thinking (Gollwitzer and Bargh 1996). For example, during inner-city riots in the United States in the 1960s, many people attributed riot participation to viewing such behavior on television. Viewers exposed to violence on television subsequently joined and imitated the demonstrated behavior. Similarly, television programs have been blamed for luring people into committing copycat crimes by showing them how to commit them (Hearold 1986).

Knowledge of information-processing makes it clear that the imitation effects attributed to audiovisual presentations can and do occur, but serious television-induced crimes are rare for most viewers, including children. How individuals interpret the images shown on television hinges on the entire stock of memories on which they draw for processing as well as on their personality traits. A child or adult whose schemas classify committing violence as bad is unlikely to imitate behaviors that carry strongly negative connotations. Viewing such behaviors is more likely to evoke revulsion and motivate actions designed to stop the violence. However, for susceptible individuals, the graphic presentation of details, in which audiovisuals excel, may well be a stronger stimulus for imitation than would purely verbal stories. Behaviors on the borderline of social acceptability, such as fighting and bullying among children, are among the most likely television-induced imitation problems.

QUALITY ISSUES

Efforts to overcome the prejudice against audiovisuals face their greatest obstacle from the undeniable fact that many television broadcasts are abysmal in content and format. As will be discussed in more detail in the next chapter, in many respects televised news has lived up to its worst publicity. The potential power of audiovisuals to convey significant meanings has remained underdeveloped and underused. Unlike movie producers who have mastered the art of creating virtual realities through audiovisuals, most journalists still tell their stories in words and use pictures merely as adjuncts to the words, as they were taught to do. The rich storytelling potential of audiovisuals is rarely exploited to its fullest.

As table 4.3 shows, when coders were asked to record their evaluations of contributions made by the pictures in 189 nonfeature television news stories, they concurred with only minor disagreement that only 29 percent of 2,002 visual scenes contained in the stories contributed entirely new information. An additional 10 percent of the pictures helped to identify people and places that might otherwise be unknown, and 6 percent added clarifications that made the story more readily comprehensible. A mere 4 percent of the pictures provided

Table 4.3   Picture Contributions to Verbal Themes in Routine Nonfeature
              News Stories (%)

Picture Contribution	ABC	CBS	NBC	PBS	All
Irrelevant information	21	33	41	40	32
Redundant information	30	15	10	15	19
New information	34	24	41	10	29
People or object identification	10	2	—	30	10
Clarification	3	13	5	5	6
Addition of emotional components	2	13	2	—	4

NOTE: N = 189 stories, 2,002 visual scenes (camera turns to new subject). ABC = 61
stories, CBS = 46 stories, NBC = 42 stories, PBS = 40 stories.

emotional content that was not readily apparent from the verbal text.
Thirty-two percent of the visual scenes added no information at all beyond what was verbally conveyed, while 19 percent merely reinforced
the text (Graber 1986). Stated in more positive terms, nearly a third of
the pictures were important, another third were useful, and almost a
third were a waste.*

The belief that audiovisuals are poor carriers of important political
information has become so ingrained in conventional wisdom that it
has throttled research. Most social scientists have ignored pictures in
their television content analyses, treating the messages as if they consisted only of verbal texts. In tests of what viewers learn from television
news, scholars have usually asked only for recall of the verbal message,
assuming that the visuals mirrored the verbal texts or conveyed no significant substantive information at all. Similarly, social scientists have
rarely used pictures as stimuli to test people's attitudes. Studies like those
of Nayda Terkildsen (1993), who measured racial attitudes through reactions to pictures, and the work of John Lanzetta and his colleagues
(1985), who measured reactions to various types of facial expressions,
remain the exception. Hence there is a dearth of evidence about learning attributable to audiovisuals that has lent further support to the
myth that audiovisual messages lack substance. The situation is roughly
parallel to what happened for media studies in general after Joseph
Klapper's study, *The Effects of Mass Communication* (1960), was interpreted as support for a "minimal effects" theory. Social scientists in
droves abandoned media research, fearing that they were wasting their
time by studying an inconsequential phenomenon. Minimal effects

*A later study yielded higher picture contribution scores. See pages 194–96.

Table 4.4   Real and Imagined Picture Contribution (%)

Picture Contribution	After Exposure to Audiovisuals	After Exposure to Audio without Visuals
Additions		
Reality	34	19
Clarification	16	14
Emotion	13	6
Information	11	9
Memory	3	5
Interest	—	11
Wallpaper		
Nothing	13	18
Substandard	5	3
Distraction	4	6
Duplication of schema	—	8
Variable/depends	—	1

NOTE: $N = 263$ responses for audiovisual group; 263 responses for audio-only group.

theories were ultimately disproven, and media studies are again attracting many social science researchers. But the same has not yet happened for studies of audiovisual information transmission.

Even audiences have accepted the myth. During one experiment, I exposed a group of twenty-four respondents to a series of televised news stories in full, while a matching group heard only the audio portion. In midstream, the treatment regime for the groups was reversed, so that the audio-only group became a full-exposure group and vice versa. When audio-only subjects were asked to imagine the visuals that they had failed to see and estimate what they might have contributed to the story, they attributed very little substantive content to them (table 4.4). But when these same subjects had seen a similar story with audiovisuals only minutes earlier, they reported a lot of substantive picture content. Obviously, descriptions of the imagined visuals matched their false stereotype that pictures are largely devoid of separate meanings even though they had described major visual contributions by audiovisual scenes they had viewed just minutes earlier (Graber 1993).

The low regard in which learning from audiovisuals is held (which is partly justified by poor quality) is also reflected in television viewing patterns. Video-surveillance studies reveal that viewers often combine television watching with other activities, such as eating, housework, childcare, and even newspaper reading. Such distractions lower attention to the television message and create the myth that audiovisuals are ill suited for conveying important political content (Basil 1994).

Audiences tend to describe television as primarily a medium of rapid, superficial surveillance of the environment—a headline service—or a medium of entertainment that does not warrant close attention or even undivided attention. By contrast, it has become customary to praise printed information in all of its many forms as the chief medium for transmitting serious information. The myth that television, by comparison, is an intellectual lightweight thus prejudices judgments about the merits of audiovisuals. This happens despite the public's preference for television watching and despite people's claim that television is their chief source of serious information, including political news.

THE BURDENS OF PAST NEGLECT

Unwillingness among intellectual elites to grant that current audiovisual capabilities are well suited for conveying political information has serious consequences. It perpetuates the myth that print media are the modality of choice for conveying political information, and it retards development of more effective political television offerings. Failure to take advantage of the public's preference for audiovisual fare by presenting excellent political programs has reduced public interest in political news, especially among younger generations. Most damaging is the failure to tell the fascinating stories of politics audiovisually, which harms preteen and teenage children during the years when they are most receptive to exploring new knowledge realms. Educationally impoverished adults throughout the world are also harmed. As mentioned, effective print literacy is not nearly as widespread as commonly assumed, even in societies with highly developed educational systems. This is where the capacity of audiovisuals to convey complex information shines, while print information sources have little to offer.

There is yet another reason for making the development of audiovisual message transmission a high priority. The audiovisual mass media currently make up the bulk of the world's common symbolic environment. When it comes to pictures, the language journalists use for stories is quite similar everywhere. As discussed, visuals are analogic in the sense that they show particular scenes exactly, whereas words must represent these images by arbitrary signs. For many phenomena, such as the thousands of hues of colors, words are entirely lacking or are unfamiliar to most people. But the pictures have universal meanings. The commonality of audiovisual message transmission holds promise that media with a worldwide reach, like CNN, can contribute to the homogenization of news throughout the world.

Creating a shared conception of reality in modern society is an essential element for mutual understanding. Many political situations defy the human imagination and require visual proof to be believed. The enormity of genocide in Cambodia, in Rwanda, or among the Kurds of Iraq was not evident to distant observers until pictures of piles of corpses or barely alive, skin-and-bones survivors were publicized. Even then, people found it hard to believe what they saw. But they shared these gruesome impressions and made them part of internationally shared collective memory. The fact that memories of the Holocaust remain vivid decades later for people throughout the globe proves how profound such impressions can be even when they are not regularly refreshed.

My plea for tailoring political information to the needs of nonliterate and functionally illiterate adult and child populations should not obscure the fact that the nonliterate cannot live well without acquiring literacy, or at least verbal fluency. The pictures that individuals store in their brains cannot be transmitted visually to the brains of others. Human thought transmission requires words; sketches are inadequate. To the extent that people lack language to express themselves, they cannot share their thoughts. Although it is feasible to store words in spoken form, there are still very great advantages to storing them through written symbols as records of the past and resources for future use.

THE FINAL SCORE

The capacity of audiovisual news to transmit political information accurately and effectively has been challenged on many grounds. This chapter presents and analyzes the major indictments. For the most part, it also refutes them, pointing out how they are contradicted by available evidence and how audiovisuals are unparalleled in their ability to illuminate unfamiliar situations. In many instances, the assumptions underlying the indictments fail to take into account the ways human brains process complex information. Where the charges are valid, the problem generally refers to television news production, rather than inherent characteristics of audiovisuals.

Television news production problems are shared to varying degrees by all modalities, including print news. However, they may be more serious when they occur in television news because of the potency of audiovisual formats. Concern about adverse effects of audiovisuals on the public's thinking often obscures the fact that positive consequences are more likely. While television may show children too much of the seamy side of life, it is also a major source of learning (Fowles 1992). Thanks to television, average Americans of all ages are far more worldly-wise than ever before. But wisdom has its dark side, along with its bright face.

The chapter also lays out some of the deleterious social and political consequences springing from the denigration of audiovisual news presentation. The most serious is the retardation of the development of more effective news presentations that would enrich the information environment of the world's illiterate and functionally illiterate millions.

While televised news is far better in many respects than its public image, it currently is far worse in actuality than it should be, given the technological resources that are now available. In the next two chapters, we will assess the qualities of current television content, emphasizing how it could be improved to become a more valuable resource in the United States and elsewhere.

5

THE BATTLES OVER
AUDIOVISUAL CONTENT

A BIRD'S-EYE VIEW OF TELEVISION

"This instrument [television] can teach, it can illustrate; yes, it can even inspire. But it can do so only to the extent that humans are determined to use it to those ends. Otherwise it is merely lights and wires in a box" (Kamalipour 1994). This comment, attributed to famed journalist Edward R. Murrow (and uttered in 1956), epitomizes the conclusions reached in this chapter. A close examination of the alleged major weaknesses of television content, as well as its claimed strengths, makes it clear that most of the valid complaints do not relate to the inherent nature of audiovisuals in general and television in particular as a medium of information transmission. Rather, they spring from sins of omission and commission in the use of the medium.

Television, as one critic points out, "is merely a blank canvas . . . on which an incredible variety of people get to paint" (Johnson 1998b). The cure for most of its political ills is therefore quite obvious and feasible—namely, allow responsible, civic-minded journalists to use the medium's audiovisual potential to paint as accurate and complete a picture of politics as is possible and curb the current abuses. The many highly praised, widely watched political programs that have been produced over the years are testimony to the medium's potential for intelligently and effectively mirroring the ever-changing political world. They also demonstrate that television appraisals require a full palette of colors. A paintbrush saturated in black ink will produce little more than caricatures.

Our discussion in this chapter will encompass the entire panoply of politically informative programs through which average Americans learn about politics. Besides over-the-air and cable television news, that panoply includes full-blown documentaries, mini-documentaries, and news magazine broadcasts. It also includes numerous entertainment programs that deal with basic political concepts and values, such as freedom of speech, submission to authority, and tolerance of fellow citizens who belong to different subcultures (Delli Carpini and Williams 1994a, 1994b). Studies of the political information supply that ignore the full range of media are seriously flawed because average Americans are far more likely to witness discussions of political issues when viewing non-news rather than news shows during their many hours of daily television viewing. Women, it seems, actually prefer to get political information from entertainment programming, while men prefer news formats (Jensen 1995).

SOME CAVEATS ABOUT TELEVISION IMPACT ON VIEWERS

The basic complaint about television broadcasts, leveled most strongly against news programs, is that the content is unsatisfactory and that it harms various publics socially and politically. Before detailing the specific allegations, the limitations on impact predictions that were briefly outlined in chapter 4 need to be explained more fully in order to put the complaints about television content into a realistic perspective. Media impact tends to be misunderstood and often exaggerated because hypodermic theories remain rampant. According to these discredited theories, people exposed to messages adopt and interpret them exactly as presented, akin to medical patients who are treated with a disease-specific vaccine.

If one can provide evidence, for example, that a viewer's behavior resembles a scenario shown on television, hypodermic theories predict a single cause-and-effect sequence—namely, that the show motivated the behavior and is likely to motivate similar behavior in other viewers. Such an interpretation ignores the fact that multiple cause-and-effect sequences are far more likely because various audience members filter messages through their particular prisms of information and experiences. The viewer who allegedly imitated a behavior, such as driving his car at excessive speeds, may, indeed, have learned this behavior from the broadcast. But he or she may already have been disinclined to obey speed limit regulations prior to seeing drivers do so on television. The broadcast may have been an added incentive, or it may not have been a factor at all in subsequent unlawful behavior.

Most speculations about the effect of particular television offerings also ignore the fact that the impact of the same story may vary for different viewers or even for the same individuals under different circumstances. Moods matter, as do recently experienced events. "[T]he influence of television and the role it plays in our lives depends as much on how we watch as on what we watch. It is possible to watch the same television stimulus in radically different ways, and to get different things out of it" (Condry 1989, 49).

For example, when thirty participants in an experiment were asked through a Q-sort procedure about their interpretations of an episode of the television program *Law and Order,* they interpreted the program in four different ways.* The episode depicted a racial incident that occurred in the Crown Heights section of Brooklyn in 1991. One group thought that the key message of the broadcast was that a narrow focus on justice for individuals may conflict with the best interests of the community. There was disagreement about whether this was good or bad because group members could not agree about whether individual or community welfare deserved priority. A second group thought that the episode focused primarily on the behaviors of various individuals involved in the situation. Again, the group members disagreed about which individuals had acted appropriately or inappropriately, as shown in the broadcast. The third group thought that the broadcast highlighted the issue of individual responsibility and various inadequacies of the criminal justice system, while the fourth group interpreted the episode as illustrating race tensions and group hysteria.

Obviously, the way the story had been framed in the broadcast limited the range of possible interpretations. Nonetheless, it left enough leeway to permit multiple judgments about what the key issue was in the broadcast. It also left room for different conclusions about what constituted justice and fairness in the situation (Carlson and Trichtinger 1997).

Even the physical setting in which exposure to stories takes place, including the people present at the time, can affect a story's impact. Messages are interpreted differently when they are received in a living room setting as compared to a workplace or school or when they are watched in a group setting or alone. Furthermore, viewers vary widely in their sensitivity to the many latent cues through which television conveys many meanings. For instance, a politician may be shown in a full-screen facial close-up to indicate her importance, or she may be photographed

---

*In a Q-sort, subjects rank order statements about an issue or a person to indicate how well the statements reflect the subject's views. Factor analysis then reveals the principles underlying each subject's pattern of preferences.

against the background of family pictures to indicate her love of family values. Such symbolism, which supplements the message's manifest content, is often overlooked or construed in disparate ways.

The impact of most stories is fleeting for the vast majority of viewers unless these stories become medialities—uniquely memorable events that leave an exceptionally large mark because they are featured prominently over and over again in nearly identical versions. A good example of a mediality is the Chappaquiddick incident in which a young woman on Senator Edward Kennedy's staff drowned under circumstances that cast suspicions on the senator's conduct. Repeated broadcasts of that story over a multiyear period kept the public's memories of the incident alive and doomed Kennedy's chances for the presidency. When prominent political or entertainment figures die in spectacular accidents or contract dreaded diseases, publicity about the situations tends to ignite the public's concerns quickly and massively, with lasting effects. When less prominent people are involved, if there is any impact at all, it is apt to be much milder and briefer.

The practice of focusing research on the impact of single stories, rather than on the collective impact of multiple stories over time, has also led to misjudgments about media effects (Jensen 1995). While the threshold for arousing the audience's attention is rarely reached with single stories that appear during a brief span of time and then disappear, it may be reached if there are multiple stories on the same theme, such as corruption in the legislature or incidents of medical malpractice. For example, triggering changes in the consumer index, which records the public's confidence in the economy, usually requires repeated "bad economy" stories. Even multiple "bad economy" stories may lack punch when contemporaneous "good economy" or other "good news" stories serve as a counterweight.

Stories may prime the thinking processes, so that subsequent stories will be interpreted in line with the thrust of the priming story, as discussed in chapter 2. The earlier story may also serve as an interpretive frame that accentuates some aspects of a perceived reality in ways that promote a particular problem definition, causal interpretation, moral evaluation, and/or treatment recommendation (Entman 1993). The framing phenomenon goes beyond the impact of particular priming stories. All images that people accumulate and store throughout their lifetime and then bring to bear on incoming information become part of the interpretive frame for that information. The real significance of particular stories for audience members becomes apparent only when one looks at them within the large body of experienced and mediated news in which particular groups of people have been immersed over long periods of time. That large body includes the collective memories of various communities, which are usually taken for granted by the modern storytellers who produce televised news. These mental supplements, which storytellers anticipate, are just as much a part of the audiovisual texts as what is actually presented, assuming that the storytellers judged their audience correctly.

Though it is usually difficult to link people's images with any particular televised presentation, the fact remains that television does provide powerful stimuli that add to and alter the images already stored in memory. The cultivation studies undertaken by George Gerbner and his associates (1982) provide ample evidence that people's perceptions of many aspects of political reality have been shaped by television images. Polling evidence likewise confirms that long-time exposure to various types of television programs influences the viewers' attitudes and values (Page and Shapiro 1992). However, the occurrence, degree, and duration of change depend on the nature of the issues involved, the framing of the media stories, and the viewers' personal and collective predispositions as well as on the historical forces at work at a particular time.

MAJOR PROBLEMS WITH CURRENT TELEVISION OFFERINGS

Keeping these caveats in mind, what are the particulars in the bill of indictment of current television fare? We shall focus on five major charges to which we have not yet paid attention. We have already discussed the complaints about numerous content flaws, such as deception and excessive emotional stimulation as they relate to the characteristics of the audiovisuals. And we reserve discussion of user-hostile attributes for the next chapter. Here are the five charges, briefly stated:

1. Television programs fail to cover content that audiences feel they want and need.
2. Television programs fail to educate the public about the real nature of politics. Even when stories address important issues, they often dwell on inconsequential dramatic aspects and sensationalize them to attract a large audience. Consequently, television routinely caricatures the political world.
3. When television features entertainment, it is usually lowbrow, "cheap" fare, rather than high- or middlebrow. This deprives

the audience of the type of entertainment that nourishes the spirit and the imagination.

4. Television programs pay excessive attention to violent behaviors, socially risky behaviors, and illicit activities. Such programs inspire asocial, often criminal, behaviors.

5. Television watching, irrespective of program content, displaces other worthwhile endeavors, such as reading, work on community projects, and vigorous recreational activities, like playing, that stimulate the imagination. In fact, the couch potato syndrome spawned by lengthy television sessions is a major cause of the epidemic of physical obesity and intellectual sluggishness among Americans at the turn of the twenty-first century.

Let's examine these complaints against the backdrop of the economic and legal environment in which television operates in the United States. American over-the-air television is largely supported by fees that advertisers pay to reach peak numbers of potential customers for their services. To keep numbers large, most over-the-air television programs have been geared to nationwide audiences. That requires featuring programs that can keep the attention of widely diverse groups that include many people of limited education and interests. The formula developed by the television industry to attract such heterogeneous audiences emphasizes the human-interest aspects of stories, such as conflict and violence, love and sex, and triumph and tragedy. This audience-catching formula, which has been used throughout history by literary giants like William Shakespeare and the writers of Greek tragedies, remains highly successful because it resonates with basic human needs and desires. The spread of cable television and other new subscriber-paid technologies has removed some of the strictures created by mass-market concerns because it has made narrowcasting geared to various intellectual and interest levels feasible and common. Still, the stories cast in dramatic human-interest formats prevail because most audiences flock to them.

Now to the first major complaint.

1. Television programs fail to cover content that audiences feel they want and need.

What are the facts? Evidence abounds that the vast majority of Americans like much of current television programming and find it beneficial. How else can one explain why average Americans spend a huge chunk of their leisure time with it and why they tell pollsters that

Table 5.1   Satisfaction with Television Programming, 1998 (1994) (%)

Question: Generally, how satisfied are you with the choice of things you can see on television these days? Are you very satisfied, fairly satisfied, not too satisfied, not at all satisfied? And how satisfied are you with the choice of *news* programs available to you on television these days? Are you very satisfied, fairly satisfied, not too satisfied, not at all satisfied?

Satisfaction Level	All Television Programs	Television News Programs
Very satisfied	16 (14)	35 (43)
Fairly satisfied	45 (43)	50 (43)
Not too satisfied	28 (29)	9 (7)
Not at all satisfied	10 (11)	4 (4)
Other: don't know, etc.	1 (3)	2 (3)

NOTE: Data for 1998 from surveys conducted by the Pew Research Center for the People and the Press 24 April–11 May 1998. 1994 data in parentheses are from surveys conducted by the Pew Research Center in February 1994.

they like most programs? During a typical year, American adults who are eighteen years of age or older average twenty-eight hours and twenty minutes of weekly television viewing (*Public Perspective* 1995). These figures have remained constant in the 1990s, except for a moderate dip for a fraction (24 percent) of the small group of viewers who are spending substantial time surfing the Internet (Pew 1998d). Television viewing occupies roughly 40 percent of the average person's leisure time, often at the expense of other activities, including socializing and sleeping.

Table 5.1 shows that a majority of viewers (61 percent) claim to be Very Satisfied or Fairly Satisfied with television offerings in general, and overwhelmingly (85 percent) satisfied with news offerings.* Similarly, when asked, "How good of a job does the evening news do in summing up the events of the day?" 18 percent of the respondents in a 1998 nationwide poll gave it an Excellent rating, and 50 percent called it Good, while 21 percent said it was Only Fair and 4 percent labeled it Poor. Seven percent gave no ratings (Pew 1998d). A follow-up poll in the late spring of 2000 that measured satisfaction only of frequent viewers showed slightly lower satisfaction ratings overall (Pew 2000b).

Why is television so popular? In chapter 2, we explained its popularity in terms of its reliance on audiovisual messages, which are well suited to human information-processing capabilities. But there are also

---

*Satisfaction levels with general programming have risen four percentage points since 1994, while dropping one percentage point for news programming, when Very Satisfied and Fairly Satisfied ratings are combined.

many environmental factors, including the fact that it is readily available in nearly all homes and requires almost no effort and skill to operate. Even two-year-olds can learn to switch on the power and press the buttons to change channels. Though detractors would like to argue that ease of operation is its chief attraction, that is obviously not the case. Roderick Hart (1994) calls television a "seductive" medium, with sights and sounds and messages that intrigue and fascinate viewers. In the pretelevision and pre-modern-radio era, people who wanted news or entertainment had to seek it largely outside the home. They often joined organizations simply for companionship, rather than for their lofty purposes. Now the information/entertainment center is largely in the home, where many more people can enjoy it.

Surveys show that most Americans claim to derive more pleasure from television than from sex, food, hobbies, religion, money, or sports (Kubey and Csikszentmihalyi 1990). When people are asked to designate the mass medium that they would miss the least, television is rarely mentioned (Winick 1988). When given the option to take only one information source with them while stranded on an imaginary mid-ocean island, television is the medium of choice, although college students prefer their audiovisuals via a computer. When audiences have to miss television, they find it painful. For example, media scholar Charles Winick contacted 680 households comprising 1,614 people whose television sets were broken (81 percent) or stolen (19 percent) and who were without television for an average of six weeks. Based on extensive interviews, he found that in 24 percent of the households, family members had experienced mourninglike reactions, 39 percent of the families reported anxiety syndromes, and 29 percent noted moderate psychological discomfort symptoms. Only 8 percent reported suffering little distress (reported in Fowles 1992).

2. Television programs fail to educate the public about the real nature of politics. Even when stories address important issues, they often dwell on inconsequential dramatic aspects and sensationalize them to attract a large audience. Consequently, television routinely caricatures the political world.

Given television's heavy focus on entertainment, it should come as no surprise that observers who want television to be primarily a medium for civic education share the views of former Federal Communication Commissioner Newton Minow that television is "a vast wasteland." By 1995, Minow called television fare "toxic," explaining that "[i]n 1961, when I called television 'a vast wasteland,' I was thinking of

an endless emptiness, a fallow field waiting to be cultivated and enriched. I never dreamed we would fill it with toxic waste" (Minow and
LaMay 1995, 7). Minow particularized his complaint in his famous
1961 speech by saying: "You will see a procession of game shows, violence, audience participation shows, formula comedies about totally
unbelievable families, blood and thunder, mayhem, violence, sadism,
murder, western bad men, western good men, private eyes, gangsters,
more violence, and cartoons" (Minow 1964, 52).

Minow's scathing accusation notwithstanding, television does devote substantial slices of time to informative stories about important
happenings in the viewers' world. The point becomes quite evident
when one searches the content of television news broadcasts for stories
that deal with significant domestic and foreign politically relevant issues. The data presented in table 5.2, recorded in minutes and seconds,
were drawn from early evening national newscasts on ABC, CBS, CNN,
and NBC during the November 1997 through May 1998 period. They
represent one constructed week—which means that successive weekdays were analyzed for successive months—on assorted "free" channels. (Comparablé data about late evening local broadcasts—the most
widely watched news source—are presented in the next chapter.)

Over the course of the week, viewers would be exposed to roughly
forty-three minutes of foreign news; thirty-two minutes of general domestic stories; thirty minutes of news dealing with social issues, including health; twenty-four minutes of news about the environment,
including the weather; and sixteen minutes of economic news. A viewer
who watched the nightly thirty-minute over-the-air network newscasts
six days per week and a sixty-minute CNN newscast once a week would
get a serious political lesson lasting two hours and twenty-four minutes.
That is almost equivalent to the weekly classroom time of a student en-
rolled in a political science college course, except that the viewers'
"course" meets year-round and the information is far more concentrated on factual data. More important than these differences is the
fact that the viewers' course lacks supplementary readings and an important incentive for learning—namely, exams and a final grade.

Table 5.3 shows how many hours of politically relevant programming in a variety of formats is available around the clock in a typical
week in a major metropolitan area (Chicago) on over-the-air and cable
television. Sixteen over-the-air and thirty-nine cable stations were
monitored between April and July 1998 in a randomly constructed
week pattern. The data, separated into cable and over-the-air channels,
are reported under three category headings. The News category includes

Table 5.2 Politically Informative Segments on Typical Nightly National Newscasts, 1997–98

Data/Source	General Domestic	Economic	Social	Environmental	Foreign	Daily Total
Sunday CBS	Employment 2:50	Stock market 0:20	Births 4:20	Historic sites 2:00	Iraq; Japan; South Africa 8:30	17:40
Monday NBC	Major crimes 6:40	Stock market 0:20	Flu; cancer 5:20	Storm damage 6:30		18:50
Tuesday ABC	Navy personnel 2:10	TV show buys; stocks 2:20	Aging; women 5:00	Winter 0:30	UN/Iraq; Italy; Russia 4:40	14:40
Wednesday CBS	White House problems; crime 5:40	New cars; stocks 3:00		El Niño harm 3:20	U.S./Iraq; Italy; Indonesia 4:40	16:40
Thursday CNN (60 min.)	White House problems; campaign funds 11:50	Stock market 0:10	Hepatitis; women 3:30	Lunar ice; weather; floods 5:20	Yugoslavian strife; UN/Iraq; Russia; NATO; China; Europe 17:10	38:00
Friday NBC	V.P. Gore charities 2:40	Stock fraud; market 5:20	Space flights 2:40	Storms; relief 6:00	Russia; UN arms control 2:30	19:10
Saturday ABC	Minnesota tobacco deal 2:30	Lettuce crop 1:50	Alcoholism; civil rights 8:50	Weather 0:20	Indonesian unrest; Mideast peace 5:30	19:00
Weekly totals	31:30	15:50	29:40	24:00	43:00	144:00

NOTE: Broadcast time is listed in minutes and seconds. The respective dates for the constructed week are 11-23-97, 12-29-97, 1-13-98, 2-11-98, 3-5-98, 4-17-98, and 5-9-98. The CNN broadcast is 60 minutes; all others are 30 minutes.

Table 5.3 Hours of Politically Relevant Programming on Weekdays and Weekends

| | Over-the-Air Television | | | Cable Television | | | |
Time	News	Talk	Public Affairs	News	Talk	Public Affairs	Total
Weekdays	14	6	9.5	10	3	8	50.5
Weeknights	16	9	5	14	12	33	89
Saturday day	3	2	5	8.5	3	10	31.5
Saturday night	7	—	8	13	6	24.5	58.5
Sunday day	9	7	8.5	10	4	8	46.5
Sunday night	9	—	5.5	7	7.5	14.5	43.5
Subtotal	58	24	41.5	62.5	35.5	98	319
Weekly total[a]	178	84	99.5	158.5	95.5	262	877.5

NOTE: Based on one constructed week drawn from the April–June 1998 period. N = 55 channels. Daytime = 6:00 A.M. to 5:59 P.M. Nighttime = 6:00 P.M. to 5:59 A.M. Broadcasts were monitored around the clock.

[a] Weekly total figures multiply findings by five to cover a full week, excluding Saturday and Sunday.

all programs that were labeled in *TVWeek,* the *Chicago Tribune*'s weekly program guide, as news. *TVWeek* also served to identify Talk shows. However, only three of the seventeen listed talk shows—*Today, Good Morning America,* and *This Morning*—are included in the table. The others, such as those hosted by Oprah Winfrey and Maury Povich, were deemed to be predominantly nonpolitical, although they cover many politically relevant social problems, such as out-of-wedlock pregnancies among young students, the purity of food supplies in supermarkets, and deficiencies in the criminal justice system. Similarly, in composing the Public Affairs category, all soap operas, movies, and sportscasts were excluded despite their intermittent coverage of the types of social and political issues that the talk shows feature fairly regularly.

The Public Affairs category includes serious programs that focus on analysis of politically salient past and current situations in history, government, the economy, and science, providing data and interpretations. Overall, the numbers in table 5.3 should be considered broad approximations, rather than firm figures, because there are no widely shared guidelines for categorizing the political information content of programs. Moreover, many programs are mixtures of serious information and fluff. Many talk shows and entertainment programs regularly interrupt for brief headline reports or breaking news stories or intersperse programs dealing with significant social issues in a lineup that is primarily light entertainment. The largest number of contributions to the Public Affairs category came from CNN, the cable news network; C-SPAN, which focuses on the official activities of the federal government; and PBS (public television), which features a large number of public service programs. Other major sources were public service stories aired on news magazine shows and on specialized cable channels like the Discovery Channel, the History Channel, the Learning Channel, and the Disney Channel.

Despite our exclusion of most television programs that cover politics peripherally, the totals shown in table 5.3 are impressive. However, in weighing the scores, one must consider a number of factors that make it impossible for viewers to take full advantage of such a rich information base. Time slots are a major hurdle. Many of the programs are broadcast simultaneously. However, no viewer needs to forgo news or public affairs programs because of schedule conflicts; they are available at every evening hour between 6:00 and 11:00 P.M. The broadcast day begins at 3:30 A.M. and runs for a full twenty-four hours, with some of the longest news and public affairs programs broadcast after 11:00 P.M. and before 7:00 A.M. Many of these programs exceed one hour. Because the majority of viewers are unlikely to be watching at these hours, their audience numbers are relatively small, however. Most Americans are not hungry enough for political information to sacrifice other wee-hours activities for them. The appeal of many programs is also reduced because they are repeated throughout the broadcast days, so that each presentation covers precisely the same information or only slightly altered versions. While it is helpful to hear important stories more than once, many viewers have no taste for such repetitions.

We have established that political news abounds on over-the-air and cable television. The figures presented in table 5.3 would more than double if we added political news available on the Internet. Sites sponsored by the major news organizations feature audiovisual political news around the clock, often in great depth. To assess the scope of Internet offerings and compare Internet fare to conventional news, political scientist Brian White and I analyzed audiovisual news coverage of an important event—the announcement of the verdict in President Clinton's impeachment trial—on conventional news media and the Internet. We found that the Internet offerings were infinitely richer and more diverse (Graber and White 1999).

What stood out about the websites was the corollary materials that accompanied the main stories. MSNBC, the website of the NBC network, for example, provided links from stories on the impeachment vote to stories on Linda Tripp, Ken Starr, and Monica Lewinsky, who were important players in the Clinton saga. Other links led to a politics bulletin board for readers' comments and to an on-line survey where readers could evaluate fifteen prominent participants in the impeachment as "winners and losers." Links remained available on the site as the day's news progressed. There were even links to stories from the prior ten days. The site also allowed visitors to e-mail their senators directly via a link from the story. Links to MSNBC correspondents' reports were also available, many in streaming audio and video, so visitors could actually hear and see the comments of the analysts almost as they were being broadcast.

A number of these reports were still available several months later on a site devoted to the impeachment, allowing visitors the opportunity to review for themselves the tone and attitude of the correspondents and pundits. Of course, the ability to update information is not limited to the Internet sites. Television news programs regularly update their broadcasts. Yet doing so, while retaining previously provided information, is far more difficult in conventional media. It often requires cutting off coverage of current or breaking news.

In sum, the information available to average citizens on the Internet, while in many ways similar to that available elsewhere, and certainly framed in similar terms, is richer and is packaged in ways that let the visitor control what he or she reads, hears, and views. This goes beyond selecting particular stories to allowing visitors to do keyword searches for particular story aspects. Conventional media lack these facilities. They are also generally unable to feature more than one story or one voice at a time. Usually, they cannot add information to existing newscasts because the size of their coverage is determined by set amounts of air time. The web suffers no such limitation. It can add and add and add, while keeping older stories and information on-line as close as a click of the mouse. It is a nearly boundless treasure trove of political data.

The quantity of available political news seems almost limitless, but what about the quality? We turn to election news coverage to answer that question.

National Election News Flaws. In the field of politics, national election news has been the most frequent target of complaints about a misdirected emphasis on froth over substance. Media scholars charge that conventional television dwells on insignificant news and slights significant stories. The critics' complaints are generally louder than warranted because they fail to put them into the context of election events and because they neglect to mention that there is much excellent election coverage along with the chaff. Nevertheless, there are ample reasons for complaints about coverage quality.

By and large, coverage inadequacies spring from efforts to please audiences who do not care very much about serious political news. Instead of repeatedly delving into detailed analyses of policy issues, as the critics would like, broadcasts dwell on horse-race and hoopla stories, which seem fresh and exciting to viewers, personally appealing, and otherwise attractive. Generally, such stories are also easier to compose and may require fewer personnel resources. Linking stories to familiar human themes demands little background knowledge and is much easier than explaining complex political, economic, and social issues in the one- to three-minute time slots normally allotted to television news stories. Besides, "[p]olitical reporters tend to be politics-wonks rather than policy-wonks" (Schudson 1995, 10).

Following are the common indictments of election news coverage for which examples abound. Most of them are based on the assumption that the news should dwell primarily on policy issues and that citizens are ill served if other topics gain the lion's share of attention. This assumption is debatable, as pointed out in chapter 3, where we questioned whether citizens can and should engage in complicated comparative analyses of the issue stands of the candidates. Nonetheless, leaving this issue aside, there still is ample evidence that election news, as well as other political news, brims with stories that are short on substance.

The strongest criticism is leveled against the heavy emphasis on the horse-race and hoopla aspects of the race and the excessive attention to strategy and tactics and opinion polls at the expense of discussion of policy issues. That criticism of news quality is certainly warranted. However, many of the justifications given for this state of affairs have merit even though they do not make reforms unnecessary.

Journalists defend the emphasis on horse-race and hoopla news as good and popular journalism because breaking events produce the freshest and hence most attractive news. They point out that the typical American presidential election campaign drags out over many months. Substantive issues are usually covered in the opening phases. That makes them "old" news later on even though many viewers missed them initially because attention to election news peaks only during the final weeks of the campaign. Another incentive for choosing horse-race and hoopla news is the need for pictures for television stories, which privileges events for which pictures are easy to get over more important ones that require more elaborate preparations for audio-visual coverage. It is very simple and economical to shoot pictures of what politicians are physically doing on the hustings compared to hunting for pictures to illustrate possible outcomes of proposed actions.

Critics also complain that the quality is low when television broadcasts cover serious news stories about issues and about the professional qualifications of the candidates. Such stories tend to cover a very limited array of policy concerns and qualifications, usually the most controversial ones, even when other issues and qualifications are more important. Selective coverage of issues and qualifications frequently and unduly diminishes or enhances the images of particular candidates. Again, the charges have merit, but so has the explanation that time constraints on television news force superficial coverage. On average, 80 percent of the stories are covered in less than three minutes in typical newscasts; 33 percent take less than one minute. That leaves little time to report the facts, along with contextual and explanatory information.

There is even a flip side to the complaints about superficial coverage of political news stories. James David Barber, among others, has criticized television news for being too sophisticated, rather than not sophisticated enough:

> The trouble with television news is that it is too good—too intellectual, too balanced. It passes right over the heads of the great "lower" half of the American electorate who needs it most. If those who would reform television stopped thinking in terms of turning the network news into the *Encyclopedia Britannica* or the *New York Times,* it could realize its enormous, unexploited potential for reaching and enlightening voters who now do not know what it is talking about. (1979, 14)

Barber's analysis is probably correct for many viewers, especially when they watch the more sophisticated newscasts that take a lot of prior knowledge for granted. The "chatting classes"—intellectuals, including media professionals—may well have become alienated from the concerns and modes of communication of average folk because the working-class, apprentice-trained reporters of old have been replaced by middle-class, well-educated newspeople. Being politics buffs as well as journalists, they tend to provide their audiences with a confusing array of facts. In particular, the norm that news should be well balanced by presenting clashing viewpoints has encouraged the concoction of news stews that unsophisticated viewers find indigestible.

Television campaign coverage has also been accused of fostering a dangerous "politics of personality" by constantly bringing the images of candidates for the highest office in the land into people's living rooms. Facial close-ups—which are standard for 70 percent of all television stories—presumably encourage viewers to judge candidates based on the impressions gained via these pictures, rather than on the policies that they claim to espouse. Personalization of politics may turn it into a synecdoche: "It comes to stand for the entire human struggle. Each evening on the nightly news, Greed, Lust, Envy, and, occasionally, Honor stride the boards. The drama of statecraft becomes the human drama, and politics is reduced to a theatrical convenience" (Hart 1994, 50).

The merits of these charges about a picture-based politics of personality are debatable. One can counter them by arguing that audiovisual cues are helpful because they provide evidence of character traits, such as strength, compassion, and trustworthiness. Most people are experienced in making sound judgments based on such cues. By contrast, to judge the comparative merits of complex policy proposals and to assess how likely it will be that a particular candidate will, indeed, be able to implement the proposal are well-nigh impossible tasks for average voters. Nonetheless, it is irrefutable that campaign news should offer voters clear information about the candidates' issue positions along with information about their personal qualities.

There is substantial merit to the charge that television often typecasts candidates early in the campaign and perpetuates these stereotypes even when they no longer fit the situation. Typecasting facilitates the rapid coverage that is needed to compress a maximum of stories into the available time slot. Subsequent stories can then be framed in line with these simplistic stereotypes, thereby perpetuating them. Pack journalism—the tendency for journalists to copy each other's stories and frames—thereafter makes the stereotypes uniform throughout numerous broadcast outlets. The damage to candidates and to voters' ability to appraise them properly can be immense.

Excessive negativism is another serious, and entirely deserved, accusation. Although the majority of broadcast messages are neutral, there is an abundance of heavily negative messages compared to the positive ones. Candidates' flaws are amply and often overly harshly covered, while their strengths are given short shrift. The heavy emphasis on the strategic aspects of campaigns makes campaign activities seem contrived and designed to fool citizens. Political reporters act like cynical insiders; theirs is news with a smirk. Whatever is done is attributed to self-serving reasons—namely, political advantage and power and, above all, the desire to win elections.

For example, when President Reagan flew to Louisiana in 1983 to inspect sites of flooding and to arrange for federal aid, television showed him helping to fill sandbags to stem the flood. But the commentary, instead of praising his efforts, suggested that he had come primarily to create the impression of being an empathetic chief executive. Reporters claimed that picture-taking had actually interrupted flood control efforts. Much of the public's cynicism about electoral politics, and the political process in general, has been rightly or wrongly attributed to negative mass-media coverage.

Of course, journalists have solid reasons for cynicism about politicians' actions and motives. Many leading figures are not pure as the driven snow, as an overidealistic public may claim to expect. It may therefore be unfair to blame journalists for depicting politicians, warts and all, merely because such reports enhance public cynicism. However, journalists can be blamed for overdoing their insinuations, especially when they know that viewers are likely to take their remarks at face value and the visual "proof" presented on the screen enhances this effect.*

Critics correctly complain that many important stories are omitted because journalists fear that they might bore the audience, which then might switch to a different program. For example, minor candidates, including third-party candidates in presidential elections, routinely receive inadequate coverage because the majority of voters probably are not interested in them. Similarly, state and local elections receive insufficient coverage in the national and local media because the public has shown little concern about most of these elections in the past. Even the major candidates' pronouncements are slighted or paraphrased by journalists who believe that their own statements are superior and untainted by the self-serving bias that might be expected from candidates. Nonetheless, although there is broad agreement that many significant stories are omitted, there is little agreement about which stories are most significant and should be featured when coverage space is limited.

---

*When viewers were asked in a 1998 survey about the credibility of well-known anchors and reporters, 75 percent gave high ratings to Peter Jennings and Tom Brokaw. The figure for Dan Rather was 74 percent. Comparable ratings for President Clinton and Vice-President Gore were 45 percent. Television talk-show hostess Oprah Winfrey (64 percent) outranked Secretary of State Madeline Albright (42 percent) (Pew 1998d).

Whatever choices are made, they will always be praised by some observers and condemned by others.

Other Areas of Blame. Complaints are similar about other types of political news—inadequate attention to crucial topics, such as foreign affairs and economic issues, and stunted coverage of many important groups, such as labor unions. When important issues are discussed, coverage often lacks context and realism. For example, the horrors of political violence, including war, are all too often sanitized so that they seem innocuous. Here, too, coverage is criticized for being unduly negative, emphasizing the self-interested motivations of politicians and other leaders at the expense of explaining the substance of policies (Cappella and Jamieson 1997). Many of these complaints are amply justified, of course. But there are also many baseless charges about the frivolity of political news that have become mantras among prominent professional and academic elites (Graber 1998). Frequent repetition has transformed them into seemingly unchallengeable truths.

The harm done to the image of television by adverse comments about the quality of news and public affairs offerings has been compounded by similar complaints about entertainment. We now turn to these complaints.

3. When television features entertainment, it is usually lowbrow, "cheap" fare, rather than high- or middlebrow. This deprives the audience of the type of entertainment that nourishes the spirit and the imagination.

The condemnation of current entertainment features on television as lowbrow and cheap is part of the old debate about the respective merits of high and low culture. The human dramas that critics like Newton Minow condemn so sweepingly are and have been common to even so-called high-culture offerings since time immemorial. They are as omnipresent in slapstick comedies and soap opera tragedies as in acclaimed ancient and modern literary classics and in most grand operas. One may argue about the quality of treatment of these eternal human themes in particular presentations, but it seems unwarranted to condemn most dramatic television stories as numbing and of no long-term benefit while assuming that printed works that cover the same themes are likely to be liberating and mind-stretching.

Television, as Roderick Hart (1994, 11) points out, "is a people's medium, after all, and it celebrates that fact each day. It celebrates people's joys in its game shows, their strivings in its sports programs, their lusts via the Playboy Channel." Isn't that the way it should be? Elites have forever tried to impose their cultural tastes on mass publics, and mass publics have forever resisted. Ironically elites, too, choose to watch many of the types of presentations that they condemn as low culture and unworthy of attention.

In the past, radio entertainment programs and most of the popular movies have also been stigmatized as vulgar. Public service broadcasting was initially set up with a high-culture focus to counter popular vulgarity. Not unexpectedly, that emphasis declined when slim financial support from the public sector forced public television stations to seek support from commercial advertisers. Inevitably, this brought about a concern with the size of the audience and hence a need to appeal to popular tastes—and popular tastes lean toward light entertainment, especially in the evening when people are ready for recreation.

Most prime-time evening programming is therefore light and fluffy, designed for casual viewing. Akin to light background music—these shows can form a backdrop to other activities like fixing or eating a meal, cleaning the house, or even reading the newspaper. Even though many people complain about an excess of violence and graphic sexual materials in entertainment shows, they select such content in massive numbers. Literally millions of people pay money to watch programs that have been X-rated, which usually means that they involve graphic scenes of violence and sexual activities as well as foul language. Subscriptions to magazines featuring such content by far exceed subscriptions to "serious" magazines, especially those with political content. On the Internet, hard-core sex sites draw the largest crowds and constitute the largest share of the pay-for-view market, which yields billions of dollars annually.

In a 1992 Roper poll, interviewers asked: "People have given us various reasons why they watch television. Please tell me if you think each of them explains your use of television very well, somewhat, or hardly at all?" (*Public Perspective* 1995). Forty-seven percent of the respondents indicated that they used television primarily to be entertained. However, this was followed closely (46 percent) by people who claimed to use television primarily "to obtain information about what is happening in the world." Several other entertainment options also were mentioned as best explanations for viewing, but by smaller percentages. These included using the medium "simply to relax" (35 percent), "to fill spare time" (26 percent), and "for companionship when you're alone"

(23 percent).* Judging from the many hours that people routinely devote to watching entertainment shows, they must feel at least partially satisfied.

Another serious charge follows.

4. Television programs pay excessive attention to violent behaviors, socially risky behaviors, and illicit activities. Such programs inspire asocial, often criminal, behaviors.

Many television critics claim that the content of current entertainment fare is personally and socially harmful in many ways. They are especially concerned about the impact on children and about the danger that criminal behavior will be imitated. Violent television, they contend, creates scripts in people's minds that may be activated when a suitable opportunity arises. As explained in chapter 4, despite some frightening incidents, these concerns, for the most part, are not warranted. Information-processing research shows that the majority of viewers, including children, rarely imitate criminal behavior because they have powerful countervailing schemas that constitute formidable inhibitions. Imitation effects are considerably stronger for undesirable behaviors, such as health-damaging use of alcohol or automobiles and various daredevil activities. The reason is that children, as well as many adults, have no strong learned inhibitions against such behaviors. When they do, viewing asocial behaviors may lead to catharsis and revulsion, rather than imitation.

What about situations when events pictured on television have inspired viewers to commit violent acts as a protest against social injustice? This does, indeed, happen for the small number of people whose thinking is receptive to such behaviors and who lack strong countervailing schemas. Protest activities may be regrettable when they are based on misinformation or unduly inflammatory comments by journalists. The blame then belongs to the storytellers, rather than the medium. Not uncommonly, story framing is flawed, failing to show the full situation or misinterpreting it. For example, in 1991, street violence

---

*Jib Fowles, in his 1992 book *Why Viewers Watch,* claims that the appetite for content is allocated as follows: 10 percent for information about the real world; 15 percent for soap operas to make people feel good; and 75 percent for fantasies that help to release tensions for adults as well as children. He reports that people prefer fantasy release to release created by watching real-life events.

followed a judge's decision to grant probation to a Korean woman who claimed self-defense as the reason for shooting an African-American teenage girl during a shoplifting incident. The broadcasts reporting the incident had omitted pictures of the tall, heavyset teenager repeatedly knocking the small, slight merchant to the ground. Absent these pictures, it appeared as if a grown woman had wantonly killed a defenseless young girl in an argument over a bottle of orange juice.

Similarly, when rioting erupted in Los Angeles in 1992, following a report that an all-white jury had exonerated all but one of the white police officers accused of brutally beating a black man during an arrest for a traffic violation, television coverage suggested a citywide conflict, rather than a localized situation. The intersection where most of the violence was concentrated was called "ground zero," implying that it was the center of a much wider zone of combat. Commentators showed scene after scene of rioting but gave little chance to officials, such as the chief of police, to put these pictures into perspective. Given the impressions that were conveyed about the justifications for the violence, it was not surprising that scores of people rushed to the scene to join the fight and copycat rioting erupted in other communities around the country.

When false stories circulated that Korean merchants in the area had set fire to their own stores, pictures of stores in flames lost their emotional appeal, and firefighting help diminished. Throughout, reporters' comments often revealed great ignorance of the Los Angeles situation. The pictures then came to mean something quite different from what they actually showed because "[v]ideo images never speak for themselves. They are contextualized by the discourse that presents them, and they are interpreted based on the associational cues they elicit" (Dobkin 1996, 91).

We now must consider the final claim.

5. Television watching, irrespective of program content, displaces other worthwhile endeavors, such as reading, work on community projects, and vigorous recreational activities, like playing, that stimulate the imagination. In fact, the couch potato syndrome spawned by lengthy television sessions is a major cause of the epidemic of physical obesity and intellectual sluggishness among Americans at the turn of the twenty-first century.

One of the most serious charges leveled against television is that it displaces civic participation (Putnam 1995). As discussed in chapter 1, political scientist Robert Putnam raised eyebrows nationwide when he charged in 1995 that television watching harms civic life because it impairs social trust and discourages citizens from joining groups. He claimed that people who rely primarily on newspapers for news belong to 76 percent more civic organizations than people who get most of their news from television, irrespective of education and income levels, age, race, place of residence, work status, and gender. Heavy users of television seemed most afflicted by this loss of civic energy. Putnam attributed the phenomenon to television's seductiveness, which keeps viewers from engaging in the type of socially interactive entertainment, like bowling, that, he argues, fosters civic engagement. Television, says Putnam, has become a primarily solo activity that isolates people physically and psychologically from their neighbors.

In a related vein, media scholar Roderick Hart (1994) argues that television distracts people from analyzing the substance of political issues. Broadcasts engage them psychologically and dupe them into believing that they are playing an active role in politics, when, in fact, the act of watching television from home distracts from actual participation. When the public sphere is brought so vividly into everyone's living room, people no longer feel compelled to seek it outside the confines of their homes. Politics becomes "refeudalized," as Jürgen Habermas (1989, 141) sees it. Genuine community, Habermas contends, requires physical interaction.

The charges that television watching reduces civic participation have been refuted on numerous grounds. It remains highly questionable whether there is, indeed, a connection between membership in a variety of social and sports organizations and serious participation in politics (Mondak and Mutz 1997). Bowling partners do not routinely argue about politics as part of the sports outing. Furthermore, television viewers are not markedly asocial when it comes to membership in organizations. To the contrary, the evidence runs the other way (Ladd 1996). The vast majority of American television viewers have continued to participate in a miscellany of old and new organizations related to religion, education, social welfare, the environment, and various professional activities. In fact, when the full range of group activities is considered, civic participation in the United States is on the rise; it is also far more common than in most other democratic societies. While voting has ebbed, most other forms of political participation, such as contacting public officials and working on community problems, have risen. Additionally, rather than isolating people, television provides them with scores of virtual neighbors throughout the global community (Norris 2000).

Television also stands accused of depressing the reading of worthwhile books and stifling the imagination. These charges, too, are questionable. There is no evidence of a decline in inventions, scientific discoveries, or the creation of artistic innovations. Quite the contrary! Reading has also increased during the television era (Fowles 1992). Market data, which are an indirect measure of reader interest, show that more books were published annually at the turn of the twenty-first century by a greater variety of publishers than ever before, even if one ignores the flourishing industry of desktop publishing made possible by computers.*

The impact of television watching on students' reading scores and habits is less clear. Reading scores have been fluctuating since the advent of television (Condry 1989). At first, they went down, but then they moved up again. A lot seems to depend on what students watch and how much time they spend in front of the television set. Robert Kubey and Mihaly Csikszentmihalyi (1990) found that the amount of time spent watching television correlates positively with academic success. They argue that children can learn a lot by experiencing reality through television. There is also massive, convincing evidence that educational programs enhance the social, intellectual, and educational development of young children. They foster increased school readiness and higher achievements in English, mathematics, and science when the youngsters reach high school (Huston and Wright 1998; Anderson 1998; Neuman 1991). Of course, any major new diversion tends to produce reallocations of time. Time spent watching television has taken away time from other things like conventional sports or reading or socializing. Television exercise classes, web page reading, and Internet chat rooms may be substitutes. Whether such changes are beneficial or harmful to individuals and their communities is a complex question for which there is no single definitive answer, other than "it depends."

SUMMARIZING THE INDICTMENT SCORE

What has the dissection of the bill of indictments leveled against current television fare revealed? The final score is mixed. Some of the charges have merit; others do not or are exaggerated.

*However, there are twice as many video rental outlets as bookstores (Schudson 1995).

The first charge, that television programs do not accord with viewers' tastes, is obviously wrong if one considers the public as a whole and grants that there will always be sizable exceptions. By and large, people are pleased with much of current television fare. A vast variety of news, talk, and public affairs (broadly construed) programs makes serious information about current affairs and problems available at all hours of the day and night. They contain much of the content that viewers mention when asked what new offerings they would like to see. As is true of all private and public goods, mismatches between supply and demand are more often due to lack of information about what is available, and where and when, than to shortages of the desired goods. Rote repetition of commonly voiced complaints is also a factor in exaggerating the impression of widespread audience dissatisfaction.

The second charge, that journalists often choose poorly when it comes to political content and that they make serious errors in the framing and tone of news, is correct, although the flaws are not as universal as the critics suggest and many negative ratings of journalists' judgments are controversial. When only a small fraction of available political information can be squeezed into television's time slots and when very diverse audience tastes need to be satisfied, the wisdom of nearly every story choice becomes contestable. Television does present a caricature of the political world, as charged, but that is the nature of the broadcast beast. When selection is necessary, distortions are inevitable.

Whether or not the third complaint—that television entertainment is too lowbrow—has merit hinges on one's views about which tastes should prevail in the marketplace. Should it be the elites who prefer so-called high culture or the general public to whose tastes much of the current entertainment fare is geared? In the age of "the common man," a judgment in favor of current practices seems appropriate to me, especially since an ample supply of highbrow entertainment is also available. Besides, the question is moot in many ways because the public votes with its proverbial feet. It shuns elite recommendations most of the time and turns to more congenial programs.

The fourth charge—that television programs pay excessive attention to asocial behaviors—has won a lot of support among elites, as well as the general public, though the definition of "excessive" is a matter of judgment, rather than provable fact. However, the claim that such offerings lead to the spread of such behaviors generally has been far too sweeping in light of what is known about information-processing. Still, considering the widespread expressed dislike of such displays, there seems room for substantial cutbacks even though audiences flock to these offerings in massive numbers, despite condemning them. In 1999, for example, more than 70 million viewers tuned in to an interview with Monica Lewinsky in which she discussed her illicit sexual affair with President Clinton. Polls had indicated that most Americans were disgusted with media fixation on this story throughout the preceding year.

Finally, concern has been expressed about the opportunity costs that the public incurs when it stays in front of its television sets for many hours each week. That concern raises questions about the appropriateness of time allocations that individuals make as well as questions about the long-range consequences of these choices. These are highly controversial matters, as shown by the debate about the impact of heavy television watching on political participation. There are no firm philosophical answers to such questions about the slices of time that individuals should allocate to various activities or to questions about where the balance should lie between low- and high-culture offerings or between television watching and reading. It is not even certain that the epidemic of obesity that concerns American physicians can be blamed to any measurable degree on a television-inspired couch potato syndrome.

TELEVISION'S MAJOR SOCIAL CONTRIBUTIONS

Besides attracting adverse criticism, television has had its share of accolades for its contributions to public life. For the sake of a balanced analysis, these deserve as much attention as its shortcomings. Even as severe a critic as Newton Minow (Minow and LaMay 1995) concedes that television has been socially useful, quite aside from the generally highly praised children's programs like *Sesame Street*. Here are examples of the types of benefits reaped from broadcasts. For the most part, these benefits have substantially enhanced the quality of political life in the United States and abroad.

1. Television fosters the growth of social and political movements by making them visible to large numbers of potential supporters, lending them importance and often legitimacy.

The Civil Rights movement is an American example. Showing physical assaults on peaceful civil rights marchers or snarling police dogs keeping black children out of school aroused powerful support for the

Civil Rights movement throughout the United States. In fact, in the age of television, there have been hardly any successful counterestablishment movements in the United States that did not get their first publicity boost from audiovisual messages. Antiwar protesters, antinuclear protestors, environmentalists, Earth Day celebrants, antiabortion demonstrators, and women's rights advocates all have been able to bask in the television limelight, thereby attracting attention to their causes.

Regardless of whether television exposure ultimately legitimates or delegitimates the movement, and regardless of the movement's merits, the exposure gives its adherents a chance to tell their story to a wide public of potential supporters and opponents that would otherwise be beyond their reach. Despite all of the complaints about civic apathy, television has been an effective mobilizing agent that has helped such movements to grow and prosper or has hastened their demise. In the age of the Internet, resort to the mobilizing power of audiovisuals has already risen dramatically, and the growth rate is accelerating. The impact on politics is likely to be profound.

Television has been especially important in totalitarian societies, where, before the age of the Internet, it has had relatively few competitors vying for the public's attention to political matters. Time and again, television has been the handmaiden to revolution in such societies. The liberation of Eastern Europe from communism is an example. When Russian television gave Soviet citizens a ringside seat at a parade that showed opponents of the regime openly defying it, without being stopped, it was clear to all that protest movements had become viable. Within a very short time, the Soviet empire collapsed (Mickiewicz 1996, 1998). The last chapter has not been written as yet in the revolution that started in China's Tiananmen Square in 1992. The picture of a lone student placing his slight body in the path of a slow-moving tank in hopes that it would stop has been etched into the minds of Chinese freedom fighters and their supporters throughout the world. It may yet foster a major turn toward democracy in China, especially with the help of countless websites that are beyond any government's censorship controls.

2. The publicity provided by television can be an important tool in propelling a major policy to success or failure. It mobilizes potential supporters and opponents and spurs public opinion formation.

Television, however transmitted, often deserves major credit for lending vital support to the forces favoring or opposing key public policies.

As discussed in chapter 4, the precise impact of television on official policies—the CNN effect—is hard to measure in complex situations, but at the very least it seems clear that television has often played a significant role that many—though by no means all—analysts have deemed beneficial. For instance, television coverage of Vietnam War opponents in the United States hastened America's exit from that country in the late 1960s and early 1970s. Television in its many forms also helped the American public in making sense out of the impeachment hearings during the waning years of the Clinton presidency.

The collapse of Wisconsin Senator Joseph McCarthy's witch-hunt for communist sympathizers, following televised Senate hearings in 1954, and the fall from political grace of President Richard Nixon are other examples. The Nixon impeachment debates in the House Judiciary Committee in 1974 were broadcast live on television to a large audience of average Americans who had been averse to the idea of ousting a president. The television coverage of the Senate Watergate hearings and the House Judiciary Committee the following year was crucial in bringing about a change in the public mood. However, as Gladys Lang and Kurt Lang (1983) detail in their careful dissection of Watergate politics, it is generally wrong to ascribe major developments to a single force. Congress and the executive branch were major players in the Watergate situation, along with the media. The precise influence of each partner to such a symbiosis is usually impossible to gauge.

Powerful documentaries about conditions of the poor, sanitation, control of chemical and nuclear weapons, and other social issues have also influenced policy-making. Edward R. Murrow's "Harvest of Shame" (1960) on *CBS Reports* called the attention of Congress and the public to the dreadful conditions in migrant labor camps in Florida, as did a 1961 *CBS Reports* program that dealt with hunger in Mississippi. CBS has also reported extensively on RU-486, the French abortion pill, and opposition to the pill by the right-to-life movement (1991). It has discussed the controversial Norplant method of birth control and the legislative action that was contemplated to induce poor women to use it (1991). Well-executed documentaries on race relations, gun control, and a slew of public health matters have influenced people and swung votes in elections and in legislative assemblies.

3. In times of natural disasters or manmade crises, such as wars or violence against government leaders, the media, including television, become important teammates of government in efforts to restore public order, safety, and tranquility.

Ample and excellent television coverage of breaking events has been credited with calming the public's fears in the wake of the assassination of President John F. Kennedy in 1963. Comments by Wisconsin Senator William Proxmire are typical: "Not only was the coverage dignified and immaculate in taste, it was remarkably competent and frequently it soared with imaginative, if tragic, beauty. The intelligence and sensitivity of the commentary and continuously expressed dedication to this country's strength and solidarity in its hour of terrible grief were superb" (quoted in Fowles 1992, 178). Television provided excellent surveillance of breaking developments and reassurance that the authorities had the situation under control.

Shedding light on war situations, acts of terrorism, and hostage crises traditionally has been an important public service rendered by television, which can clarify hard-to-imagine situations through on-site pictures and graphs. For example, *60 Minutes* did numerous programs on Gulf War issues in 1991, including an interview with General Norman Schwarzkopf, commander of allied troops in the Persian Gulf, about likely scenarios in case of a poison gas attack on American ground forces. Other programs examined the likelihood that thirty-five Americans had been killed by "friendly fire," as charged. The role played by Israel in the Gulf War and the use of Patriot missiles and other weapons systems were also examined. However, while coverage can enlighten, it can also obscure. In the Gulf War, for instance, media coverage unduly glorified the precision of American aerial strikes and withheld pictures of Iraqi casualties out of fear that they might generate sympathy for the enemy (Bennett and Paletz 1994).

In natural disasters, such as floods or tornadoes, or even ordinary wintertime snow and ice hazards, television can clearly identify dangerous locations and help guide people to safety. It can show the locations where immediate assistance is needed to avoid further harm. It can monitor the progress of rescue efforts. These matters are "political" because they involve government services and decisions by elected leaders and public bureaucracies.

4. Television can provide superb coverage, either live or retrospectively, of cultural differences and of major events in political history. It can even realistically reconstruct and present events that occurred long before the age of television.

Most television fare relates to America's mainstream cultures, so that minority cultures often feel like the Eskimo elders in Canada who called television "an atomic bomb that leaves buildings intact, but destroys the lives and souls of the people" (Brooke 2000). But this need not happen. Culturally appropriate programming produced by cultural minorities and beamed to cultural enclaves has mushroomed. It enriches the lives of cultural minorities by catering to their needs and by helping them to preserve their unique cultural values. But it also allows them, as well as members of the majority culture, to visit with each other vicariously, thereby cementing a sense of common humanity and shared political interests.

The capacity of television to bring events to life in America's living rooms extends to events in the distant past, like the fall of Troy or the fall of the Roman Empire; events of the near past, like major battles of World War II or the horrors of the Holocaust; or recent events, like various aspects of space exploration or presidential travels. Such events are often presented by the highly popular electronic magazines, such as *60 Minutes, 20/20,* or Ted Koppel's *Nightline.* Three-quarters (76 percent) of the public agreed in 1998 with the statement in a Pew survey that news magazines like *60 Minutes, 20/20,* or *Dateline* "help me to really understand an issue" (Pew 1998d).

By 1994, there was at least one magazine show on television every single night. News magazines took up twelve hours of prime-time television weekly—three on CBS, four on ABC, and five on NBC. Electronic magazines draw large audiences, averaging 10 million viewers for programs that give more time to individual political stories than is possible on newscasts (Mifflin 1998b). Some of the shows are primarily entertainment, but many contain a great deal of serious news. For example, the television networks have repeatedly examined the slayings of President Kennedy, civil rights leader Malcolm X, and controversial labor leader Jimmy Hoffa.

60 Minutes reported at length in March 1993 on the shoot-out at a religious compound of the Branch Davidians near Waco, Texas. The standoff, in which several law enforcement officers perished, ended when a fire killed most of the residents at the compound. The incident made major political waves and may have been the spark that ultimately produced the bombing of a federal office building in Oklahoma City in 1995. Reports on hate crimes have covered the activities of the Ku Klux Klan, attacks on gay and lesbian citizens, and anti-Semitic and anti-Arab violence. Problems faced by the Drug Enforcement Administration (DEA) in dealing with the smuggling of heroin, cocaine, and other dangerous drugs on a worldwide basis have been graphically illustrated.

How powerful visuals can be under such circumstances is clear from descriptions by *New York Times* television critic Walter Goodman (1992) of scenes of atrocities committed during the breakup of Yugoslavia.

> Two small corpses (one a Serbian infant, an ethnic-cleansing bullet having evidently gone astray) after an attack on a busload of children trying to escape the killing ground; mourners scattered by mortar fire at the funeral for the two children, a mother running from her 32-month old daughter's grave, a grandmother injured; civilians dashing across dangerous streets to do their daily chores, like people seeking sanity in a madhouse; cities destroyed and families who have left everything behind coming up against closed borders. . . . The message strikes like a mortar shell: Less than 50 years after the destruction of Nazism, the doctrine of racial purity is again on the rampage in Central Europe.

Such scenes are harrowing to watch; they are far more powerful than the words available to describe them, except when these words evoke images of previously watched scenes from memory.

5. Casting political issues into dramatic formats effectively conveys their meanings to mass audiences likely to forgo reading. It is especially useful for audiences short on formal education or deficient in language skills.

Entertainment fare can be a superb teacher about political problems by creating illustrative fictional case studies. This is why Population Communications International (PCI), a New York–based, privately funded nonprofit organization, assists developing countries all over the world in educating their people through television dramas, apparently with very encouraging results (Elber 2000). The plots of many dramatic programs, situation comedies, and soap operas are borrowed from contemporary controversies. PCI-assisted programs, for instance, have covered family planning, gender equality, domestic violence, and AIDS prevention.

Script writers often do extensive, careful research to capture major arguments. One of the earliest television examples of a situation comedy designed to illuminate major social problems was producer Norman Lear's *All in the Family* in 1971. The show dealt with racism, abortion, homosexuality, and women's rights—all "hot" and important social topics. By the end of the 1971–72 season, it was the most popular show on television (Schudson 1995). Similarly, *M*A*S*H* dealt with

Vietnam War issues, although it transplanted them to Korea. *Lou Grant,* a popular program in the 1970s and early 1980s, used a newsroom scenario to deal with foreign policy problems, such as dumping hazardous wastes in Third World countries.

THE BALANCE SHEET

In this chapter, I have put the major complaints against television content into perspective to show to what extent they are valid, invalid, or only partly valid. I have also pointed out that television, despite its many serious shortcomings, makes major contributions to political action and to the public's understanding of political issues. All of the flaws have their bright side, as well as their mitigating circumstances, and all of the strengths have their dark dimensions as well. The study of television, like the study of other social phenomena, is a study in contrasts.

Before turning attention to policies that would enhance television's strengths and diminish its weaknesses, we need to examine one final problem area—user-friendliness of audiovisual presentations as seen from an information-processing perspective. That story is told in the next chapter.

6

MAKING NEWS SELECTION, FRAMING, AND FORMATTING MORE USER-FRIENDLY

Average Americans deserve to be called "Teflon-coated news consumers." Despite ample exposure to video, audio, and print information about local, national, and world events, most of the news about local, national, and world events to which they are exposed fails to leave a mark on their minds. What explains this phenomenon? In this chapter, we go beyond the human physiology basics already described in chapter 2, beyond actual public affairs knowledge discussed in chapter 3, and beyond the availability of political information discussed in chapter 5. In chapter 6, we look at learning obstacles springing from the substance and presentation of political information on television news.

MAJOR OBSTACLES TO LEARNING FROM AUDIOVISUAL MESSAGES

Content analyses of print and electronic media, coupled with research of the ways in which people acquire and process political news, indicate that the answers to the Teflon puzzle lie primarily in four interrelated problems areas. All of them involve mismatches between the ways journalists choose, frame, and present the news and the ways average Americans would prefer to have it chosen, framed, and presented.

The first major problem lies in the choice of news topics. Information-processing research shows that, much of the time, average Americans pay close attention only to news about significant topics that clearly relate to their lives and experiences (Graber 1993, 1994b; Gamson 1992; Conover and Feldman 1984, 1989; Rahn et al. 1990; Norris et al. 1999). Many news stories fail to meet these criteria. They cover news that is of peripheral interest to the public. Even when there is significant linkage to people's concerns, stories often fail to make the link clear enough. The news also presents a heavy dose of fluff stories, which capture the audience's attention and distract it from the more serious fare.

A second barrier to learning relates to the level of political sophistication required to comprehend complex television news stories. Many stories about weighty governmental issues, such as tax plans, social insurances, and levels of military preparedness, are presented without sufficient context and interpretation to make them understandable for average Americans. Sometimes reporters supply a fairly adequate context when an issue surfaces initially but fail to repeat it when the story reemerges after an interval that is long enough to allow average viewers' memories to fade. For ordinary news stories, fading of detail is usually substantial by the time two months have elapsed (Graber 1993). Reporters tend to assume that audiences still remember the information long after most of it has actually been forgotten. Without an adequate review of the story's context and prior events, its meaning becomes hazy.

A third obstacle to learning about politics from television news is the unattractive manner in which the most serious aspects of political stories are framed. During elections, for example, horse-race and hoopla news is couched in expressive audiovisual language. By contrast, journalists miss many opportunities for effective audiovisual presentations of the issues at stake in the election. Average citizens ignore many political news stories because they find the presentation unattractive and boring compared to watching the highlights of sports events or seeing close-ups of local celebrities (Valkenburg et al. 1999).

Finally, audiences find it difficult to process televised information because message formats are not user-friendly. Words and pictures are thrust at them helter-skelter, often at unmanageable speeds. That makes it too much trouble to extract information that is deemed boring and not particularly relevant to people's daily lives.

MISMATCHES IN STORY SUBSTANCE

From the perspective of ease of learning, the topics covered by many political stories do not match the audience's chief interests. Rather, many stories cater to the concerns of politically sophisticated elites, including media elites, who follow political events closely. Stories about free trade zones around the world, changes in capital gains legislation, expansion of membership in NATO, and evidence of atmospheric damage in Antarctic skies are hardly likely to excite most Americans unless the connection to their lives is made clear. That does not happen routinely. Similarly, the public is not generally intrigued by political infighting within the Beltway, or even scandals involving misconduct by the president, or by the savings and loan association debacle that produced huge losses for the government (and ultimately the taxpayers) in the 1990s. It does not help that such stories are usually framed for knowledgeable elites.

As table 6.1 demonstrates, a majority of Americans claimed to have paid *close* attention to fewer than 5 percent of the major news stories featured prominently during the 1986–2000 period. That amounted to a mere 35 news stories out of a total of 763 about which they were questioned. The table compiles the responses to an ongoing survey that asks a randomly selected national sample of respondents how closely they followed specific important news stories during the previous month. Respondents were asked if they were following these stories "very closely, fairly closely, not too closely, not at all closely."

Half (eighteen) of the stories that attracted very close attention covered natural and manmade disasters. The list includes floods, earthquakes, and hurricanes as well as explosions and crashes involving planes, cars, and boats. Their major attraction was the fact that they involved danger to or loss of life of average citizens. Most people can identify with that and can imagine themselves in similar situations. Eleven of the memorable stories covered potential disasters in the form of military activities that put average Americans in harm's way. Four stories dealt with increases in the price of gasoline—which is an important pocketbook issue for most Americans—and the remaining two referred to the 1996 presidential election and the Supreme Court flag-burning case.

Table 6.2 presents thirty-five stories that were also featured prominently but received very close attention from less than one-third of the audience. Stories that attracted close attention from less than 5 percent of the audience have been omitted from the story pool from which the examples were drawn. Judging from the subject matter of these stories and their prominence in the news, many social scientists, especially political scientists, would expect them to arouse substantial interest among average Americans. What happened and was it predictable?

There are many explanations for this lack of attention to such national and international news stories. Most Americans regard television primarily as an entertainment medium to be enjoyed at the end of the

Table 6.1 High Public Attentiveness to Major News Stories, 1986–2000

%	News Story
80	Explosion of the Space Shuttle *Challenger* (July 86)
73	Destruction caused by the San Francisco earthquake (Nov 89)
70	Verdict in Rodney King case and following riots and disturbances (May 92)
69	Crash of a Paris-bound TWA plane off the coast of New York (July 96)
69	Little girl in Texas who was rescued after falling into a well (Oct 87)
68	Shootings of students and teachers by two students at a Colorado high school (April 99)
67	War's end and the homecoming of U.S. forces from the Gulf (March 91)
66	Hurricane Andrew (Sept 92)
66	Iraq's invasion of Kuwait and deployment of U.S. forces to Saudi Arabia (Aug 90)
65	Floods in the Midwest (Aug 93)
63	Earthquake in Southern California (Jan 94)
63	Iraq's occupation of Kuwait and deployment of U.S. forces to Persian Gulf (Oct 90)
63	Iraq's occupation of Kuwait and deployment of U.S. forces to Persian Gulf (Sept 90)
62	Iraq's occupation of Kuwait and presence of U.S. forces in Persian Gulf (Nov 90)
62	Recent increases in the price of gasoline (Oct 90)
60	Invasion of Panama (Jan 90)
60	Destruction caused by Hurricane Hugo (Oct 89)
59	Events following the shooting of students and teachers at a Colorado high school (May 99)
59	Iraq's occupation of Kuwait and presence of U.S. forces in Persian Gulf (Jan 91)
58	Recent increases in the price of gasoline (March 2000)
58	Oklahoma City bombing (June 95)
58	U.S. air strikes against Libya (July 86)
57	Explosion of a pipe-bomb at the Atlanta Olympics (July 96)
57	Plight of American hostages and other Westerners detained in Iraq (Sept 90)
57	Recent increase in the price of gasoline (Aug 90)
56	Recent increases in the price of gasoline (Sept 90)
55	Outcome of the 1996 presidential election (Dec 96)
54	Death of John F. Kennedy Jr., his wife, and his sister-in-law in a plane crash (July 99)
54	Death of Princess Diana (Sept 97)
53	Crash of a United Airlines DC-10 in Sioux City, Iowa (Aug 89)
52	Deployment of U.S. Forces to Somalia (Jan 93)
52	Alaska oil spill (May 89)
51	News about cold weather in Northeast and Midwest (Jan 94)
51	Release of American hostages and other Westerners from Iraq and Kuwait (Jan 91)
51	Supreme Court decision on flag burning (July 89)

SOURCE: Excerpted from Pew 2000a.

NOTE: Table shows percentage of people who claimed to follow the story "very closely."

Table 6.2 Low Public Attentiveness to Major News Stories, 1986–2000

%	News Story
32	NATO air strikes against Serbian forces (May 99)
32	Clinton administration's health care reform proposals (Sept 94)
31	Impeachment trial of President Clinton in the Senate (Feb 99)
30	Trial of Timothy McVeigh for bombing in Oklahoma City (May 97)
30	End of Gorbachev's rule; Commonwealth replaces Soviet Union (Dec 91)
29	Proposals to reform the Social Security system (Jan 97)
26	News about the candidates for the 2000 presidential election (March 00)
26	Debate in Congress over welfare reform (Aug 95)
26	Bush/Gorbachev summit meeting in Helsinki (Sept 90)
25	Proposals in Congress to reform the IRS (Nov 97)
24	Debate in Washington about how to reform the Medicare system (June 97)
22	Congressional hearings about U.S. Persian Gulf policy (Jan 91)
22	Reunification of Germany (Oct 90)
21	Debate about NAFTA (Oct 93)
20	Debate in Washington over regulating the tobacco industry (April 98)
19	Legality of campaign contributions to Democrats by foreign business (April 97)
19	Proposals to eliminate affirmative action programs (Aug 95)
18	Latest Mideast peace agreement between Israel and the Palestinians (Nov 98)
18	Economic and political instability in Russia (Sept 98)
18	Congress examines federal raid of Branch Davidian Waco compound (Aug 95)
16	Government recommendation to break Microsoft into two separate companies (April 00)
15	Deepening financial crisis in many Asian countries (Jan 98)
15	Ethics committee's investigation of Speaker of the House Jim Wright (May 89)
14	President Clinton's trip to China (July 98)
13	New ratings system for television programs (Jan 97)
12	Recent political turmoil in Indonesia (June 98)
11	Resignation of Russian President Boris Yeltsin (Jan 00)
10	Chinese President Jiang Zemin's visit to the United States (Nov 97)
9	Debate over U.S. policy concerning global warming (Nov 97)
7	Controversy over including right-wing political party in Austrian government (Feb 00)
6	Pres. Clinton and Russian Pres. Boris Yeltsin summit in Helsinki (April 97)
5	Expansion of NATO to include Poland, Hungary, and Czech Republic (March 98)
5	Ethnic conflict in Kosovo, Serbia (March 98)
5	Britain's Labor Party defeats the Conservative Party in general elections (May 97)
5	Conflict between the Yugoslavian republics (Dec 91)

SOURCE: Excerpted from Pew 2000a.

NOTE: Table shows percentage of people who claimed to follow the story "very closely."

Table 6.3 Selective versus Routine News Attention, 1998 (%)

Level of News Mentioned by Respondent	Routine Watching	Stories Selected Only if Important/Interesting	No Answer
Local community news	61	38	1
National news	52	46	2
International news	34	63	3

SOURCE: Excerpted from Pew 1998b.

workday, rather than as a demanding intellectual exercise. Other factors are boredom with an important story like Medicare reform that has been in the news repeatedly; competition from other concurrent events, including other news stories; and unattractive story formats. But the main reason illustrated by the data presented in table 6.3 is the fact that average Americans are far more attentive to news from their own backyards than to international and national news.*

Self-reports on patterns of attention to various types of news two years later, depicted in table 6.4, show the same trends of preference for local information albeit less strongly. Poll figures on responses to questions about a variety of political issues also underline this trend. When survey questions focus largely on public attention to national and international news, they are probing the slimmest areas of public knowledge. Political elites think that the public should give preferred attention to these areas of politics, but public choices run in different directions.

Television audiences also are far more complimentary about the quality of local news compared to national news. When asked in an open-ended question in 1998 about the one word that best described their impression of the national media and the local media, respectively, the ranking term for national media was "Biased," while the ranking term for local media was "Good." Compared to national news media, local media received double the number of favorable comments and half the number of unfavorable ones. Overall, the balance for comments about national news media ran 56 percent favorable and 44 percent unfavorable compared to 85 percent favorable and only 15 percent unfavorable for local news media (Pew 1998d).

---

*The data in tables 6.3 and 6.4 are based on responses of a random national sample of 3,002 and 3,142 adults, respectively, eighteen years of age or older who were interviewed via telephone by Princeton Survey Research Associates between 24 April and 11 May 1998, for table 6.3 and between 20 April and 13 May 2000, for table 6.4. Sampling error rates are plus or minus 2.5 percentage points.

Table 6.4 Close Attention to Various News Topics, 2000 (%)

Question: How closely do you follow this type of news either in the newspaper, on television, or on radio: very closely, somewhat closely, not very closely, or not at all closely?

News Topics Followed Very Closely and Somewhat Closely	Follow Closely	Breakdown	
		Very	Somewhat
Crime	75	30	45
Health	74	29	45
People and events in your community	73	26	47
Local government	63	20	43
Science and technology	63	18	45
News about political figures and events in Washington	60	17	43
International affairs	59	14	45
Consumer news	57	12	45
Entertainment	56	15	41
Religion	53	21	32
Sports	52	27	25
Business and finance	50	14	36
Culture and the arts	42	10	32

SOURCE: Excerpted from Pew 2000b.

Average audiences ignore or quickly forget most of the facts of news stories that do not seem to be relevant to their concerns (McGraw et al. 1990, 1991). In fact, most viewers' main purpose for watching news is surveillance to make sure that their world is intact and safe. To do that, two-thirds (67 percent) claim to look for general information about important happenings in preference to news narrowly focused on their own concerns (Pew 2000b). Once that is done, they have little further use for the information (Graber 1993). Besides inability to recall much, if anything, about these stories, that also means that people do not develop rich schemas for processing this type of information whenever it reappears in future news. As noted, television news stories commonly tap into viewers' memories to draw out contextual details that cannot be presented in full by the story because of time constraints. When reporters during President Clinton's impeachment trial mentioned that lawyers relied on constitutional interpretations developed during similar proceedings against President Nixon, they assumed that most viewers could draw on memories from the earlier situation. Considering the passage of time and moderate initial interest in legal minutiae, that is a very questionable assumption.

Journalists find, and experimental research substantiates, that it is very difficult to make most international and even national political news stories relevant to ordinary Americans. "The attempt to relate the abstractions of national political debate to one's immediate life circumstances is a complex, delicate, subtle, and often frustrating process" (Neuman et al. 1992, xiv). It therefore should come as no surprise that well over half of all adults say that government is too difficult to understand and that they are little interested in politics. The continued willingness of the public to expose itself regularly to large amounts of political information, including national and international news, nonetheless suggests that people, though frustrated with run-of-the-mill politics and political news, are not alienated from the political process. They are eager to learn information when its salience is clear (Key 1965; Popkin 1994; Page and Shapiro 1992). In fact, 87 percent of the public actually claims to enjoy keeping up with important news at all levels "a lot" or "some," even though most of it does not interest them (Pew 1998a).

Why are mismatches between journalistic and audience perspectives about what constitutes the most desirable news so common? At the heart of many of the mismatches about content and format lie hallowed journalism norms, which have become straitjackets into which most news stories are laced. The hunger for prized scoops, for example, prompts journalists to ignore audience tastes and concentrate on the freshest news even when it is less important than other stories and when crucial evidence is still missing. The desire to be "objective" leads journalists to feature contradictory story interpretations that confuse many audience members, and their fear of engaging in inappropriate editorializing explains why they often shun interpretations. Other reasons for mismatches are ingrained idealistic, but unrealistic, notions of what citizens ought to learn and like and the realities of the news-gathering and news production business. Audience preferences are considered, of course, but they are often misconstrued or outweighed by the other concerns.

Pleasing advertisers by attracting as large an audience as possible is one of the main news business concerns. Reporters often abandon serious political news and pander instead to voyeuristic instincts to guarantee large audiences because such programs attract serious viewers as well as fans of racy fare. Other stories are uninteresting to the audience, short on intellectual content, and often repetitive because journalists are either lazy or overwhelmed with work. Lifting stories verbatim from general wire-service reports and scanning the daily police blotter for news are examples of low-effort reporting.

Table 6.5   Profile of 10:00 P.M. Network Newscasts in Chicago, 1997

Commercials	11 min.	Politics/government	2 min. 36 sec.
Crime/justice system	3 min. 44 sec.	Promotions/lottery scores	2 min. 11 sec.
Sports	3 min. 41 sec.	Living/features	1 min. 49 sec.
Health/medicine	2 min. 54 sec.	Money/business/consumers	1 min. 15 sec.
Weather	2 min. 38 sec.	Other (under 1 min. each)[a]	3 min. 7 sec.

[a] Includes disasters, accidents, national news, foreign news, religion, arts, education, urban affairs, media, science, and technology.

A great deal of time on "news" programs is actually devoted to information other than political news. A content analysis of the 10:00 P.M. network news in Chicago during the 1997 fall season demonstrates just how much time is typically spent on news of little substance even in well-rated newscasts (Johnson 1998a, 1998b). News analysts generally deem Chicago news "better than average" compared to other big-city markets, according to a February 1997 news survey sponsored by Rocky Mountain Media Watch. The survey covered 100 cities in fifty-five markets in thirty-five states. Chicago news is also five minutes longer than average. Nonetheless, its basic configuration is typical in terms of the sequence of stories within the broadcast, the substance of featured stories, and the time allotted to individual stories. In Chicago, as elsewhere, the 10:00 P.M. local news is particularly important because it captures the largest nightly news audiences—1.1 million people in the Chicago area.

The content analysis of the sixty broadcasts shown by three local affiliates of the national networks in the fall of 1997 revealed that nearly one-third (31 percent) of the broadcast time, eleven minutes out of a thirty-five-minute total, was devoted to commercials. Table 6.5 details the average time allotted to various types of news topics in these 1997 newscasts.

To coax the audience to sit through the large dose of commercials, two minutes and eleven seconds—or 9 percent of the "news hole," the technical name for nonadvertising time in a newscast—were used for "teasers" to announce upcoming news.* Sports and weather combined received another 26 percent of the news hole. While popular, these stories preempt a disproportionately large share of the broadcast. In the

---

*In typical prime-time half-hours, commercials account for only 23 percent of the broadcast time, and much less time is squandered on teasers.

national news, sports stories receive far less attention, but weather news is equally prominent.

After subtracting time for commercials, teasers, sports, weather, and lottery scores, only fifteen minutes and twenty-four seconds were left for news even in a thirty-five-minute newscast. How did journalists use this tiny slice of broadcast time? Crime and criminal justice system news plays a prominent role in the 10 o'clock news broadcasts. Audiences avidly consume it, as shown in table 6.4, even though they complain about excessive emphasis on crime news. Crime news is also plentiful on national broadcasts, but compared to the local news, it is far more focused on political wrongdoing and white-collar crime than on the run-of-the-mill crimes featured at night. Combined with accident and disaster news (0:56), "mayhem" news fills almost five (4:40) minutes of the 10:00 P.M. news hole. Nearly half (twenty-six) of the sixty newscasts began with a murder, rape, or accidental death story; five other openings involved nonviolent crimes, adding to the impression that crime is rampant even though the winter of 1997 was a period of declining crime rates and there were plenty of interesting stories of greater and more lasting significance to the Chicago audience that could have been featured.

Another five (4:43) minutes go to health and medical news and other lifestyle matters. The remaining time is split among business and consumer items, domestic government and politics news, and a miscellany of other types of news with varying relevance to governmental issues. Analysis of the two-minute-thirty-six-second time slice of news devoted to government and politics stories showed that several topics were conspicuous by their sparse treatment. In a month when school reform was a major political issue in Chicago, as well as in the Illinois legislature, none of the newscasts included in this sample gave even a full minute to the topic. The same held true for state news in general, for urban affairs, for science news, and for foreign news, which is a heavy favorite in the national newscasts. One-third of the news hole at the national level is devoted to foreign affairs.

Despite the fact that the 10:00 P.M. news is billed as "local" news, it covers local political events only lightly. One reason for sparse attention to local government affairs in the Chicago area is the discrepancy between the boundaries of television markets and local community boundaries. Television markets cover portions of many different communities, forcing stations to present "local" newscasts that interest all of these communities, rather than a single community. Cable television,

Table 6.6 Nonadvertising Time Distribution in Chicago, 1997 (%)

Crime/justice system	15.6	(10.6)	Promotions/lottery scores	9.1	(6.2)
Sports	15.4	(10.5)	Living/features	7.5	(5.2)
Health/medicine	12.1	(8.3)	Money/business/consumers	5.2	(3.5)
Weather	11.0	(7.5)	Other (under 1 min. each)[a]	13.0	(8.9)
Politics/government	10.8	(7.4)	(Advertising share = 31.5)		

NOTE: Calculations in parentheses include advertising times.

[a] Includes disasters, accidents, national news, foreign news, religion, arts, education, urban affairs, media, science, and technology.

which covers smaller markets, brings some relief on that score, as does the Internet.

While there were grave deficiencies in coverage, the monthlong broadcast sample contained twenty-two in-depth, lengthy (more than three-minute) stories covering serious issues that had public policy implications. Many of these were hard-edged investigative reports by experts in the respective fields. They were featured as the lead story on seven occasions and constituted 12 percent of the leads. The issues covered by these stories often related to mundane local problems, such as public safety concerns or municipal services, rather than major national issues, but they provided information that the audience could use. Such coverage of issues related to people's daily lives helps to explain the public's high regard for local newscasts.

In table 6.6, the focus is on the percentage of the news hole allotted to various topics exclusive of advertising. The figures in parentheses indicate the percentages if advertising is included in the calculation. In an average newscast, broadcast time was divided among 14.5 stories. To allow some of these to run for a minute or two, or even longer, requires that others be kept below thirty seconds, which is generally inadequate to do justice to their messages.

HURDLES TO STORY INTERPRETATION

The fact that audiences find it difficult to understand news stories and relate them to their lives often springs from reporters' failure to supply internal and external contextual information that would clarify the story's meaning and its impact on the totality of politics (Bennett 1997; Entman 1989; Iyengar 1991). Societal forces that shaped the reported events are left unexplained. If such information were included, stories would become more informative and easier to process, and far more interesting. Comparisons with related events and appraisals of the story's significance for various groups are examples of helpful contextual information that is often missing. Such information is especially important for complex stories, like stories about economic conditions. Linking specific stories to their larger themes also helps comprehension. For example, for the average person a story about campaign funding irregularities becomes an illustration of her or his evolving "crooked politician" schema (Lodge et al. 1990). Journalists would facilitate processing if they would stress this theme or whatever other theme the story might illuminate.

Many news stories present multiple facts about complicated issues in a confusing manner. Coverage of the 1993–94 health care reform debate in the U.S. Congress provides numerous examples (Jamieson and Cappella 1998). The press identified alternative health plan proposals by their sponsors' names even though names are hard to remember and the plans could have been classified according to their basic structure. Worse, identifications were used inconsistently. The twenty-seven reform proposals that had been introduced were labeled with over 100 different names. Audiences found it difficult to cope with such puzzling complexity (Cappella and Jamieson 1997).

When journalists reported the consequences of the various reforms, they mentioned a broad spectrum of possibilities. Audiences find such stories confusing. For them, it is much easier to process a limited number of clearly explained likely outcomes than to make sense out of a large number of cryptically stated contingencies (van Dijk 1988). Similarly, audiences can judge more easily what is most and least important when the consequences are prioritized. As mentioned, journalists generally avoid doing so, lest it be considered inappropriate editorializing. Encased in the straitjacket of veneration for what passes for objectivity, they avoid expressing evaluations and feelings, except as they creep in through the choice of particular words and audiovisuals.

Because American journalists prize objectivity, they have adopted the convention of presenting opposing sides in controversies, preferably featuring experts of equal prominence. This can be very perplexing for audiences, contrary to the romantic notion that average people can easily discern what is correct and what is false if they are told "the facts" about the situation. Most people, most of the time, need help with evaluating how the pluses and minuses add up and what the bottom line is when their personal experiences are insufficient to judge a particular political situation (Lodge et al. 1990). But journalists rarely provide adequate help. This does not mean that journalists should make evaluations for audiences; rather, it means that they should supply audiences with usable evaluation criteria. In many instances, these criteria can be drawn from politicians' claims about the rationales undergirding their policy proposals. Reporters tend to shy away from these pronouncements because they distrust politicians' statements, often with good reason.

A further common news-framing problem is the use of unfamiliar, undefined technical terms. Many people do not know the meaning of "indexing" tax rates to inflation or "capping entitlements" in the budget or "regulating emission rates." The ABC news story on the AIDS crisis in South Africa (10 July 2000, see the next page) is a typical example of journalistic rhetoric in broadcast news. Based on WordPerfect textual analysis, the story has 309 words, of which 54 (17.4 percent) are unintelligible for average readers. According to the Flesch-Kincaid Grade Level Formula, the grade level of the AIDS story is 10.4 compared to a 4.0 grade level for a Hemingway short story and a 10.5 grade level for income tax form 1040 EZ. A grade level score between 7.0 and 8.0—meaning that a U.S. seventh or eighth grader can understand the document—is considered most suitable for general audiences.* Using the Flesch Reading Ease Score, which runs from zero (the most difficult) to 100 (the easiest), the AIDS story scores 51.2. That puts it in the "fairly difficult" range (50–60). A large number of news stories fall into that range or close to it, with television texts slightly easier than newspaper texts. In terms of sentence complexity, where 100 is the highest, most complex score, the AIDS story is at 37 compared to 14 for the Hemingway story and 27 for the income tax form. For vocabulary complexity, where a 100 rating is again the most complex score, the AIDS story rates a 27, the Hemingway story a 5, and the income tax form a 42.

The choice of examples that are meaningless for average persons is another problem. Most Americans cannot conceptualize the enormity of figures running into millions and billions and even trillions of dollars, although they can relate to homespun examples and comparisons.

---

*The formula for the Flesch-Kincaid Grade Level Formula is $(0.39 \times ASL) + (11.8 \times ASW) - 15.59$, where ASL is the average sentence length (the number of words divided by the number of sentences) and ASW is the average number of syllables per word (the number of syllables divided by the number of words). The formula for the Flesch Reading Ease Score, using the same abbreviations, is $206.835 - (1.015 \times ASL) - (84.6 \times ASW)$.

LANGUAGE COMPLEXITY IN BROADCAST NEWS

On 10 July 2000, ABC's Nightline *aired a program called "South Africa's Deadly Debate." During the program, Aaron Brown, a Washington-based ABC reporter, interviewed three scientists: Dr. Anthony Fauci, director of the National Institute of Allergy and Infectious Diseases in Washington, D.C.; Dr. Peter Piot, executive director of the joint United Nations program on HIV/AIDS; and Dr. Hoosen Coovadia, professor of pediatrics and child health at the University of Natal. The scientists were responding to the doubts expressed by South Africa's President Thabo Mbeki about the linkage between HIV and AIDS. The selections below represent the scientists' concerns.*

Dr. Fauci: . . . I was really quite disappointed in the fact that the president of South Africa, Mr. Mbeki, really, I believe, lost an opportunity to—to make some definitive statements in a very specific way about what could be done and what opportunities now are available with regard to drug companies talking about donating drugs for a considerable period of time, the idea of mother-to-child transmission, perinatal transmission. There were many specific things that could have been said. He indeed did mention HIV and AIDS. And he said some very good things that really were very important and he's brought attention to it. So I don't fault him for that, but I believe the opportunity was present to do something even more and lead the way for all of Southern Africa. And, unfortunately, that opportunity was squandered.

[Turning to Dr. Piot, Aaron Brown asks whether the opportunity has vanished forever.]

Dr. Piot: I really don't think so. Because when I look at what's being presented here at this conference, I find that the solutions for this terrible problem in Africa, this major development crisis, are also in Africa. We're hearing about very positive experiences. A country like Uganda where today there are at least 50 percent less new infections than five to 10 years ago, particularly among young people. The same thing is happening in a country like Zambia, in Central Africa and in a country like Senegal where they manage to keep the level of infection very low thanks to very early intervention. This is the kind of experiences that are being exchanged here.

[Aaron Brown then asks Dr. Coovadia whether AIDS in Africa has unique characteristics.]

Dr. Coovadia: There are local differences in HIV/AIDS. And that's not unexpected. The problem is, I think, that individuals who are—who help government don't realize that's a common phenomenon. I've looked at children for more than 30 years now, and measles was not entirely the same in the United States as it was in Africa. Polio wasn't the same and hepatitis B is certainly not the same. So there are local and regional variations in childhood diseases and in diseases of adults which we know about, we accept as a normal pattern in the differentiation of human diseases for very many other diseases other than HIV. So are there differences? There are. But HIV's fundamentally one single disease with regional variations.

When lavish military spending is discussed, for example, lay audiences can readily see that it is wasteful to spend $100 or more on toilet seats or hammers. But they are not certain whether it is extravagant to spend millions on an aircraft navigation system or billions on a fleet of aircraft carriers. People tend to think of the cost of government programs as cheap or expensive or as a waste of money or worthwhile in terms of the value received—but news stories rarely match such frames. It is far more meaningful to state that the combined annual spending at all levels of government—federal, state, and local—equals nearly half the value of goods and services that Americans produce each year than to report multibillion-dollar expenditure and gross domestic product figures. When information is framed to parallel how ordinary people think, it can be processed more easily, as explained in chapter 2 (Graber 1993; Ottati 1990; Ottati and Wyer 1990; Wyer et al. 1991). All too many stories fail to meet this criterion (Graber 1993; Buscemi 1997).

That a disjunction exists between the way journalists frame political stories and the way audiences frame them for specific issues has been documented by Neuman and his colleagues (1992). Their analysis of news framing of five issues—South Africa, the Strategic Defense Initiative, the stock market crash of 1987, cocaine and drug abuse, and the AIDS crisis—revealed five major frames used both in media stories and by interview respondents. But as table 6.7 shows, the percentages of discussion devoted to each of these frames varied considerably. Journalists dwelled far more on conflict, and audiences dwelled far more on the human impact of the stories and their moral implications.

Table 6.7 Journalists' Frames versus Audiences' Frames for Five Stories (%)

Framing Concept	Journalists	Audiences
Powerlessness against superior forces	33	22
Conflict; politics as contest	29	6
Human impact of events	18	36
Economics; profit and loss	16	21
Moral values inherent in stories	4	15

SOURCE: Adapted from Neuman et al. 1992, 62–75.

Presidential debates are another good example of significant differences in framing. When ordinary citizens frame the questions about future policies, most audience members report that they can identify much more readily with the questioners than when journalists frame their typical questions about campaign strategies and candidate shortcomings. The town hall–style presidential debate in 1992 has been characterized as reflecting "all the qualities of 'Oprah' dropped in the middle of C-Span's intensely sober coverage of a town meeting" (McNulty and Daley 1992). "Oprah" style, named after the popular television talk-show hostess, means dealing with people's gut-level concerns in a style that is compatible with their manner of thinking. It does not necessarily mean a hollowness of substance or minimal follow-up probing (Stevens 1992). When "town hall" formats have been used in the past during public meetings or call-in television, the outcome has been comparable. The thrust of the questions and the manner of framing have differed substantially from the usual journalist-dominated interchange. Audiences have responded enthusiastically.

THE QUEST FOR INTERESTING, APPEALING NEWS

If news is not cast in interesting ways, many citizens will shun it. This is why interest is a major factor in learning about politics. It can even compensate for limited information-processing skills. There is ample evidence that people whose cognitive skills are low but whose interest in various news topics is high learn as much about these topics as disinterested people whose cognitive skills are high (Neuman et al. 1992; Graber 1993). Of course, people's reactions to particular stories vary, often considerably, because interest is partly a matter of each person's internal motivation and partly a matter of story appeal (Liebes 1988). This is why the manner of storytelling must be geared to the tastes of particular audiences.

Average news stories are structured to answer *who, what, where, when, why,* and *how* questions. Interview data reveal that people want to know about all these story elements, but are most interested in the *why* and *how* (Graber 1993). As one experienced news director explained it during an interview:

> [T]here is an implied question in the viewer's mind about how did it happen. And you need to answer that in a story because people are going to want to know, for example, if, could it happen again, you know, could it happen to them? Is this a freak occurrence, or is this some serious misdesign in the system? Even though the answers aren't known, you have to acknowledge in the story that you asked those questions, too. . . . You pique the curiosity by showing a train wreck—look, what happened? How did it happen? Anybody hurt? You know, the questions that immediately come to mind have to be answered. And, as much as you can answer with real people who are here at the scene of the crash, or who are helping people out, or whatever, all the better. (Quoted in Graber 1994a, 491–92)

Yet a content analysis of word and picture messages in a sample of 350 randomly selected television news stories (feature stories and snippet news were excluded) showed that coverage of the *why* and *how* questions and story contexts was poor. By contrast, over 90 percent of the stories reported clearly *who* and *what* were involved and *where* and *when* it happened (Graber 1997). Table 6.8 shows that only half (51 percent) of the stories explained *why* the situation was occurring. In some news categories, such as law enforcement stories, only one-third (30 percent) of the stories provided reasons. The *how* question, which is answered by information about the successive events in an unfolding story, fared even more poorly. On an average, only one-third (34 percent) of the stories supplied this type of information. For inclusion of contextual data, the range varied between a high of 82 percent for stories about public officials and lows of 43 percent for stories about Western bloc politics and 48 percent for stories about economic conditions. The overall average was 65 percent.

In most cases, it would not be difficult for journalists to answer the *why* and *how* questions and thereby retain the audience's interest. When we asked news directors how they might add *why* and *how* information to a story about legislation to curb drunken driving, they acknowledged that the typical approach was boring when it cast this

Table 6.8 News Element Coverage in Broadcast Stories

	Who (%)	What (%)	Where (%)	When (%)	Why (%)	How (%)	Context (%)	Number
Events abroad								
East bloc politics	100	100	95	95	30	30	60	20
West bloc politics	100	100	90	100	35	20	43	12
Mideast problems	100	100	100	95	55	35	72	15
Third world unrest	100	100	100	95	52	45	76	10
Foreign/defense policies								
Foreign policy	100	100	93	85	60	30	72	13
Defense policy	100	100	94	94	62	46	73	15
Economic issues								
Economic conditions	80	100	75	80	60	32	48	15
Fiscal policies	95	100	90	86	60	5	73	25
Non-economic issues								
Public officials	100	100	100	100	45	48	82	18
Law enforcement	100	100	100	100	30	43	65	15
Miscellaneous	100	100	90	95	38	45	59	24
Private-sector news								
Business news	85	100	90	90	68	30	52	10
Health/medical news	95	100	90	95	67	32	73	15
Average score	97	100	93	93	51	34	65	207

NOTE: Numbers represent the percentage of stories in each group that covers the question. End column = *N*s. 143 stories were excluded from this analysis because they were less than twenty seconds long or were lengthy features.

news as a purely verbal announcement or showed legislators discussing the problem. Instead, they suggested casting it with pictures that demonstrate the serious sociopolitical consequences of drunken driving and animated graphics that put the monetary costs into perspective. A real or simulated example of how such legislation would work in practice and the degree to which it might infringe civil liberties would also be interesting, as would comparative accident data from states with tougher laws.

Most American audiences are attracted by vivid information, which means that "it is (a) emotionally interesting, (b) concrete and image-provoking, and (c) proximate in a sensory, temporal, or spatial way" (Nisbett and Ross 1980, 45). The concept of vividness can refer to the story's subject matter or the manner of portrayal or both. Audiovisual information, as explained, has great potential for vividness. Nonetheless, journalists often fail to make it appealing. For example, they may discuss a politician's welfare proposals from the dull safety of the newsroom, casting it as a "talking head" event, rather than presenting audiovisuals where pictures make the problems come to life. In our content

Table 6.9   News Content Attractions in Television, Newspapers, and Magazines
(per 100-word average)

Attraction Factors	Television	Newspapers	Magazines
Number of pictures	6.7	0.1	0.2
Human interest examples	0.4	0.2	0.2
References to specific people	2.2	1.3	1.3
Causal (why) information	0.9	0.8	0.7
Consequences (how) information	1.3	1.2	1.1
Definitions	0.3	0.3	0.2
Context information at story start[a] (%)	47	31	31

SOURCE: Adapted from Neuman et al. 1992, 52–55.

[a] Percentage of information devoted to context in first section (20 percent) of average story. The remaining coverage includes facts, opinions, and analysis.

analysis of 350 news stories, conflict was the most common dramatic element. Seventy-two percent of the stories involved conflict. By contrast, only 39 percent showed emotional scenes, 41 percent showed people interacting with each other, and 33 percent presented situations with which average viewers might be able to identify.

Whatever the shortcomings of televised news are when it comes to dramatic casting, the situation is worse in other media. When the authors of *Common Knowledge* compared the audience appeal features of television, magazine, and newspaper stories, they found that television news ranks above the others. Not only is it proportionally far richer in attention-grabbing pictures, as table 6.9 shows, but also it has twice as much human-interest content and almost double the references to specific people. When it comes to "context factors," television leads in mentioning causes and consequences of the events in the stories and in referring to policy implications (Neuman et al. 1992). This is why, despite its many flaws, audiences consider it the most interesting, attention- and emotion-arousing, and relevant mode of news presentation.

But is vividness feasible for the many routine stories that are not inherently dramatic? Content analysis indicates that most stories in the average newscast are routine. It also shows quite clearly that the answer is "yes." In our sample of 350 nightly political news stories, 60 percent of the stories were run of the mill. Nearly half of these stories were actually dramatic or could have been through featuring close-ups of people, showing their facial expressions and revealing their body language, or picturing conflict or extreme contrasts in social or political conditions. Many of these stories emphasized human interactions, such as friendliness or hostility, or strong emotions, such as joy, grief, anger, or fear.

Digital television and other new technologies will make dramatic presentations ever easier. As discussed more fully in the next chapter, the new digital spectrum allows stations to bring viewers movie-quality high-definition pictures and sounds, which will greatly enhance the attractiveness of audiovisuals. Virtual reality simulations are now possible, which come very close to actually "being there." Advanced search technologies allow viewers to focus on those scenes that are of greatest interest to them and observe them from various perspectives and focal lengths, almost as if they were physically there and had privileged access to the scene, beyond what is usually granted to ordinary citizens.

As holds always true, technologies must be used responsibly, lest they do harm. Television producers need to guard against using exciting footage that distorts the factual content of stories or takes them out of their context (Milburn and McGrail 1992). For instance, in riot situations, when the unrest is localized, viewers need to be reminded that most of the community is peaceful, and they need to be told about the causes of the riot. But even when emotional footage skews a situation, the benefits may still outweigh the disadvantages. Dramatic framing attracts many viewers who might otherwise ignore the news entirely. Average Americans, whose attention to political news has been waning, are willing to spend many hours of scarce time watching television if the story arouses their emotions. Audience figures collected during the live coverage of the bombing of Iraq during the 1992 Persian Gulf War give ample proof. CNN, for instance, reached its largest ever audience— roughly fourteen times the normal audience—during the event, topping even the major networks and their affiliates (Gutstadt 1993).

Dramatic presentations also increase viewers' emotional involvement with significant political issues and may stimulate them to care and become politically active. Unfortunately, the spike in interest may be short-lived, as happened when the Gulf War drama ebbed. "[A]s soon as the dramatic, dangerous, and suspenseful focus of the news had died down, and despite the politically and historically critical nature of the stories that continued to air, the American public was ready to turn its attention to other areas" (Gutstadt 1993, 402).

USER-HOSTILE FORMATS

Format—the specific verbal, aural, and visual techniques used in delivering messages—also has a strong impact on attention to television programs and comprehension.* Matters such as the ampleness of language and images, the pacing of segments, and special visual effects like dissolves or panning or low or high camera angles are important. "[C]ontent and structure interact in important ways to influence the meaning and ultimately the way people remember television messages" (Geiger and Newhagen 1993).

Formats are all too often user-hostile because they ignore the viewers' information-processing capabilities. For example, news stories presented at the start of a broadcast are often blocked out by later stories that follow them too rapidly. Formats may obscure the correct meaning of messages inadvertently or intentionally. Designers of election campaign advertisements are routinely accused of deliberately formatting their messages deceptively to extol their candidate and vilify the opposition. Stuart Hall has pointed out that broadcasters often subtly embed "preferred readings" and parameters for a range of interpretations in television texts. For example, they make smoking an undesirable behavior by showing a homely person puffing on a cigarette, rather than showing a glamorous individual, as in cigarette advertisements. Such formatting may consciously or subconsciously influence audiences and deter them from making unbiased interpretations (Hall 1980).

Brevity and Pace

Several structural aspects of current television news presentations are particularly user-hostile. The brevity of most stories is a major culprit (Graber 1990). Three out of four television news stories last less than three minutes. Nearly a third run for less than one minute. During news conferences or presidential debates, conventions of brevity commonly force participants to limit their answers to three minutes or less. Such brief snippets are hardly sufficient to provide adequate information about most political happenings, including essential facts, contexts, and guides for interpretation.

Insufficient story details also make it more difficult for audiences to process the information. Locating schematic information is easier when messages provide multiple cues, so that viewers have a better chance of finding a relevant schema. This is particularly helpful for

---

*Nelson and Boynton, in *Video Rhetorics: Televised Advertising in American Politics* (1997), dissect formatting techniques verbally and with a videotape to lay bare the interactions between images and sounds and the nuances of various combinations that have been used in political advertising.

viewers with little education whose limited reservoir of schemas is diffi-cult to match. Compared to longer stories, brief ones are less redundant and less likely to repeat facts in follow-up stories. Redundancy, of course, aids memorization. Furthermore, unless viewers tape broadcasts and re-view them, they cannot readily repeat portions that they did not hear or understand initially. Print media and computer-transmitted audio-visuals are much more user-friendly in that respect.

Even within individual television news stories, the pace is usually hurried to cram in as much information as possible. Viewers are then confronted with an overload of information, considering the brief time available for processing. Pictures that carry important, information-rich messages appear on the screen in extremely rapid succession. Three-quarters of the visual messages are visible for no more than twenty sec-onds at most. The quantity of visual cues is frequently excessive, con-sidering the sparse time for processing (Caldwell 1995). Videographers also vary the picture focus far more frequently than would occur when people normally view a situation, requiring extra mental efforts from the viewer. Slow motion tends to be used in many situations when it does not enhance understanding and consumes valuable time that could be used to better advantage.

Similarly, dialogue is often overdone. News directors seem to fear si-lence. Because time is so short, verbal messages are often broadcast ex-tremely rapidly, so that comprehension suffers. To make matters worse, in many instances picture and word messages that are presented simul-taneously are uncoordinated. Rather than reinforcing each other, they may be different, even contradictory. Processing such divergent mes-sages simultaneously is difficult at best, and often impossible. But even without that, coordinating pictures and words into unified cognitions requires more effort than many viewers are willing to make, especially when their attention is divided between watching the news and carry-ing out other attention-grabbing tasks. "Cognitive busyness"—ex-posure to multiple visual and aural stimuli—makes it difficult for politically unsophisticated viewers to process televised information efficiently (Rahn, Aldrich, et al. 1994; Rahn and Cramer 1996).

Because of the hurried pace, there are few pauses within newscasts to serve as "stopping points," which are essential for processing informa-tion that has just been presented. Story follows story or advertisement in rapid succession, registering only momentarily in short-term mem-ory. No student would be expected to learn subject matter well in a classroom where information was presented in capsules that rarely ex-ceeded three minutes, note-taking was impossible, and twenty different

subjects were broached in a thirty-minute span. The pace of story presentation was not always so hectic. In the late 1960s and early 1970s,
images and sound bites were markedly longer, and they would often be
followed by two or three seconds of silence, allowing the message to
sink in. Now presentations are much more rapid-fire.

The reasons for brevity of individual news stories are partly structural
and partly strategic. Structurally, the space allotted to hard political
news is small because competing soft news stories and commercials are
deemed more profitable. Strategically, there is a perception that viewers
lack patience to sit through longer stories, except when extraordinary
events are happening, and that they will not tolerate more than a half-
hour of news at a stretch. If it runs longer on an ordinary news day,
their reaction is a switch of the dial to more entertaining fare. The generally low viewer counts for lengthier news programs on public television, C-SPAN, and CNN seem to bear out this perception.

Sequencing

Another problem that hampers information transmission is the often
illogical sequencing within newscasts, as shown in table 6.10. International, national, and local political, economic, and social news stories
are assembled in crazy-quilt fashion, interspersed regularly with unrelated advertising breaks. Like dream sequences, newscasts are "a dis-
jointed procession of images and doings. . . . There is little that is
orderly about the sequence of material" (Fowles 1992, 39). When disparate topics follow each other in rapid succession, viewers are forced
to leapfrog erratically among unconnected schemas. Learning suffers
(Crigler et al. 1993). Staying focused on even a single topic becomes
arduous when the broadcast is interrupted by lengthy, eye- and ear-
catching commercials (Geiger and Reeves 1993a, 1993b). Table 6.10
shows that the typical thirty-minute nightly newscast has four breaks,
each averaging slightly more than two minutes in length. That leaves
less than twenty-two minutes for news.

The processing hurdles created by illogical sequencing within and
between news stories are not the only sequencing problem. News directors also need to be concerned about priming effects to which they
are exposing audiences. Information dispensed during an entire newscast, as well as the sociopolitical conditions at the time of the newscast,
affects how individual story messages are likely to be interpreted. The
context can readily suggest improper inferences. The Ruby Clark case
(*Clark v. ABC*, 684 F.2d 1208 [6th Cir. 1982]), discussed in chapter 4, is

Table 6.10 Typical News Sequencing and Breaks

Sunday, 23 November 1997, CBS—30 minutes
   Septuplets; U.S./Iraq relations—1:50 break
   Asia Pacific summit/Japan economy; U.S. labor shortage—2:00 break
   Death of Cuban leader; South African Winnie Mandela hearing—2:20 break
   Fertility treatments—1:50 break
   Gettysburg commercialization

Monday, 29 December 1997, NBC—30 minutes
   Hong Kong flu; airline turbulence; winter storm—2:00 break
   Unabomber trial; hospital murders—2:20 break+
   Airline turbulence—2:20 break
   Cameo reports about famous people; Oklahoma City bombing trial—2:30 break
   War on cancer

Tuesday, 13 January 1998, ABC—30 minutes
   Biological clock; weapons inspection in Iraq—1:30 break
   Navy dismissal of gay sailor; global stock market—2:20 break
   Death penalty for women—2:10 break
   Winter weather; Russia's President Yeltsin; Sicily volcano—2:20 break
   Television and football

Wednesday, 11 February 1998, CBS—30 minutes
   U.S./Iraq relations; White House sex scandal; independent counsel to investigate
     Interior Secretary—1:50 break
   El Niño weather update; cable car accident—2:50 break
   Abortion clinic bombing; carjacking chase; rights of disabled golfer; American
     investors; Indonesia demonstrations; stock market report—2:10 break
   Winter Olympics—2:20 break
   Cars of the future

(*continued*)

in point. The jury ruled that Mrs. Clark had been improperly labeled as a prostitute when her picture appeared on screen during a television broadcast in a neighborhood that had just been identified as a place frequented by prostitutes. Though the narration never mentioned her, the sequencing of the story implicated her (Grimes 1990). In a similar vein, television networks routinely suspend air travel advertisements when major aircraft accidents are in the news. Concern about the priming effects of disaster news are the reason. Political scientists Shanto Iyengar and Donald Kinder (1987) have demonstrated such priming effects in a series of experiments that show that prior stories can influence subsequent political appraisals.

Considering the diversity of stories in a typical newscast, it is difficult to avoid damaging sequencing. Furthermore, suggested remedies are subject to the caveat that one can never be sure what associations will be evoked for individual viewers or what events will be at the top of the public's agenda at the moment when a broadcast airs. Such uncertainties may be the reason why so little attention has been paid by news

Table 6.10   (continued)

Thursday, 5 March 1998, CNN—60 minutes
  Ethnic violence in Yugoslavia; weapons inspection in Iraq; Clinton sex scandal;
    campaign fund-raising abuses—3:30 break
  Sri Lanka terrorism; Russian rightist parties; Chinese economy—2:50 break
  Moon exploration—3:50 break
  Clinton sex scandal—3:10 break
  Pakistan floods; Australia floods; California land slides; blood transfusion
    contamination—3:00 break
  NATO expansion; Secretary of State in Europe—3:40 break
  Boxer sues promoter; female space shuttle commander

Friday, 17 April 1998, NBC—30 minutes
  Tornadoes in Tennessee; space shuttle launch—2:00 break
  Russian internal politics; weapons inspection in Iraq—2:20 break+
  Mutual funds—2:20 break
  Global warming; vice-president's charitable contributions—2:50 break+
  Tornado in Alabama

Saturday, 9 May 1998, ABC—30 minutes
  Mideast peace proposal; Minnesota tobacco settlement—2:00 break
  Texas weather; binge drinking in colleges; Ku Klux Klan rally; shooting of traffic
    offender; death of Nixon friend—2:30 break
  Mud slides; Indonesia unrest—2:10 break
  Lettuce shortage; charity drive; gun violation in grade school—1:50 break
  Homeless New York actor

SOURCE: Compiled by the author from the Vanderbilt Television News Abstracts, 1997,
1998.

NOTE: One randomly constructed week drawn from ABC, CBS, NBC, and CNN nightly
news between November 1997 and May 1998. Length of commercial break is reported
in minutes and seconds. The plus sign indicates brief news item component, such as a
stock market report.

producers to juxtapositions of stories beyond efforts to produce a con-
tinuous flow of stories that keeps viewers tuned to a particular program.

   Given the learning hurdles created by the prevailing formats of television news presentations, it is not surprising that average Americans
fail to learn much from the massive amounts of political information
to which they are exposed year in and year out. The real surprise is that
they learn as much as they do.

LESSONS FROM TWO BROADCASTS

What can be done to make better use of the information transmission
strength of audiovisuals? To stick closely to the bounds of reality, we
will peg our discussion on communications scholar Michael Griffin's

(1992) analysis of two actual television news stories. One of the stories made reasonably good, though by no means perfect, use of the audio-visual potential of the medium; the other did not. Both stories were broadcast on NBC news on 26 January 1990. They concerned an airline crash involving Peru's Avianca airline and the U.S. government's legal case against Panamanian General Manuel Noriega. As is typical of news stories, both were constructed by patching together image fragments and sound bites and counting on viewers to supply missing parts of the story by drawing on their memory banks.

Typical pictures taken for news stories include "establishing shots," which identify relevant scenes and locations; "cut-ins," which can serve to illustrate story details; and "cut-aways," which can be used for transitions (Millerson 1992). Only a fraction of all available picture footage will be used. The main purpose of visuals in most stories is to signify that a particular event is important and that reporters were on the scene and gathered information that validates their spoken report. The information content of the pictures and their artistic quality are generally secondary because the words are still considered the main carriers of the message.

It is rare to have actual live coverage of unplanned events, such as car crashes or police chases. Videographers therefore mostly go to the scene of action after the event has occurred and shoot pictures of the aftermath in line with their preconceived ideas about the usual course of events in similar situations. Many of these shots are so generic that they can be archived for future use. The Avianca air crash represents the type of event where live footage of the consequences of an important happening is often available. Nonetheless, such footage tends to be ignored. "Even when an incident like a plane crash affords the greatest opportunity for the visual presentation of 'actualities,' reports tend to be dominated by 'talk about' the event rather than images of the event. They are constructed as interview segments with corroborating 'representative' images, rather than as visual 'documentaries' of ongoing activity" (Griffin 1992, 136).

Most television stories begin with an introduction by the anchor, who sets the frame and then introduces the reporter stationed at a particular location related to the story. The location is identified through an establishing shot, which pictures or symbolizes the scene. The narrative that follows interweaves visual image bites and script. The visuals validate the report because they allow viewers to "see for themselves" that the reporters and anchors are telling an accurate story. The ubiquitous commercials, which interrupt the flow of messages, disturb the audience's processing of the story and may suggest that the political news is trivial because commercials are allowed to intrude. Closing overviews of the entire scene are common, as is a final picture of the reporter and anchor.

The Avianca Story

Like many other stories, the story started with a visual teaser designed to hook the viewer. In this case, it was a zoom-out from the broken fuselage of the plane to a shot of a young child in the arms of a paramedic. A voice-over by anchor Tom Brokaw then asked: "Is it possible the Avianca airliner ran out of fuel? The crash killed more than sixty." The story, which took an exceptionally long five minutes and forty-five seconds overall, was then presented in three segments. The first of these, lasting three minutes and fifteen seconds, covered the crash site and included vistas of the wrecked plane and its location, which allowed viewers to comprehend the effect of the disaster on people, equipment, and the crash site.

The segment also included a host of meaningless pictures that served as backdrops for the narration. Among these were several views of the anchor broadcasting from a typical studio and split-screen views of the faces of NBC's aviation expert and the on-site reporters. There were also twenty-two seconds of meaningless stock footage of an unidentified airport where passengers were checking luggage and then boarding a plane that was sitting on the tarmac. Using visuals as symbols to signify that routine activities are going on, such as reporters visiting the scene or passengers embarking on unrelated air trips, is largely a waste of precious visual resources. Among the more informative pictures, often shown too briefly to absorb detail, were several views of the wreckage, including some close-ups of crash investigators, an aerial overview of the site, and a ground-level pan shot of the fuselage. A total of twenty-five seconds was given to four action shots taken the previous night that showed firemen trying to pull victims from the wreckage.

A full minute was devoted to illustrating a helpful discussion about the possibility that the plane might have run out of fuel. It was a mixture of computer graphics and still photos designed to explain U.S. rules on fuel reserves and link them to the plane's flight path, along with a graphics simulation of a cockpit where pilots and flight controllers conducted a paraphrased dialogue. During these shots, a narrator's voice described the plane's problems and reported the pilot's last message. These scenes ended with a dissolve and the standard return to the crash scene, the reporter, and the anchor.

The second segment, which lasted two minutes and ten seconds, focused on the rescue operations and the victims. It included interviews with hospitalized survivors and shots of injured children being pulled from the wreckage, which symbolized the utter horror of the event. To open the segment, the anchor introduced the on-site reporter who "was there last night." A collage of pictures then appeared on the screen, but again they were shown too briefly to allow inspection. They included views of volunteer firemen and emergency workers pulling people from the wreckage or carrying them away on stretchers; a hospital entrance, along with a snippet interview with a hospitalized survivor; and a somewhat longer interview with a rescue worker who told of saving a little girl whose bloody face was shown. Finally, there was a brief interview with a tearful father who was looking in vain for his seven-year-old child, followed by an announcement that the child was dead.

The final segment was a twenty-second purely verbal postscript that was not well integrated into the crash story. The anchor reported that one victim had rubber cocaine containers in his stomach. To make this addendum meaningful, the link between the crash and cocaine smuggling could have been clarified. It may also have been possible to illustrate the cocaine discovery with X-rays.

The Noriega Story

While the majority of the visuals in the Avianca story were informative, most of the pictures in the Noriega story were "wallpaper"—decorative but adding little to make the story come to life for the viewer. The pictures were drawn from stock photographs, file footage, and graphics. Documents shown as evidence of Noriega's misdeeds were indistinct, as were the fleeting pictures of the main actors in the story. Genuine visual inspection was thus impossible. Yet producers commonly use such marginal visuals, preferring them to showing the faces of journalists and their sources—"talking heads"—for lengthy periods of time.

The Noriega story, which took less than three minutes, began with a view of anchor Tom Brokaw in the network studio along with a graphic enclosed in a box that displayed a picture of Noriega, his name, and a symbolic figure of a blind goddess of justice holding her scales. When Brokaw reported that Noriega had appealed to President Bush for reclassification as a prisoner of war, a picture of a correspondent in front of the White House appeared to signify that the story involved presidential action. Then followed indistinct images of Noriega's letter of appeal, file footage of Noriega accompanied by police and in court, and a close-up of a drawing of the general. None of these pictures allowed viewers to observe the general closely and gather clues from body language. The reporters' discussions of the legal situation were accompanied by pictures presumably showing the prosecutor and lawyers, but their identities were not clear.

When the narrative turned to the search for evidence in Panama, footage of cars backed up at an entry checkpoint for a U.S. air base in Panama was used as a backdrop to suggest that the location had switched to Panama. The base was identified by a sign, followed by a glimpse through a chain-link fence at an unidentified building. It was unclear how the building might be connected to the story. A telephoto shot then showed four unidentified men in short-sleeve shirts and jeans walking across a parking lot to a parked car, while the reporter commented that U.S. drug agents at the base had been studying Noriega evidence. Again, it is not clear whether the unidentified men were investigators.

Several indistinct shots then showed papers, passports, credit cards, and piles of paper money, presumably hoarded by the general. When the reporter mentioned that Noriega owned a condominium in Paris, viewers saw the Eiffel Tower—which has become an icon for France—and a very brief cut to the exterior of a high-rise building and a street sign. The reporter questioned whether this property was bought with drug money but provided no evidence to support this suspicion. Then he mentioned that another figure linked to Noriega had been arrested. The pictures showed a distant shot of a man in handcuffs walking along a sidewalk and then up a long staircase. The story ended with a brief wrap-up by a reporter placed in front of a Miami courthouse who reported that Noriega was doing well in prison, followed by a final word from the anchor.

Obviously, the audiovisuals in the Noriega story convey little beyond the spoken words, unlike the audiovisuals in the Avianca story. The two stories are fairly representative of the mixed audiovisual quality of U.S. television news fare. This is confirmed by data from a content analysis designed to test the contributions made by visuals in television news stories over and above what was told by the verbal account (Graber 1991). In 150 network news stories, drawn from ABC,

CBS, and NBC national news, 32 percent of the visual information proved irrelevant; it was little more than wallpaper. Eighteen percent of the information was redundant, with the pictures providing essentially the same information as the words. But the remaining 50 percent of the pictures presented valuable information that was not covered by the spoken story. The Avianca story thus was somewhat better than average, while the Noriega story was somewhat worse.

A fifty/fifty score when it comes to the effective use of pictures amounts to the proverbial half-empty/half-full glass. There is much room for improvement, but the situation at the turn of the century is by no means as dismal as it is often bemoaned by critics like Newton Minow (1964; Minow and LaMay 1995). Chapter 4 has told that story.

THE CATCH-22 SCENARIO

In *Out of Order* (1993), Thomas Patterson argues that Americans expect their news media to achieve goals that are conflicting and out of sync with the nature of American media. To a substantial degree, the *Mission: Impossible* theme fits this chapter's recitation of problems of news selection, framing, casting, and formatting. These problems are serious, and most have been acknowledged. It is also clear that only moderate changes can be expected, given the dilemmas inherent in news presentation. Americans idolize intellectual news that presents sophisticated analysis but, at the same time, want it to be simple, personalized, and entertaining, though not too blatantly fluffy. They want in-depth, contextualized coverage as long as it can be crowded into snippets measured in seconds and the whole newscast does not delay them from other pursuits for more than thirty minutes. But the snippets are then condemned for being intellectually indigestible because they cram too many words and pictures into too small a package and contain too few moments of silence to allow the information to sink in. Journalists share the scholars' ideals about the seriousness with which political news should be handled in a democracy, but they find it difficult to reconcile the demands of creating complex news presentations with the demands to produce news quickly, cheaply, and entertainingly so that it earns advertising profits for their organization. And so it goes. It is a classical Catch-22 scenario.

In the next chapter, we turn to the prospects for audiovisual news improvements in the twenty-first century. We shall highlight what can be changed to make news processing easier, more palatable, and more productive, always keeping our vision within the bounds of the realities of our age and the constraints imposed by the human brain, body, and spirit.

7

PEERING INTO THE CRYSTAL BALL: WHAT DOES THE FUTURE HOLD?

Television remains the most widely used, and hence most influential, medium for presenting political information to average Americans. It is true that, at the turn of the twenty-first century, the television networks' prime-time news audience figures had plunged to 25 percent from a high of 57 percent in the 1970s and 1980s. But, overall, attention to televised news has not declined; the audience simply has switched its news-watching time or has gone elsewhere. The "elsewhere" is the many new information venues, mostly cable or satellite television, and increasingly the audiovisual presentations on the web from late night news shows to early morning offerings (Kirk 1999).

Despite losing more than half of their nightly news viewers, the established networks, as a group, still garner the largest slice of the audience and therefore come closer to being a "national" medium than cable and satellite television, their younger competitors. At the turn of the twenty-first century, the most popular cable news programs still attract less than a third of the audience captured by the most popular network news television programs. Over-the-air television remains king of the information market by a wide margin (Pew 1998c).

Projecting current trends beyond the year 2000 has led to estimates that average Americans, over the period of a month, will watch, on average, 69 hours of television, 60 hours of subscription video services, 51 hours of basic cable, 3 hours of on-line programs, and 3 hours of video games (Jones 1997). That amounts to 186 hours of exposure to audiovisuals—a bit more than 6 hours per day. If these projections are accurate, the lion's share—37 percent of the total time—will still be devoted to over-the-air television, 32 percent to subscription video, 27 percent to cable, and 2 percent each to the fastest-growing audiovisual offerings—on-line programs and video games.

The continuing dominance of audiovisuals as carriers of political information for most Americans underlines the importance of discussing how the many weaknesses described in this book can be overcome and how the considerable strengths of political television, which have been detailed as well, can be enhanced. Will it be possible to build on existing strengths and overcome the genuine weaknesses so that this highly popular information medium will serve the public's need for civic information? My answer is a cautious "yes." The human and material resources are largely in place; what is needed is the will to use them for effective democratic governance.

Making the necessary reforms will hinge on several interrelated factors that depend on the joint efforts of television journalists, the owners of television media, politicians, and the viewing public. (1) Television journalists must see to it that political news programming becomes more audience-driven, privileging audience wants over the news preferences of various elites, including journalists, and over cost-cutting concerns. (2) Journalists and their employers must also be willing to make full use of technology changes, especially narrowcasting, to multiply offerings tailored to the tastes of new generations of audiovisually sophisticated viewers. (3) To make sure that adequate funding is available to produce excellent news, the owners of television media must return to their more public-minded past. In years gone by, supplying the public with adequate political information was deemed an important public service primarily and a money-making enterprise only secondarily. (4) Politicians, too, must make the public's need for information a top priority. It must be given precedence over their own immediate political advantage, which may lie in concealing or distorting information or in keeping it ambiguous. (5) Last, but not least, the public must broaden its sense of civic responsibility so that it ranges beyond each person's immediate personal interest sphere. All of these changes are feasible.

THE "NEW" TELEVISION AUDIENCES

What kinds of programming preferences will the television journalists of the next few decades have to satisfy? Answering that question requires discussion of the major changes in attitudes toward political information between the baby boomer generation and their parents, on one hand, and the Internet generation, on the other. The early twenty-first century will belong to the Generation Xers, born in the 1960s and 1970s, and their offspring, who were immersed in televised information

Table 7.1 Interest in Technological Innovations by Generation (%)

Type of Innovation	GenXers	Parents	Grandparents
Skip TV stories at will, as in newspapers	74	69	49
Click button for more information on story	66	61	38
Select news mix (politics/sports/weather)	54	53	32
Design program from story menu	50	49	27
Have instant access to news any time	50	45	30
Choose from 100+ channels	43	33	14

SOURCE: Excerpted from News in the Next Century 1996, 67.

from infancy onward. While it is always hazardous to project generational changes, it seems quite likely that the children of GenXers, raised in the age of audiovisual plenty, will continue the trends in audiovisual information-gathering set in motion by their parents and grandparents. What do studies of GenXers tell us about their choices of political information and their preferred information delivery systems?

GenXers have spent more time watching the world unfold on audiovisual monitors than in any other waking-hours activity. They have learned from infancy on to prize the creation of virtual reality that visual presentations make possible. GenXers like a great deal of control over their information supply, rather than patiently watching what newscasters have assembled for them in a newscast. GenXers are not intimidated by the technologies that need to be mastered to get information from multiple sources. As table 7.1 shows, three out of four GenXers like to skip television stories at will, and two-thirds enjoy selecting additional information for stories of their choice. Many relish having hundreds of different news sources at their fingertips. They also are perpetual surfers who move quickly from program to program unless a presentation truly engages them. When it comes to political information, half indicate that they want instant, round-the-clock access to news at times of their choosing.

GenXers like to participate in shaping their information menu. Half of them, according to table 7.1, enjoy assembling their own television programs, picking and choosing among stories. They also demand interactivity. This is the "talking back to your television" concept that first surfaced in the 1960s. But, above all, GenXers are niche viewers. They want to limit their news consumption, including news about politics, to the information that interests them most. They resist being told what information they ought to consume. That means that they skip stories they do not like and are eager to get more information about

Table 7.2 News Interests by Generation (%)

News Topic	Generation X (18–29)	Boomers (30–49)	50 + and Older
Local community, hometown	59	71	67
State, place of residence	53	63	57
U.S., country as a whole	47	55	64
Weather	45	51	59
Health or fitness	34	33	37
Sports	29	22	23
Other countries, the world	23	18	29
Consumer products	23	24	25
Entertainment, movies, TV, celebrities	23	12	9
Computers/technology	18	20	11
Religion	17	19	29
Politics and government	11	23	36
Business, stock market	6	14	17

SOURCE: Adapted from News in the Next Century 1996, 49.

preferred stories at the punch of a button or the click of a computer mouse. Modern technologies make it possible to indulge all of these preferences. The supply of political information has grown exponentially, thanks to cable television, the Internet, and a bevy of new digital television channels. Viewers are able to collect these riches at will.

Even though studies of generational changes in interest show that curiosity about some aspects of politics has diminished, GenXers retain an appetite for political news. More than half claim high interest in news about their local communities and their state, and nearly half say they are interested in news about the entire country.

Table 7.2 shows the types of programs in which GenXers claim to be "very interested." These programs should therefore be priorities for information suppliers, as long as expressed interests continue to be corroborated by audience statistics. Local community events rank at the top of news preferences for all generational groups. In fact, 45 percent of GenXers watched local news regularly in 2000 compared to 17 percent who watched network news (Pew 2000b). Events in one's state of residence are second, and news about the country ranks third. At the turn of the twenty-first century, average Americans, including GenXers, by and large, are most interested in politics close to the grassroots. When news focuses on events abroad rather than events at home, interest drops sharply. Only 23 percent of GenXers express keen interest in international news—on a par with their interest in news about consumer products and about entertainment and celebrities. Interest in day-to-day reports about the minutiae of politics and government in the nation ranks near the bottom, with a mere 11 percent of the GenXers—compared to 23 percent of their parents and 36 percent of their grandparents—saying they are "very interested."

Overall, the numbers in table 7.2 are encouraging for observers who are worried that young Americans are alienated from politics because they read and watch and listen less to the kind of political fare preferred by prior generations. If we use the grandparent generation represented in table 7.2 as a point of departure, rather than the parents of GenXers who were stirred by the turbulent sixties, the intergenerational drop in interest for local, state, and international news is below 10 percent. The sharpest drops—as high as 25 percent—come in national news, especially Beltway gossip. That suggests that Beltway gossip should shrink in favor of the types of local news that audiences find relevant to their lives. If the news supply becomes genuinely attuned to the changing needs and desires of news audiences and if the quality of the stories improves, it is quite likely that the numbers of viewers of political news will rise again.

In an age where the accuracy of audience research has reached new heights, journalists should have no trouble ascertaining continuously what types of stories will attract their viewers. Research tools to assess audience needs and capabilities include depth interviews, skillfully run focus groups, and various psychological and psychophysiological tests, such as heart rate and galvanic skin response measures and checks of eye and other facial movements. Psychographic models, which were developed to segment audiences for marketing or analysis purposes, have pioneered many analytical techniques for scientific segmentation. These techniques use responses to a battery of questions in order to identify people with similar interests (Wells 1974; Myers 1996). The seminal work, reported in chapter 2, that has shed light on the real nature of information-processing is also a major resource for producing audience-friendly program designs. The journalism community, schooled in social-scientific procedures through "precision journalism" training, is already familiar with many of these tools.

While progress in judging the audience's preferences has been great in some areas, it has lagged in others. For instance, few audience analyses appraise the knowledge base that particular audiences bring to political information. If this were done more frequently, journalists would be less likely to overestimate what audiences know and might recall to round out the sketchy information presented in news stories. Reporters would then be more likely to provide adequate contexts for news stories. When reporters write serious stories, they all too often tailor them to suit their own tastes, forgetting that their audiences' information backgrounds are generally far more limited. Stories about the need for reforming the welfare system, for example, convey little meaning when viewers are unfamiliar with the nature of the critical problems in the existing system.

NICHE PROGRAMMING: ADVANTAGES AND DISADVANTAGES

New digital technologies make it ever easier to satisfy the Internet generation's demand for news offerings that meet the special interests of various audience sectors. As has been true for radio, where the audience realms of giant stations splintered into tiny, specialized fiefdoms, so the audience realms of giant television networks are splintering into increasingly smaller configurations. While older viewers, especially women, have remained among the most loyal network television fans, younger viewers across the demographic spectrum are moving elsewhere (Pew 2000b). Television journalists therefore are less concerned about developing programs that please large, heterogeneous audiences, which previously forced them to offer much television fare pegged to the lowest common denominator. The trend toward narrowcasting began with the emergence of cable television. It has progressed to the digital technology stage, which allows a single television channel to carry multiple programs simultaneously.

The Internet has further extended the possibilities for niche programming. It allows people to select, at times and places of their choosing, from a seemingly endless array of multiple types of political information available worldwide. Even when Internet messages are substantively or technically flawed, they nonetheless diversify the political information pool—and the opportunities for glimpsing diverse views—far beyond past boundaries. Jürgen Habermas's (1989) funeral oration for the public sphere may have been premature after all. While economic constraints and lack of technical skills will prevent the vast majority of the world's people from using the Internet for the foreseeable future, these constraints are shrinking in technologically developed countries, where the first generation raised in the computer age is taking the helm (Pew 1998c, 2000b).

The Discovery cable channel is an example of what can be done by widely available television systems that serve a broad range of audience interests.

> For an aviation buff, the Discovery Wings cable channel is a dream come true—programs about planes and flying all day long. Replace the aviation aficionado with the health nut hungry for the latest medical news (tuned to Discovery Health), or do-it-yourselver immersed in home renovations (Discovery Home and Leisure), or a schoolchild exploring ancient worlds (Discovery Civilization)—Discovery has a channel for each. (Mifflin 1998a)

Television diversification has followed two distinct paths. The established television networks have chosen to address their offerings to selected demographic groups splintered along cleavages of age, gender, and ethnicity. For example, CBS has targeted older Americans, while Fox has aimed for a younger crowd. Some networks direct programming toward African Americans, and others target Spanish-speaking Latinos. Cable channels, by contrast, have ignored explicit demographics and have concentrated instead on interest fields, such as science, history, cooking, or mechanics.

Threats to Democracy

Narrowcasting does raise concerns about the viability of American democracy. If citizens do not drink from the same well of information, will they splinter into communication ghettoes? Will interactions diminish sharply among people whose backgrounds and matching preferences vary? Evidence of increasing fragmentation along various interest, lifestyle, age, income, religion, and ethnicity cleavage lines is mounting. A 1998 survey of audiences for entertainment shows, for example, showed that African Americans were flocking to newly available shows featuring African-American actors, while Caucasian Americans watched shows oriented toward white audiences. Fifty-one percent of African Americans followed crime news very closely in 2000 compared to 27 percent of whites and 32 percent of Hispanics. Figures for health news are 45 percent, 27 percent, and 29 percent, respectively (Pew 2000b). In the 1970s and 1980s, when fewer narrowly targeted choices were available, audience self-segregation along demographic lines was much less common (Sterngold 1998). As channel capacity grows, niche programming tends to progress into niche-within-niche offerings that make the splinter audiences ever tinier. They may be more satisfied by these specialized programs but also more disconnected from others in their community whose interests differ.

Niche programming may also be socially dangerous because it supports the Internet generation's penchant to limit their information diet to their special interest topics, creating a nation of people who know more and more about less and less. It may also mean that much of the public largely ignores entire areas of politics to which they gave at least passive attention in the past. Large numbers of people may be tempted to ignore civic information entirely if specialized news channels offer alternative program choices in competition with broadcasts of civic events, which most of the audience finds boring. Audience tallies show that this does happen (Pew 2000b). Attention to major political broadcasts, such as presidential addresses, declined sharply when other programs became available simultaneously.

Overall, the trends evident at the start of the twenty-first century do not bear out the nightmarish vision of large numbers of people isolating themselves from public affairs. The vast majority of citizens, including the Internet generation, have continued to attend to more general information sources, even when they devote substantial time to narrowcast fare (Pew 2000b). Moreover, many of the news choice options on different programs are like peas in a pod, often low-intellectual-calorie peas at that. Such programs do restore some commonality to the political information supply, but they waste the chance for diversifying it.

Whenever major national events have loomed, such as key decisions in the impeachment case against President Clinton, viewing levels for general news programs have risen sharply. For example, on 19 December 1998, when the House of Representatives voted to impeach the president, CNN news scored its highest single-day rating of the year. Other broadcast outlets reported similar audience peaks, although these were below the levels of attention lavished a few years earlier on the verdict in football legend O. J. Simpson's murder trial or the events connected to the accidental death of the widely cherished Diana, Princess of Wales. However, CBS, which covered a major football game (New York Jets versus Buffalo Bills), attracted more than 12 million viewers on the day of the Clinton impeachment vote, surpassing the audience levels of all political news programs combined.

The Shrinking Scope of News

If news production is audience driven, will news offerings supply the political information that the public needs? For example, lack of interest among viewers has been cited as a major reason for the sharp reduction in the number of stories dealing with events outside the United States following the end of the cold war. The focus group data presented in chapter 3 suggest that citizens will continue to demand political information about the broad range of issues that they deem salient to their lives. But citizens' interests do not necessarily encompass all the issues that elites deem important for average citizens. This portends a shrinking of the scope of news for individual citizens, though less severely than some observers fear, depending on the skill of journalists in clarifying the relevancy of seemingly remote issues.

The idea of allowing consumers of political news to guide the choice of information presented to them for immediate attention has been partially implemented already by print, television, and radio outlets in the United States that follow the tenets of "public" (or "civic") journalism. The staffs of papers like the *Charlotte Observer* in North Carolina and the *Wichita Eagle* in Kansas try to ascertain the interests of their readers through devices such as polls, focus groups, or town meetings. They then prepare stories that cover these concerns in exceptional depth. For instance, television programs can show how other communities have dealt with particular problems and provide guidelines for making fact-based comparisons between the local and the remote situations. Advocates of this type of journalism believe that it restores the role of the media as the mobilizer of civic action and the voice of public opinion. Journalists respect the public's choices, rather than derogating them. Opponents, who are plentiful and include prominent mainline journalists, argue that public journalism abandons the press's hallowed leadership role in setting the civic agenda, that it shamelessly panders to shallow public tastes, and that it leads to neglectful and dangerous silence about many important issues (Schudson 1998).

Leaving aside the question whether journalists know better than ordinary citizens what information belongs on the civic agenda, we do need to ask the "to what avail" question. If journalists supply information that is unwanted and largely ignored, while covering areas of strong demand sparingly, what is accomplished? It amounts to preaching to an empty church. If people do not want much international news but crave local news, shouldn't the demands of the mass audience be heeded, especially when specialized media, tailored to the preferences of elites, are available? A public that is exposed to political information that is of little interest is unlikely to be motivated to political thinking and action. "[I]t is not an informed public . . . with the motivation or frame of reference or capacity to act in a democracy" (Schudson 1995, 26–27).

Regardless of what journalists do, in the end it is the audience that determines whether or not the content will lead to civic enlightenment and political participation. Attempts to force-feed audiences with news they do not care about are apt to fail when the audiences have alternative program choices (Entman 1989). However, it is within the grasp of journalists, as well as the political leaders who are their sources, to whet the public's appetite for important news stories. If it can be made clear that the story is, indeed, important and relevant to the audience's concerns and if story presentation is appealing, sizable audiences will be attracted. The presidency and other visible public offices have often served as the bully pulpit that can draw nationwide attention to important stories.

THE CLIMATE FOR CREATING A USER-FRIENDLY JOURNALISM

Journalists' Inclinations

In chapter 6, I discussed the many framing and format barriers to user-friendliness that hurt the transmission of political information and drive audiences away. The prospects for overcoming these hurdles seem bright for several reasons. High on the list is the eagerness of journalists to improve their performance. For example, in a series of interviews in which television news directors discussed story presentation, they complained that current news conventions stifle their creativity (Graber 1994a, app.). They were especially concerned about the severe time pressures that prevent insightful coverage and jeopardize the goal of keeping audiences watching. As one director put it, "I personally feel that the quality of news presentation at this point is so shoddy, slash, economical . . . the material is so shallow, it is so diffused, there is no density to it. So people don't particularly pay attention." He thought that it was possible to do much better. "What I try to do is to find ways to get around the . . . predictable. . . . It is empty and devoid of any content." In the opinion of another director, current news production styles did not meet the standards of serious journalistic work. Serious work would require him to "be much more ambitious. I would hustle a lot more." News directors also felt that they were covering the ceremonial aspects of politics, while ignoring the "real" story. "[T]here's nothing there of any substance . . . the real story is one that really does not get told" (Graber 1994a, 502–3).

Realistically, what can be done? There are many answers, of course. For example, the study of the 10:00 P.M. newscasts in Chicago, reported in chapter 6, led to a number of suggestions for improving the presentation of political information (Johnson 1998b). Modeling newscasts after *The NewsHour with Jim Lehrer* on PBS was one suggestion. If it were followed, more news time would go to thematic news and less to episodic news. Each broadcast would then begin with headlines of the most important news of the day, followed by three or four well-researched and well-told longer reports. To keep the audience interested, reports would be couched in the poignant news magazine styles popularized by ace reporters like Walter Cronkite and Charles Kuralt because good journalism is synonymous with good storytelling. Improvements in audiovisuals would be essential as well because good television should be synonymous with virtual reality.

A routine event, like a new movie theater opening in an inner-city neighborhood, could become a far more gripping story if it skipped the usual chitchat about the celebrities who attended the opening and focused on the impact on the people who live in the neighborhood. Pictures of the blight that strangles poor neighborhoods could graphically convey why inner cities find it difficult to attract new businesses and retain the ones that are already located there. Stories about gang-related crimes would yield new understandings and bridge the chasms between socioeconomic groups if, in addition to the grisly crime statistics, they also reported unemployment rates among gang members and showed the drug-infested slums where they spend their lives. Rather than showing the typical, meaningless picture of the exterior of the state capital, a report about planned legislation, whether for urban renewal or waste disposal sites or campaign finance reform, could depict situations that illustrate why such legislation may be needed. Expert panelists could debate the advantages and disadvantages of the new laws, and anchors could provide the context that tells viewers why they should care and how they might take appropriate action. Stories could include footage from similar communities where comparable legislation was enacted, and they could give tips for locating additional information from nonobvious sources.

To allow more time for important stories, sports reports and especially weather reports on normal days could be shortened to the most essential facts; much of the teaser information designed to deter viewer defection could be eliminated. Stories whose only claim to fame is their recency could be eliminated entirely to make room for information likely to be significant for more than one news period. The main goals of changes in broadcast formats would be to allow sufficient time for thoughtful presentations of stories that are important to the audience, to frame them appropriately for the targeted viewers, and to use the most advanced videographic techniques to make the delivery style interesting. Such changes are technically and economically feasible because the nightly news is a moneymaker, with pretax profit margins of 40 to 50 percent. This is much higher than the profit margins of most other successful enterprises. Profits would remain respectable even if media institutions invested more time in imaginative programming, rather than relying on cheap potboilers, such as gathering routine crime news at the local police station and then shooting a few routine pictures at the crime scene (Johnson 1998b).

As discussed in chapters 5 and 6, many of the pleas for changes in the news relate to the particular frames chosen by journalists. They are viewed as distorting or out of sync with the ways audiences frame problems (Graber 1994b). Framing problems are comparatively easy to correct because the choice of frames is controlled to a large extent by journalists. As political scientist Murray Edelman (1993, 232) points out, the social world is "a kaleidoscope of potential realities, any of which can be readily invoked by altering the ways in which observations are framed and categorized." Audiovisuals, we know, lend themselves especially well to a multiplicity of framings because visual fragments can be endlessly recombined to tell a story from different angles.

Journalists need to be aware of the educational and cultural levels and inclinations of various audiences in order to judge what framing approach is most likely to yield correct interpretations because it reflects the myths of a particular society. Programs should highlight those features of each situation that have meaning for the intended audience. That means that framing must be historically and culturally bound. The many print and audiovisual information sources that cater to demographically distinct audiences have blazed the way for such programming.

The Project for Excellence in Journalism

Probably the most systematic and comprehensive attempt to examine the quality of newscasts and to suggest reforms was initiated in the late 1990s by the Project for Excellence in Journalism, conducted by a group of experts on television news and affiliated with the Columbia

University Graduate School of Journalism. The project initially sponsored an extensive content analysis of two weeks of local news broadcasting (600 broadcasts, yielding 8,500 stories) by sixty-one stations in twenty cities in the spring of 1997. The study, which is ongoing, was replicated with fifty-nine stations in nineteen cities in the spring of 1999, covering 8,000 stories from 590 broadcasts (www.journalism .org/1999). The 1999 findings were essentially similar to those of the 1997 study.

Based on the 1997 data, project members identified seven areas of performance in which high-quality newscasts tend to excel and low-quality newscasts tend to flounder. Achieving the top-level standards set out for these seven areas seems crucial for improving television news offerings to serve the public's needs adequately. Three elements of *story content* are most crucial. (1) Excellent stories *focus* on a significant, informative, and interesting situation. (2) They deal with issues that affect a lot of people in major ways, rather than with ephemeral, everyday incidents that are destined to be quickly forgotten by everyone except the people most intimately involved. The *range of topics* in excellent stories is broad and covers diverse types of events that concern various segments of the local community. (3) An emphasis on *local relevance,* in addition, means a preference for stories that deal with issues that are indigenous to the area served by the broadcast.

The remaining four elements that contribute to excellence relate to the *authenticity of the story.* (4) Excellent stories result from a high *enterprise level,* which means that the news organization explored significant stories independently and pursued them in depth. (5) Excellence also requires a sufficient *number of sources* even for local stories, which often fail to identify sources. (6) Sources should reflect multiple *viewpoints* where appropriate. (7) Finally, excellent stories require *source expertise.* To be authoritative and credible, the sources whose statements are reported must be impartial, fair, and knowledgeable.

The seven elements designated by project journalists as marks of excellence represent familiar, widely accepted canons of sound journalistic practices. Regrettably, many producers of local newscasts have slighted these practices, as demonstrated by the low scores recorded for one-third (34 percent) of the stations covered by the research. Nearly half (46 percent) of the stories broadcast by low-scoring stations were trivial and lacked relevance for the viewers, let alone the local community. Sources were often sparse and poorly identified, and important perspectives from which the story should be viewed were neglected. Fully 30 percent of the stories gave no source at all. In reports about controversial issues, 43 percent of the stories presented only one side. Surprisingly, the content analysts found that scandal and sensation were the focus of only 2 percent of the stories in the study, and a mere 3 percent of the stories featured highly sensational audio or video materials.

The researchers were able to award A and B grades to 31 percent of the stations and C grades to 34 percent. A comparison with the 6:00 P.M. newscasts conducted only in 1999 showed that the earlier broadcasts earned much higher quality ratings. Three major reasons were cited: "The first is a conventional belief that viewers want quick headline service at bedtime. The second is a tendency for producers to cherry-pick from an array of eye-catching video amassed through the day [which happens to be cheap]. The third is an orientation toward late-breaking news [irrespective of its significance]" (Carr 1999).

While it is deplorable that one in three stations was rated D or F by standards developed by broadcasters themselves for their profession, it is also a reason for hope. The low grades indicate that the reforms that are needed to improve the quality of newscasts have already been en-dorsed by professional journalists and are taught to young journalists during their training. Besides, the changes required to achieve high standards are neither unduly expensive nor unusually arduous. Project sponsors summarize them as downplaying crime news and concentrat-ing instead on original stories about significant ideas and issues, with strong emphasis on core local institutions and concerns, such as school infrastructure and education policies. Stories should quote authorita-tive sources and be long enough to allow for story development (aver-age stories run under one minute).* When feasible, they should feature everyday people as story subjects or commentators, thereby building a bridge to the audience.

Even more encouraging than the fact that good political journalism is eminently feasible is the fact that the research in 1997, and again in 1999, showed that stations that practice excellent journalism tend to do well in terms of their audience ratings. Sixty-three percent of the ex-cellent stations in the project's 1997 sample had rising ratings. Com-mercial success for these stations thus does not require dumbing the

---

*The best-rated stations in the study averaged seventy-nine seconds per story com-pared to forty-eight seconds for the worst-rated stations. Overall, 70 percent of the 8,500 stories ran for less than a minute; 43 percent were thirty seconds or less. The most common story length was twenty-two seconds. Only 16 percent of the stories were more than two minutes long.

news down or hyping it up. The audience for serious, nontabloid news that flocked to the high-quality stations may be drawn from the ranks of dissatisfied viewers who curtailed their normal television news viewing in the 1990s, thereby producing precipitous shrinkage in network news audiences.

Ascertaining the appropriate intellectual level of broadcasts may require greater diligence by news enterprises in identifying the types of viewers whom their programs are trying to serve and then using the new digital channels to broadcast news that is tailored to specific categories of viewers. Centering services on consumer needs is becoming a common practice throughout the business world in the age of the Internet. The news business cannot be an exception. News consumers are empowered because an enormous number of choices are readily available to them with the click of a mouse. If they do not like what particular media offer them, they can turn elsewhere. Aside from consumer demands, audience segmentation also attracts advertisers whose products are geared to specific types of customers, rather than a general mass market.

In the opening chapters of the book, I chided the scholars who belittle the public's civic IQ for fantasizing about ideal citizens and tailoring civic IQ measurements to this image. Taking the standards developed by the Project for Excellence in Journalism as the single ideal to be followed by all newscasters would repeat the same mistake. Just as there is an audience for serious political news, there is also an audience for tabloid news that needs to be served. In the 1997 study, 57 percent of the stations that received the lowest rankings because they featured tabloid-style news also had rising ratings. These stations paid above average attention to scandal and celebrity news and covered accidents and crimes and bizarre events heavily. However, like their counterparts among the excellent stations, they also featured longer than average stories. Contrary to the beliefs of many news directors, most audiences apparently do not like snippet news, even though more topics can be covered when stories run for thirty seconds or less each than when the exposition is longer.

Tools for Better Storytelling

The reformist zeal of many important groups of journalists is not the only reason for being optimistic that major changes in tune with audience preferences can be accomplished. The breakneck pace of development of new and improved technical tools and techniques to perfect the presentation of audiovisual broadcasts is another reason for optimism (Nelson and Boynton 1997). High-definition television is breathing new vibrancy into the concept of virtual reality, bringing it ever closer to its live counterpart. Inexpensive, lightweight video cameras have opened up nearly the entire world to audiovisual scrutiny, so that viewers can be virtual bystanders to what is happening around the globe. They can even watch realistic simulations of many events that happened in the near and distant past or that may happen in the future. They "can travel in time and space to the 'not here' and the 'not now'" (Huston and Wright 1998, 19). The voyages that could be made only in human imagination in the past can now become lifelike vicarious experiences.

Developments in advertising, including campaign advertising, have demonstrated the advantage of using cinematic approaches for television because cinematic techniques tend to have much higher production standards than videographic techniques. With greater sharpness of detail and more fidelity in colors and hues, the screen has come to bear a close resemblance to life. Capturing the nuances of stories is easier when visuals include scripts of the verbal text and labels that pinpoint important visual features. Vast improvements have been made in creating charts, graphs, and diagrams with vivid colors and motion. Videographers can customize foregrounds and backgrounds as well as besting nature through techniques such as fades or folds, dissolves or morphs, explosions or implosions, and time-lapse photography. Split-screen visual techniques allow journalists to create instant interpretive contexts for stories.

The presentation of visuals can be varied in frequency, pace, or rhythm to put them in sync with the human information-processing capabilities that have been ignored in the past. For example, information-processing knowledge suggests that the ease of integrating stories across cuts depends on the relationship between the segments connected by the cuts. Integration is difficult if segments seem disparate, violating viewers' expectations. Sophisticated experimental research techniques can determine what constitutes appropriate sequencing for various audiences. Similarly, the combination of the visuals with spoken words, sound effects, and music is extremely important in conveying accurate, easily comprehensible messages. Research findings make it possible to create combinations that are geared to what people expect and find familiar (Berman 1993). The various components of broadcasts can be constructed more carefully so that they do not contradict each other, as when video delivers a message that counters the voice-over or when a bizarre shot distracts viewers from the story's substance.

There is precedent already for exchanging excellent visual sequences among news producers, making them available for multiple stories. Some of these cooperative ventures transcend national boundaries, such as the relationship among ABC News and Britain's BBC and Japan's NHK. Some smaller U.S. television stations have pioneered news-sharing agreements whereby one station pays to copy part of the broadcast of a sister station, often adapting it to better meet the needs of its particular clientele. In that way, the station that shares its footage has more money available to produce a better broadcast.

A number of stations have increased the resources needed to produce better news footage by cutting back on the number of daily newscasts in favor of fewer but better productions. When these newscasts are also aired on the Internet, as is happening more and more, viewers can watch them at times of their own choosing. Yet another tactic for improving news quality involves creating joint ventures among news titans. These arrangements are particularly important for organizations that broadcast around the clock via the Internet and therefore need ample story materials to fill the time. One such venture, created in the winter of 1999, linked the tremendous resources of *Newsweek,* the *Washington Post,* NBC News, and MSNBC and their respective websites (Barringer 1999). The superior programming that such wealthy media giants can produce reaches a potential viewing audience of millions of people, making these broadcasts attractive to advertisers eager to reach broad national markets.

PRECEDENTS FOR CHANGE

How good are the prospects for massive changes? Like most other people, journalists can be expected to resist even desired changes because change is usually costly. It requires expanding time and resources as well as breaking old habits and learning new approaches. Yet journalists are accustomed to change. They have altered many of their most prized conventions in recent decades in an effort to stay in tune with their audiences and adapt to contemporary political, social, and technological environments. Many of the changes are already moving in the directions required by changes in audiences and technologies.

For example, when ABC, CBS, and NBC discovered that they could no longer compete with the twenty-four-hour news channels in bringing the freshest news to the public, they reshaped their newscasts to produce longer, more analytical, in-depth stories. Reacting to politicians' increasingly sophisticated attempts to manipulate journalists, they became more adversarial and skeptical. They interjected more independently gathered materials to put politicians' statements into perspective, and they drew far more heavily on quotes from experts. Besides citing more conflicting views, journalists provided more of their own interpretation to counteract the slick professionalism of the public relations handlers who have become standard members of the politician's entourage.

Some of the changes run counter to the goals favored by reform-minded journalists and members of the Internet generation. For instance, as part of the shift toward a more journalist-centered form of news reporting, the time allotted to political actors to personally present their arguments has shriveled. In television coverage of presidential elections from 1968 to 1988, the average sound bite allotted to the candidates' pronouncements declined from forty-three to nine seconds. Such brevity deprives the audience of the chance to hear what the candidates want to say and to observe the candidates' body language and draw their own inferences from them, rather than hearing only paraphrases and selected quotes in contexts set by others. In response to widespread criticism, the minuscule sound bites for political candidates have lengthened again, proof that changes are reversible.

Another marked new trend in journalism is the shift toward softer news. The Committee of Concerned Journalists, a group pledged to work for journalistic excellence, documented this change in a study of news coverage from 1976 to 1997. The findings are based on 3,760 stories drawn from seven news outlets over a twenty-two year span. They represent one month of ABC, CBS, and NBC stories, one month of front-page stories in the *New York Times* and *Los Angeles Times,* and one year of cover stories in *Time* and *Newsweek.* Some of the changes have been praised by the committee, while others have earned scorn. During these decades, stories about government in the United States decreased by roughly 40 percent, from one in three to one in five, without any apparent changes in the proportions allocated to local government. Stories about foreign affairs dropped by 25 percent, from one in four to one in six. Stories about celebrity entertainment and crime tripled from one in fifty stories to one in fourteen. Whatever the topic, journalists tried

Table 7.3   Changing News Story Emphasis (%)

News Source	Traditional Political		Economic and Social		Entertainment/ Weather	
	1977	1997	1977	1997	1977	1997
ABC	71.6	44.9	15.0	33.6	13.4	21.5
CBS	67.8	40.3	17.3	41.7	14.5	18.3
NBC	54.6	38.8	21.8	36.7	24.7	24.7
L.A. Times	74.8	62.0	11.7	25.9	13.5	12.4
N.Y. Times	63.8	69.3	29.7	23.2	5.2	7.5
Time	48.1	19.2	30.7	44.3	21.1	36.6
Newsweek	46.1	25.0	21.0	48.1	32.7	26.9

SOURCE: Condensed from Committee of Concerned Journalists 1999a.

NOTE: Front pages of newspapers and network broadcasts were coded for March 1997; magazine cover stories were coded for the entire year.

The Traditional Political category combines the original categories of Government, Military, Domestic Affairs, and Foreign Affairs. The Economic and Social category combines Business/Commerce, Science, Technology, Arts, Religion, Personal Health, and Crime. The Entertainment/Weather category combines Entertainment/Celebrities, Lifestyle, Celebrity Crime, Sports, and Weather/Disaster.

to make stories more palatable by treating much of the news more like features, rather than straight news accounts. Story themes, rather than factual details, became the story essence. Over these decades, the balance moved from two out of three stories using a straight news style compared to a feature approach to a near reversal of these proportions.

Overall, the chief trend recorded in table 7.3 is a shift from traditional political news to economic and social stories, including substantially more stories about business, crime, and health care. Though decried by traditionalists, this shift is in line with changes in audience interests. The entertainment category, which includes sports and weather, has also grown but not as dramatically. Journalists attribute these substantial changes to increased competition for audiences and the realization that many soft news topics attract and retain larger audiences than competing hard news offerings.

To evaluate the impact of such changes on the overall quality of the news supply available to the American public requires looking at a combination of rivulets in the news stream, rather than examining single sources only. This will show that despite all of the criticism of particular news venues and the vocal condemnation of scores of programs, the supply of political information has never been more abundant when one considers the totality of all offerings. Gaps in one venue tend to be filled by programming in another venue. For example, there has been a

Table 7.4 Emphasis of Prime-Time News Magazine Stories (%)

News Source	Traditional Political	Economic and Social	Entertainment/ Weather
20/20	10.0	70.1	19.9
48 Hours	10.0	35.0	55.0
60 Minutes	22.3	50.3	27.8
Prime Time	13.3	46.7	40.0
Dateline	13.7	48.0	38.4

SOURCE: Condensed from Committee of Concerned Journalists 1999a.

NOTE: Shows were coded during the fall season in 1997.

The Traditional Political category combines the original categories of Government, Military, Domestic Affairs, and Foreign Affairs. The Economic and Social category combines Business/Commerce, Science, Technology, Arts, Religion, Personal Health, and Crime. The Entertainment/Weather category combines Entertainment/Celebrities, Lifestyle, Celebrity Crime, Sports, and Weather/Disaster.

substantial reduction in the number of documentaries on television. But as table 7.4 shows, prime-time television news magazines now supply many in-depth and investigative stories that network television formerly provided.

In line with the general trend toward soft news topics, the vast majority of the stories in prime-time news magazines feature economic and social news, with an emphasis on "news you can use" stories. In the print news magazines, the emphasis has also shifted to consumer and health news and celebrity entertainment and away from traditional hard news stories about governmental policies. Similarly, when the networks moved away from full coverage of political conventions during presidential campaigns, C-SPAN filled the gap and covered them gavel to gavel in greater depth than ever before. National Public Radio provides excellent political critiques, and current crises are often reported in depth by *Nightline, Frontline,* and similar investigative programs.

Despite the growth of soft news, a rich diet of hard news remains readily available, even for viewers who use neither cable television nor the Internet. Traditional hard news categories continue to dominate the front pages of newspapers, and network national news retains its strong emphasis on foreign affairs coverage. With news programs and documentaries, politically oriented soap operas, political quips on television talk shows, and the ubiquitous political advertisements that intrude over and over again into all of the popular shows, anyone who watches television is going to be exposed to hard political news. In fact, the news diet provided to ordinary Americans, in spite of its major shortcomings, is richer than ever before. The multitude of diverse political news venues available around the clock are well suited to the needs and desires of members of the Internet generation, who like to assemble their own news assortments guided by their own interests and concerns. The currents of change are moving in a propitious direction.

BOTTOM-LINE ISSUES

Thus far, we have concentrated on the encouraging prospects for making political news offerings more relevant and attractive to various audiences. We must now turn to the contributions required from the other partners to reform—the industry tycoons who own the media, the politicians who address the public via the media, and the audiences who consume the news. Many obstacles to reforming political news, including providing more in-depth political information tailored to the needs of particular audiences, relate to financing. Industry tycoons contend that profit considerations must be paramount because American media are private-sector business enterprises. This compels them to avoid costly reforms and to continue tried and true formats that produce sizable audiences and attract large advertisers. Such reasoning is not as compelling as it appears at first glance. In the past, the news divisions of networks were regarded as paying off in prestige rather than revenue, so that it was justifiable to operate them at a financial loss. Attitudes on that score have changed now, but it still may be possible to reverse the trend by appealing to the civic conscience of business tycoons. Time and again, America's business leaders have forgone substantial profits or spent millions of dollars for the sake of rendering a valuable public service and enhancing their stature in the public's eyes. In fact, the National Association of Broadcasters claims that such giving is already an industry policy. The industry donates billions for various free public service broadcasts (Jones 1999). In 1996, for example, it gave $6.8 billion.

Besides, the evidence suggests that there are direct as well as indirect financial benefits, beyond earning good will, from the type of sound programming we have discussed. On the indirect side, well-designed programming teaches citizens, including children and young adults, more effectively than has ever before been possible about the world in which they must work and make their mark. That includes learning about the values of our society. Despite the excesses of crime and sexual exploits presented in many television programs, most of them still reaffirm the basic values of American culture, which are also the values that sustain private-sector business.

In terms of direct financial benefits, if news programs are substantively sound, as well as attractive, they can succeed in their competition with body bag and sleaze journalism, as the surveys conducted by the Project for Excellence in Journalism document. The many imaginative reports produced for the mushrooming number of news magazine shows are also capturing large numbers of viewers. These programs are therefore attractive to advertisers.

The widely held belief that advertisers will buy broadcast time only on programs that allow them to reach mass audiences has become a bygone myth. Many specialized offerings attract a large enough audience of potential customers to justify the advertising costs. In an era of niche marketing, most advertisers look for specific audience traits, rather than mere numbers of viewers. For example, it may be profitable to advertise vitamins on a low-audience health-care-oriented program or computer software on a show catering to a young, upscale audience. Some specialized programs will be unable to reach a critical mass even on the Internet, which can draw on a worldwide audience pool. They can be financed through a combination of advertiser support, viewer fees, and even some public subsidies for people who are too poor to pay for the service. The United States has a long history of subsidizing mass media ventures to enrich the public's information sources (Cook 1998).

Other financial problems relate to the cost of resources for high-quality programming. To cover a broad array of political news well requires sufficient time, money, and personnel. *Newsweek* correspondent Larry Martz has described the problems created when insufficient resources are allocated for foreign news coverage. "Our remaining correspondents fly from earthquake to famine, from insurrection to massacre. They land running, as we were all taught to do, and they provide surprisingly good coverage of whatever is immediately going on. . . . [But] we miss anticipation, thought and meaning. Our global coverage has become a comic book: ZAP! POW! BANG-BANG!" (quoted in Fallows 1995, 137). Major networks have closed many news bureaus at home and abroad to lower news production costs. Company officials argue that air travel, laptop computers, and handheld filming and editing equipment allow them to cover the world with a smaller corps of headquarters-based correspondents. They disregard the huge indirect costs about which Larry Martz complains. Insufficient resources are just as common and damaging for domestic coverage, creating "a culture of superficiality and haste" (Rosenstiel et al. 1999).

There are several resolutions to this penny-pinching problem aside from the proven fact that high-quality programming pays off because it attracts audiences and the advertisers who want to serve them. When economizing becomes necessary, it can be done more judiciously than is customary in order to cut frills, rather than key information functions. As mentioned earlier, news enterprises can pool their resources, especially video footage, as long as a reasonable number of competitors remain in the field. For foreign news, networks already often share news footage with partner networks in other countries and buy footage from video news agencies, such as Reuters and the Associated Press, rather than producing it on their own. To adapt these videos to the needs of their own audiences, buyers often supply their own verbal scripts and various sound effects. Exceptionally heavy costs incurred to retain or enhance quality can be covered by viewer fees. The cable television industry has demonstrated that viewers are willing to pay for favored programs even when other programs are available free of charge. And, as suggested before, media business owners can take part of their profits for news production in the coinage of community good will and civic pride, rather than cash.

POLITICAL CHANGES

Production of political messages is not solely the work of journalists, of course. Politicians have learned to play the game of video-politics quite well. They know how to produce attractive stories that tempt media to use them without sufficient corroboration or presentation of contrary viewpoints. When politicians discuss issues, their pronouncements are often deliberately fuzzy and misleading, prompting journalists to focus on issues of candor and style, rather than the merits of various positions on these issues. Attaching partisan labels to policies while touting the virtues of partisan loyalty is an invitation to bypass critical thinking and follow one's customary herd. The remedies are clear but difficult to initiate and enforce—more responsible and responsive behavior by politicians in meeting their obligation to keep the public informed.

Persuading politicians to put the public's need for information above their own immediate political advantage is probably the toughest challenge on the road to change. It will be difficult to induce politicians to strive for full disclosure and honesty if this could cost them their job. Journalists, for their part, are not likely to pressure politicians for candor when this might offend an important news source or might expose them to the charge of undue partisanship. Journalists know that politicians can penalize cantankerous members of the press by reserving news plums for more compliant news purveyors.

Nonetheless, reforms to improve politicians' information output are not pie in the sky. A number of reform proposals have surfaced in the halls of Congress and in the press. If they can overcome the tremendous lobby pressures that face such legislation when major stakeholders fear losses, they could be quite helpful if they were passed and properly implemented. They include requiring politicians to debate political issues during election campaigns or make annual work progress reports in specified formats. Journalists could play a part by scrutinizing the accuracy of political messages similar to the Ad-Watch features in newspapers that report on inaccuracies in advertisements. The Federal Communications Commission (FCC) could require broadcasters to supply more free time for lengthy political broadcasts. As much as 85 percent of the public has expressed a desire for more substantive political news, though this imagined appetite for substance probably exceeds the capacity to watch and listen (Pew 2000b).

Politicians can also spur reforms through legislative mandates and administrative regulations. Such measures face tremendous opposition from powerful pressure groups, but some pass despite these hurdles. The 1996 Telecommunications Act and the 1990 Children's Television Act are examples of more or less welcome television reform legislation. Administratively, the FCC has ordered increased attention to educational programming and has limited the number of advertisements that can be shown on children's programs.

The advent of digital television has once again thrust the issue of public service by stations onto the public agenda. Reform advocates have proposed laws that would require devoting some of the new channel capacity to serious public service programming. They point out that other business enterprises, such as cell phone companies, pay for use of the broadcast spectrum. Less ambitious proposals would oblige stations to donate airtime to candidates only during presidential elections. Other plans have called for asking the stations to pay for the channels over and above the conversion costs that channels must already pay or for imposing new taxes on the industry and using the money to subsidize high-quality programming in general. The fate of specific proposals remains in doubt at the time of writing, but the thrust is clear. Political leaders are trying to spur investment in more civic-minded programming.

AUDIENCE FACTORS

While progress is possible and likely on many fronts, it is unlikely on others because it faces physical impossibilities or major political barriers. On the physical side, for example, the discrepancy between the availability of huge amounts of political information and the limited information-processing capacities of individuals can never be resolved. In our complex age, the vast majority of citizens will never be able to master all that they think they should know to be well informed regardless of the quality of the information, its user-friendliness, or audience diligence in attending to the information. More effective audiovisual presentations will help, but nothing can reduce the ever-growing information supply to manageable proportions.

Even if news presentation is greatly improved, it is unlikely that the lukewarm interests of average Americans in most stories about politics can ever be fanned to a lasting white heat. *Washington Post* columnist Robert Samuelson is right that the "Public Can't Stomach Abstract Politics," as the headline of one of his articles put it (1998). Americans care deeply about the freedoms they enjoy, including the freedom to concentrate on their personal affairs during times of political calm in the United States. Their families, their work, and their play are their primary concerns. It is highly unlikely that the American public will ever be eager to spend most of its leisure hours studying the multitude of major issues that crowd the nation's political agenda even in times of political calm. Theirs is a tradition of individualism and distrust of Big Government, as commentators from Alexis de Tocqueville in the 1830s onward have always pointed out. Only when politics is exciting do ordinary Americans pay close attention to it and give it priority over the many other demands on their time. When politics is pedestrian, when it becomes abstract and disconnected from people's personal interests, they tune out. The sense of civic responsibility can be heightened if news presentations are gripping and user-friendly, as demonstrated by the peak viewer levels produced periodically, and often sustained for lengthy time periods, when major news events break.

Producing top-notch programming that meets citizens' needs will require journalists to reconcile numerous basically incompatible demands and expectations. It is a dilemma all around, as pointed out in chapter 6. How can journalists provide complete information from multiple perspectives, which most citizens say they want, when these citizens are so easily confused and bored? How can journalists set forth coherent frameworks that help citizens interpret a complex universe without being accused of lacking objectivity and editorializing in inappropriate ways? How can journalists sensitize their audiences to the pains and joys of others without being chided for arousing emotions that could prevent people from making unemotional, purely calculating decisions? How can the news media serve as a forum for dialogue among citizens without being condemned for deliberate agenda-setting? Citizens expect the media to act as watchdogs that ferret out misbehavior so that government can be held accountable. But how can the media do that without being criticized for being too negative (Schudson 1995)?

Improving television will not necessarily improve its bad reputation, which detracts from its power to impart civic knowledge to viewers. Learning rates tend to reflect learning expectations. A great deal of criticism leveled against television has become a public mantra for the elite and the general public alike even though it is vastly disproportionate to the medium's shortcomings and unfair. "People tend to dismiss the medium with virtually no consideration, little feeling that they need offer evidence. TV, in this entrenched popular view, is the boob tube, the idiot box, the vast waste-land. Case closed" (Johnson 1999). While mediocrity is tolerated with grace for most intellectual endeavors, there seems to be less tolerance for it in audiovisual productions. People do not denigrate books in general because potboilers outnumber and outsell the works of Nobel laureates. But television is routinely tarred with its worst performances and receives little credit for its best. And when it is compared to other human pursuits, such as reading newspapers or books or engaging in sports or social events, the best aspects of these other endeavors are pitted against the worst aspects of television watching. Changing the adverse image is crucial because it shackles the power of television to satisfy the political information needs of the American public. If *Processing Politics* can contribute to this goal, it has accomplished its mission.

REPRISE: THE RESOLUTION OF THE PUZZLES AND THE PROBLEMS

At the outset of this book, we pondered three puzzles. Why, we asked, do ordinary Americans prefer television for gathering political information when they, as well as media experts, deride it as the boob tube or idiot box? We found that the reason for the preference is biological.

People are naturally drawn to an audiovisual medium that makes it comparatively easy, quick, and pleasant to gather and store important information and to retrieve it from memory when needed. The medium is ideal even when the messages that it transmits fail to meet high quality standards in substance and format.

The reasons for the disdain of television as a carrier of political information are more multifaceted. They rest in part on the many shortcomings of current television presentations and the stereotypes based on them and in part on the myths and stereotypes developed in an earlier age around the printed word as the key to all serious knowledge. More important, they also rest on differing conceptions of the kind of political knowledge that contemporary Americans must have to fulfill their civic duties.

These differing conceptions lie at the heart of the second puzzle addressed by this book—namely, why television-reliant citizens claim to be well informed enough to carry out their civic functions, while political scientists claim that the public is woefully ignorant about matters that it ought to know. The attempt to resolve this problem involved multiple steps. First, we tried to establish what average people ought to know to be effective citizens. I sided with the standard that most people use, which matches learning to the normal functions performed by citizens, such as voting, talking politics, and participating in lobbying for issues within each citizen's realm of concerns. The critics work by different rules. Their standards of ideal citizenship, which citizens fail to meet by a wide margin, judge knowledge needs by the totality of major problems facing the nation at any particular time. The critics believe that citizens ought to be informed about these problems because they affect the collectivity. Moreover, this knowledge should include specifics, such as names of people and locations, as well as numbers and ratios, such as the number of people receiving welfare payments and the percentage of the national budget allocated to their needs (Kuklinski et al. 2000).

It is difficult to agree about the adequacy of the public's political knowledge when the judges use such disparate measuring sticks. The second step toward resolution of the puzzle therefore involved analyzing focus group data to judge what sorts of political knowledge people do acquire when left to their own choices. These data show that the type of political information that average Americans possess is not far in substance from what the critics would like to see. It does, however, fall short of the breadth of issues that would be ideal and the detail retention that the critics cherish. The information-processing realities explained in the book make it clear that the critics' standards are unachievable. Hence we have resolved the puzzle, but convincing the critics that their standards are unrealistic remains a still unaccomplished goal.

The third puzzle encompasses a broader range of issues—how television can earn the plaudits of many observers as one of the most fruitful inventions of the twentieth century when it earns the condemnation of others as a despoiler of democracy and a danger to the civic health of the nation. The short answer to the puzzle is that both views are right. Television is fantastic in what it has already contributed to public knowledge and holds the promise of ever-greater contributions. But in all too many respects, it is, indeed, the wasteland that people deplore and the siren that lures the public from attending to the serious business of citizenship. The puzzle raised by the question is not really a puzzle after all. The real puzzle, which is addressed in several of the book's chapters and culminates in this chapter, is to identify and strengthen what is good about television as a political information medium and to identify and change what is bad.

Doing so should resolve most of the major problems detailed in response to the complaint about the merits of television. The content of political news can be vastly improved, as can the manner of presentation. News can be better matched to the interests of various audiences and to the biological equipment and psychological traits of audiences. Private- and public-sector policies can be changed to make the creation of a well-informed electorate once more a prime goal of government, as it was when this nation was founded (Cook 1998). If one can talk about the deterioration of political rhetoric, one can also talk about a restoration of high standards and a return to the best practices of the past.

And what of the citizens? Just as the image of political television has been unduly degraded, so has the civic intelligence of the public been unfairly belittled. Both have been judged by their considerable shortcomings without balancing these against the even more considerable achievements. Both have also been evaluated by unrealistic standards based on impossible expectations. I have presented evidence that average citizens can and do make sound, information-based political judgments and that average television stations can and do provide solid political news. I have also shown that new information technologies and new insights about information-processing make it easier than ever before to match the political information supply to the political information needs and demands of the American public. Given these indisputable facts, how can anyone disagree with the judgment that the Internet age is also destined to be the golden age of television (Johnson 1999)? Yet destiny is rarely self-fulfilling. Only concerted, deliberate efforts by the millions of stakeholders in American democracy will bring the goal within our collective grasp.

APPENDIX:
METHODS

The data presented in this book are based on multiple research methods. For my own research, I have relied on various types of content analysis of audiovisual and print media, on individual depth interviews, on focus group interviews, and on a variety of experiments that test what and how people learn from mass media information. I have supplemented these data with secondary analyses based on large-scale survey research projects by major survey organizations such as the Pew Research Center for the People and the Press and the American National Election Studies.

My assistants and I have also performed secondary analyses on a variety of focus group data videotapes. Some of the work has involved freestanding content analyses or freestanding audience analyses. However, for the studies that are most germane for the central themes of this book, I have relied primarily on a combined approach where audiences were tested about what they had learned—and had failed to learn—from specific information that they had encountered in experimental and nonexperimental settings. For these studies, the information supply was content-analyzed so that it could be compared to interview responses by the audiences in question and occasionally to news story diaries that they kept for selected stories. Combining content analysis of the information supply with analyses of what audiences learned from the information avoids the problems entailed in comparing audience responses with media content that was available to them without knowing that it was actually used.

Besides analyzing media content and audience responses for the subject matter that was covered or ignored, my research assistants and I analyzed and compared how political information was framed in news stories and by audiences and how complex and detailed the media and audience messages were. We also conducted experiments with small groups of people to explore the particular contributions that audiovisuals had made to learning about politics. In addition, we conducted experiments, as well as intensive interviews, with television news directors to ascertain their practices and theories about the use of audiovisuals in television newscasts.

The examples presented below illustrate how the research on which this book is based was designed and executed. Examples were chosen only from projects cited in this book. This appendix is therefore a sampling, rather than an exhaustive record of the way I have approached learning from political messages.

GENERAL INFORMATION-PROCESSING ANALYSES

Processing the News: How People Tame the Information Tide (Graber 1993; New York: Longman, 1984, 1988) is the foundation study on which all my work on information-processing is based. It was designed as a microanalysis to investigate human thought processes in depth over an extended time span. It involved exhaustive scrutiny of the past and current lifestyles, including psychological, social, and informational settings, of small groups of respondents.

For the most intensive part of the study, names were drawn randomly from an official list of registered voters in Evanston, Illinois, a university town of some 75,000 people just north of Chicago. Eighty-four percent of the 200 initial interviewees were willing to participate in the yearlong study. Each of them was classified according to interest in politics and ready access to mass-media information as well as the usual demographic characteristics. This classification allowed my research team to assess whether information-processing was affected by demographic factors, by eagerness to be informed, and/or by the effort required to obtain and use information in the face of competing demands on the respondent's time.

We developed a four-cell design that divided respondents into groups in which high or low interest in politics was each coupled with easy or difficult access to news. To keep the intensive study manageable, we selected five demographically diverse panel members for each of the four cells and identified replacements in anticipation of a 20 percent dropout rate. In the end, there were no dropouts.

Our sample as a whole included a higher percentage of college-educated people than would be found in the general population. Our *Processing the News* data as a whole therefore may reflect above-average information-processing activity levels and more intellectually sophisticated performances than one would find in the general population. However, since the panel for the study, as well as a pretest panel, encompassed several working-class people with little formal education, we could compare panelists to assess the impact of socioeconomic and educational differences.

To check whether a panel of such small size might be reasonably similar to the general American electorate in responding to political questions, we compared the panelists' responses with results from the contemporaneous National Election Studies survey conducted by the Center for Political Studies at the University of Michigan. The answer patterns were sufficiently similar to suggest that findings reported in *Processing the News* are common for demographically matching groups in the general population.

In addition to comparing some of the Evanston panel's response characteristics with those of the national sample, we matched them against the response characteristics of three panels of forty-eight respondents who were part of simultaneous companion studies. Two of the control panels represented populations from communities that differ from Evanston in size and socioeconomic characteristics. Many of the questions asked in the companion study were identical, so that direct comparisons on a wide array of answers were possible. We also used the control panels for group interviews to check on variations in response structure produced by small-group settings. Although there were some discrepancies in responses traceable to the dissimilar environments and to the group setting, the similarities were far more striking than the differences. This fact provided additional reassurance that the responses of our panelists were "normal" and that differences in the geographic location, community size, socioeconomic status, and personalities of various interviewers did not produce major variations in results. Recent large-sample studies of selected aspects of cognitive processing also corroborate the corresponding findings in our research, further easing concerns about the generalizability of our findings.

We chose to study information-processing over the course of a presidential election year because registered voters could be expected to have plenty of material for exercising their political information-processing skills in anticipation of the election. At the same time, there would be many weeks when election news would be subordinate, while the main focus would be on other political affairs.

Each panelist was interviewed ten times during the year, and the interviews were audiotaped. Interviews were spaced at roughly six-week intervals, with occasional variations to capture reactions before or following important political events that occurred during the year. Panelists did not know the interview schedule in advance. Rather, interviews were arranged on short notice, allowing little time for respondents to prepare themselves for anticipated questions.

Interviews were conducted in each respondent's home or place of business. They averaged two hours in length, so that the total data set includes approximately four hundred hours of recorded interviews, nearly twenty hours for each person. During each interview, fifty to one hundred questions were asked about a wide array of political topics that had surfaced in recent news stories. On an average, a 100-question interview yielded 1,500 to 2,000 statements in reply. This massive amount of discourse constitutes a very rich data set for observing the results of information-processing. Although not all aspects of information-processing may have been captured for each individual, there should be few significant gaps when observations across the total sample are considered.

The questions that we asked to assess information-processing probed three areas. One was the nature of information selection. What kinds of information did respondents typically extract from news stories, and what types did they typically ignore? Second, the respondents' interactions with the story were ascertained. How did they conceptualize the information, and what meanings did they assign to it? How did they fit the new information into their established belief patterns, and how did it modify these patterns? Finally, we analyzed and categorized general thinking patterns, with an emphasis on respondents' information-processing strategies, choice of perspectives for viewing the stories, and ability to draw general conclusions from specific information.

Most questions were open-ended because closed-ended questions may distort the respondents' basic beliefs and values by forcing them to fit their ideas into thinking patterns suggested by the investigator, rather than using their own approaches. To provide an added check on the reliability of our findings, we repeated many questions in successive interviews, either in the same form and question sequence or in a substantially revised form and during a different part of the interview. In this way, we hoped to guard against calling responses "typical" when they were actually unique, prompted by specific conditions in the interview setting or beyond it. Each respondent's interview protocols were independently analyzed by several coders so that coding and analysis errors could be corrected and discrepancies resolved. The main conclusions of the study are based on evidence from the combined records of all the panelists.

The interview questions covered a broad area of knowledge. It included respondents' factual knowledge and opinions about political, social, and economic issues that had been given ample recent coverage by the news media. Long-term recall was measured by inquiring about events that had happened at various earlier times throughout the year. Several questions related to media use and evaluation. These entailed queries about how often the respondent used various types of media, how well he or she liked them, and, more specifically, the sources for particular stories that the respondent recalled. Finally, there were extensive questions about the respondent's family background, past experiences, and current social setting.

Additional data about information-processing came from daily diaries in which the panelists reported what they remembered about news stories that had recently come to their attention. We asked each respondent to record at least three current events stories per day for five days of each week, along with personal reactions to the stories. The stories could come from the mass media, conversation, or personal experiences. They were to be recorded after an average lag of four hours or more to permit normal forgetting to occur. The diary forms asked for brief reports about the main themes of each story, its source and length, the respondent's reactions to it, and the reasons for paying attention to that story and remembering it. The average number of diary stories for each person was 533; the range was from 351 to 969. A majority of the panelists completed diaries on a regular five-day schedule except during periods of illness in the family and during vacations and business trips.

Panel studies raise questions about the effects of earlier interviews on later ones. To check whether significant sensitization had occurred, we conducted periodic interviews with people from the original pool of respondents who had not been interviewed except for the original screening. We found no significant differences in the answers given by panel members and outsiders. Apparently, sensitization was not a problem because so many different questions were asked during each interview that the respondents found it difficult to remember answers from prior interviews or to anticipate the types of question that might be asked in subsequent interviews. Furthermore, the yearlong time span of the study made it too inconvenient to maintain enhanced attentiveness to information.

Data Analysis

Interviews and Diaries. We used a two-stage analysis of the interview tapes and diaries to examine attention arousal and information-processing. The first round ascertained the substance of the interview responses and the diary contents. The nature of the issues that were remembered, the frequencies of mention, the positive or negative direction and strength of opinions, and similar matters were noted.

The second, and more difficult, coding task involved conceptual coding. Here coders were asked to infer thinking processes from the respondents' comments. Interview protocols were checked for such matters as conceptualizations of political situations, ability to generalize and produce analogies, cause-and-effect linkages, rationales and rationalizations, and consistencies and inconsistencies in thought. Each respondent's interview protocols were divided among three or more coders to guard against idiosyncratic coding. Each individual interview was coded independently by at least two trained coders. Intercoder reliability rates averaged 85 percent agreement on choice of statements to be coded and selection of specific codes. Intercoder reliability was equally good when coders recorded what the respondents said and interpreted what they meant and when coders noted latent features, such as the respondents' ability to generalize or their overall performance during the interview.

Print and Broadcast Media. The second portion of data presented in *Processing the News*—the mass media messages available to our panelists—came from daily content analyses of the print and broadcast media used by our respondents. Local television news was viewed, taped, and coded from the actual telecast. National news was coded from printed abstracts provided by the Vanderbilt Television News Archives. Comparisons between codings from these abstracts and codings done directly from newscasts showed only very minor differences for the information required for this study.

AUDIOVISUAL INFORMATION-PROCESSING ANALYSES

While *Processing the News* discussed information-processing in general, irrespective of the modality of information transmission, the focus was explicitly on audiovisual messages in "Seeing Is Remembering: How Visuals Contribute to Learning from Television News" (Graber 1990).

Audience Analysis

To discern what judgments television audiences would render when asked about the contributions of pictures, we conducted an experiment with forty-eight adults, evenly split between men and women, and ranging in age from their early twenties to their middle sixties. The group was selected in part to provide a best-case scenario for learning about politics from television news. Half were academics teaching social sciences, especially political or media-related subjects, in a large urban university. They were selected randomly from a pool of 282 names on the telephone rosters of relevant departments.

One-quarter of the participants were college students, selected randomly from among students entering a classroom building that houses the university's social science classes. The remaining participants were people whose employment in assorted blue-collar, white-collar, and professional jobs did not suggest uncommonly high concern with politics or unusual facility with processing political news. They were recruited from a roster of names compiled by soliciting nominations from the other participants in the experiment. The group as a whole thus represented above-average intellectual skills and interests in news, along with a liberal sprinkling of "average" news viewers.

Every participant was exposed to twelve news stories in a laboratory setting. Six stories were presented with audiovisuals and six others with sound only. Segments with and without audiovisuals were alternated. Each person was assigned to one of two demographically matched groups. The A group viewed odd-numbered stories and listened to even-numbered ones; the B group did the reverse. The procedure permitted us to observe how the two groups would vary in their reactions to a story when one group had seen it with audiovisuals and the other without. Stories had been paired according to six major themes so that each person could see the same theme with or without audiovisuals. This enabled us to compare the visuals-plus-sound and sound-only responses to the same basic theme.

We selected stories typical for the medium's nightly news. Two of the stories dealt with international trouble spots of particular concern to Americans. Other pairs of stories dealt with poverty and persecution of large population groups and with hardworking, upright, ordinary citizens caught in the throes of major misfortune by forces largely beyond their control. There were also stories about science topics and about comparatively dry economic news. The final pair of stories dealt with two politically tinged entertainment items.

Immediately following exposure to each story, each person was asked: "If a friend walked in right now and asked you to tell him/her what this story was all about, how would you report it?" The initial question was followed by several probes—"Anything else?"—intended to tap additional story elements that the individual had consciously or inadvertently withheld initially. Respondents were also asked about special meanings the story might have for them. When the story was shown with visuals, the participants were asked, in addition: "Do you recall any of the pictures in this story? Which ones? What did they show? Did they make the story more meaningful? In what way?" People who did not see the visuals were asked what the omitted visuals might have shown.

To score recall and comprehension of the audiovisual messages in each story, we identified individual verbal and visual themes. Verbal themes were defined as ideas conveyed by a single statement or cluster of statements. For example, in a story about an abortion pill, the following description of the pill was considered as a single theme, even though four sentences are involved:

Anchor: The abortion is induced by taking a pill up to two months after conception. We have this report from France.

Reporter: In size, shape, and color, it's identical to an aspirin. It's taken in pill form for four days, starting two days before menstruation is due to start.

Coded in this manner, the twelve stories contained a total of 214 verbal themes. Visual themes were defined similarly as graphics or film scenes conveying messages about a particular topic. In the abortion story, for example, the verbal statement that "experiments on laboratory animals produced a very high success rate with mice and rabbits" was illustrated with five scenes of animals. As recorded in our picture protocols, these consisted of "(a) rubber-gloved woman and man in lab coats, stroking belly of brown rabbit, apparently looking for injection site; (b) hand placing mouse into mouse cage with multiple white mice; (c) close-up of white mouse held by tail, hands visible, white lab coat in background; (d) baby chick behind cage bars; (e) pan shot of cages showing adult chickens." There were 135 visual themes. The numbers suggest the amount of information made available to the audience and the possibilities for learning.

Content Analysis

To assess the information contained in audiovisuals and the manner of presentation of television news, "Seeing Is Remembering" also reports about two separate content analyses that my research team and I had performed earlier. Two sets of newscasts were involved. The first set consisted of all political stories (189) from the early evening national news on ABC, CBS, NBC, and PBS videotaped during a two-week period. Analyzing several networks for the same period made it possible to assess different versions of the same story as covered by various journalists and at different times. To guard against the danger that the chosen two-week period might be atypical, we also randomly taped 150 national and local news stories from the early and late evening broadcasts over a four-month period that overlapped the two-week taping.

Two coders recorded routine information for each news story, such as network, date, anchors' and reporters' names, and story length. They also recorded each story's main topic; the audiovisual treatment and spin of the opening theme, which sets the tone for each piece; and all verbal and visual themes. To assess what the audiovisuals contributed over and above the themes presented by the verbal statements, the coders noted whether the audiovisuals were redundant, amplified the verbal message, or presented entirely new themes and whether they introduced judgmental and/or emotional elements. A portion of this information was correlated with data about retention of individual story themes by viewer panels.

The 2,002 visual scenes—shots of the same subject, bounded by adjacent scenes of different subjects—were classified according to their main focus. The coders further classified visual scenes as close, medium-length, or distant shots and identified or unidentified subjects, depending on whether the verbal text identified the people and scenes. These distinctions were made because audiences are likely to pay more attention to close-ups and identified elements.

Using a gestalt coding approach, the coders then assessed what kinds of information, emotions, and perspectives the visuals contributed to the story. Gestalt coding is grounded in research on information-processing that has demonstrated that television viewers concentrate on the meanings conveyed by audiovisual messages, rather than interpreting each visual cue separately. To do that, the coders first discerned a story's general gestalt or theme. Usually, gestalt identification is easy because viewers are verbally guided, particularly by the story's verbal lead-in, to the overall meaning and significance of the message elements that they are about to witness. For instance, a man running along a city street can be verbally identified as an escaping felon, a marathon runner, or a pet owner chasing his dog. Subsequent scenes will be interpreted in light of these cues. In ascertaining a story's meaning, the coders considered the context of each story within the total newscast, the manner of introducing and sequencing stories, and the meanings conveyed by sounds other than words. Other contextual factors that were recorded included the physical setting of the story, its historical and cultural context, and major contemporaneous news developments.

Extracting meanings from audiovisual and verbal themes is neither complex nor idiosyncratic because audiovisual television news language works largely through stereotypical verbal and visual discourse. The messages are designed to be easily understood because the story must quickly convey shared meanings to vast, diverse audiences. Tests in which audiences are asked about the general rather than the idiosyncratic meaning of television news stories reveal that shared meanings are, indeed, captured.

The main difference between gestalt coding and ordinary methods of coding is that gestalt coding concentrates on the meanings conveyed by word and picture combinations, rather than recording only the absence or presence of certain audiovisual features. Coding thus is holistic, focusing on the totality of the message without detailed description of visual or aural features.

To ensure coding accuracy in making gestalt coding evaluations, we routinely used two coders to cover the same material. Intercoder reliability coefficients were in the 80 percent range. Discrepancies between the two coders were resolved by a third coder, who also checked 10 percent of the uncontested coding decisions. An example of gestalt coding, drawn from a videotaped CBS broadcast anchored by Dan Rather, is shown in the box on the next page.

The accuracy of audiovisual coding schemes can be checked by asking judges to reconstruct, in brief descriptive essays, the essence of telecasts presented to them in the form of coding schedules and a topically arranged audiovisual lexicon that lists common audiovisual expressions for various situations. The reconstruction can then be compared to similar essays from people who have watched the actual broadcasts. Alternatively, the same judges can be asked after an interval of several weeks to repeat the coding operation using corresponding videotapes, rather than coding schedules. The two essays can then be compared. The normal reliability tests designed to check intercoder and intracoder reliability should also be used.

AN EXAMPLE OF GESTALT CODING

The full spoken text of the story and an annotated numbered listing of pictures precede the sample coding schedule. Message components derived from gestalt analysis are noted in parentheses.

Annotated, Full Text of Polish Priest Story

Dan Rather: The kidnapped priest was found today.

> *1. Still picture of attractive, young priest.*

The Polish regime's chief spokesman charged that the abduction 11 days ago was part of a conspiracy against the government.

> *(No visual of the official to lend authenticity to the claim.)*

Three Polish security police have been accused of the crime. The government spokesman did not say who might have ordered the kidnapping. John Shayon in Warsaw reports:

John Shayon: Polish authorities say that divers searching a reservoir in northern Poland have found the body of kidnapped priest Father Jerzy Popieluzko.

> *2–5. Pictures of (2) trucks on beach, (3) a boat, (4) rubber rafts, (5) officials in jolly mood. (Conveys notion of callousness, lack of official concern.)*

The confirmation of his death came during evening mass at Father Popieluzko's church in Warsaw.

> *6. Close-up of grieving faces of ordinary middle-aged adults, front and back views. (Suggests that average people care deeply about the event.)*

For those who had kept a vigil for their priest this was the anguish of most difficult truth.

> *7. Close-up of weeping men and women, old and young. (Arouses emotion of empathy and sympathy. Suggests that ordinary Polish people in large numbers side with the murdered priest and what he represented.)*

"There are no adequate words," the priest said gently. "It will be easier if we are together in prayer."

> *8. Picture of a priest ministering to the grieving inside the church. (Suggests that the church is on the side of the murdered priest and what he represented.)*

The anti-Communist priest allegedly killed by three members of the secret police is survived by a family living in fear that the police will come to them.

> *9. Portrait of victim displayed at altar.*

His father flees at the sight of strangers.

10. Close-up of elderly father disappearing behind closing door. (Suggests that he is afraid to be seen.)

"What they did to my son," said Father Popieluzko's mother, "should not be done to an animal."

11. Close-up of elderly distraught plainly dressed woman in simple country kitchen. (Arouses sympathy for grieving mother.)

The priest's brother hides his face for fear of being identified and becoming a target.

12. Close-up of brother, kneeling in bedroom. His face is hidden. (Suggests that he is afraid to be seen.)

"They struck down my son," said the grieving mother. "He is a martyr. And they can strike us, too."

13. Mother, back view, in kitchen. (Enhances sense that family fears persecution.)

Many ordinary Poles hold the government responsible saying that the unrelenting official attacks on the Solidarity priest created an atmosphere of hostility that encouraged his killer.

14. Group of ordinary citizens, praying in unison inside church. (Suggests that ordinary Poles and Catholic clergy are deeply moved by priest's death. No evidence that they blame the government for creating a hostile atmosphere.)

The congregation sang once again the defiant unofficial national anthem, a song Father Popieluzko had often led with the words "God give us back a free Poland."

15. Close-up of crucifixes held high during candlelight church ceremony. Close-up of hands raised in two-finger Solidarity salute. (Suggests defiance of authorities and support of Solidarity movement.)

But never before had it been sung with such pain. John Shayon, CBS News, Warsaw.

16. Close-up of grieving faces. (Heightens sympathy and empathy.)

Gestalt Coding Schedule

Hypothesis to be tested: U.S. television structures stories about Poland to put the Polish government in a bad light and arouse antigovernment sentiments in viewers.

Résumé of Historical and Situational Context: (Omitted). A single coding can be used for all stories presented within the same context. Individual stories may require supplementary codes, for example, the fact that the story precedes or follows the situation covered by the contextual coding.

Identifying Data (Omitted). These include date, channel, time, names of newscasters, names of identified on- and off-camera individuals, length of story segments.

Theme Analysis. Items 1–4 in the following list are the *four major verbal themes*. + indicates supporting pictures; − indicates disconfirming pictures. Situations are graded for intensity: a single sign = "slight"; a double sign = "medium"; a triple sign = "high."

Items 5–10 are the *six major audiovisual themes*. + indicates message clarity; − indicates lack of clarity. Situations are graded for intensity: a single sign = "slight"; a double sign = "medium"; a triple sign = "high." Picture source numbers are in parentheses.

1. Body of murdered pro-Solidarity priest was found.
2. Government disclaims responsibility; blames antigovernment conspiracy carried out by security policemen. (−)
3. Local people and clergy are saddened (+++); blame government for murder.
4. Family is saddened, fears more attacks. (+++)
5. Victim was attractive young priest. (1) (+)
6. Callousness of searchers suggests government lacks concern. Casts doubts on unsubstantiated claims that murder was committed by government opponents. (5)(+) (Pictures 2–4 contribute nothing.)
7. Average people, from all age levels, care deeply about the event and grieve for the priest. (6–9, 14, 16) (+++)
8. Average people display support for Solidarity movement, defying government. (15) (+)
9. Polish clergy ministers to mourners; sides with priest. (8–9) (++)
10. Family is grieving and afraid of persecution. (10–13) (+++)

Scoring. One point for each message. To reflect potency of message, (a) add one point for each plus sign; (b) subtract one point for each minus sign; (c) double audiovisual message points because of their potency. A summation of the scores is shown in table A.1.

Conclusion. The Polish priest story supports the hypothesis. The single progovernment theme lacks emotional impact and is partly counteracted by conflicting evidence. Neutral themes are scarce. Emotional antigovernment themes, most of them audiovisual, prevail. The audiovisual messages contribute important facts and emotional impacts that are not conveyed by the spoken text alone. The visuals relied heavily on readily codable human behavior cues.

Table A.1 Code Summation Sheet

Orientation	Theme No.	Plain Facts Impact	Emotional Facts Impact	Total
Pro-government	2	0 (1 − 1)	—	0
Neutral	1	1		
	7		$(1 + 3) \times 2 = 8$	9
Antigovernment	3		$1 + 3 = 4$	
	4		$1 + 3 = 4$	
	5		$(1 + 1) \times 2 = 4$	
	6		$(1 + 3) \times 2 = 8$	
	8		$(1 + 1) \times 2 = 4$	
	9		$(1 + 2) \times 2 = 6$	
	10		$(1 + 3) \times 2 = 8$	38

NEWS DIRECTOR STUDY

News producers' motifs and problems, viewed from their perspective, form the subject of "The Infotainment Quotient in Routine Television News" (Graber 1994a). The study was designed to assess how news producers combine the goal of informing their audiences about routine events with the challenge of entertaining them enough to capture and hold their attention. We first conducted informal open-ended interviews with more than fifty randomly chosen television news personnel responsible for various aspects of news production. We asked them about their approaches to framing specific news stories and their reasons for choosing these approaches. These informal probes were followed by intensive interviews with five experienced, Chicago-based news directors who had worked or were then working for major network organizations.

We presented identical sets of fifteen routine news situations to the five directors and asked how they would instruct a novice camera crew to cast them. We also asked them why they requested particular pictures. Their open-ended responses were tape-recorded.

The routine assignments in the hypothetical stories entailed a series of legislative controversies over the merits of social legislation and budgetary proposals. There also were reports on long-standing, familiar social problems, such as urban poverty, and reports on restoration of normalcy after strife had ended. Other situations involved peaceful demonstrations, accounts of fatality-free accidents and crimes at home and abroad, and routine symbolic governmental functions, such as breaking ground for a fair. We geared the stories to a local Chicago area focus on the assumption that these news directors would find it easier to enlighten familiar publics about information with local angles.

To classify the styles of coverage selected by our interviewees, we used categories developed by Dan Nimmo and James Combs (1985). Nimmo and Combs identified four major approaches used for telling news stories. In the *populist/sensationalist* approach, stories are depicted primarily as dramatic events. Each story stresses human interest concerns, showing how ordinary people are plagued by never-ending wrenching problems, or occasionally how they experience great joys. The story is obviously structured to arouse emotions and empathy. Alternatively, the style can be *elitist/factual,* so that stories are confined to an unemotional recounting of verifiable information told to an intellectually mature audience. This is the style that seems most in accord with the canons of democratic theory, which require knowledgeable, interested citizens who want enough factual and interpretive information so that they can make rational assessments of complex political situations.

If journalists assume that audiences are bereft of basic political knowledge, the style may be *ignorant/didactic.* This means that the information will be stripped of all complexities and divided into easily comprehensible small segments expressed in nontechnical language. Ease in comprehension is traded for precision and sophistication. Finally, the style can be *pluralist/feature.* This means that journalists place an event into a larger context, showing how it illustrates recurrent patterns. The story takes on the characteristics of a feature article. Knowing that audiences are likely to be diverse in interests and information, journalists adapt the story for a heterogeneous audience by making its appeal broad and general.

The second major feature of the design was a content analysis of local and national news stories that would permit us to assess whether the principles stated by the interviewees were, indeed, practiced. We randomly videotaped 350 nightly political news stories from the early evening national and local news on the major networks and public television and then identified routine stories. A total of 209 stories (60 percent) satisfied our criteria, after eliminating feature essays running three to five minutes in length (11 percent); high-drama stories, such as terrorist bombings, papal visits, and hostage releases (15 percent); and story snippets that were less than twenty-one seconds in length (14 percent).

To assess the full scope of the visual impact of each of the routine news stories, we recorded the nature of the opening theme and accompanying graphic and evaluated how it affected the visual message of the story. All subsequent visual scenes presented in the story were also recorded and then categorized as either close-ups or long shots. Close-ups, particularly those showing human faces, were rated as more dramatic than more distant shots.

The focus of visual scenes was further classified to indicate whether it centered on persons or on less dramatic objects, such as locations, graphics, or text, and whether it involved icons, indexes, and symbols. *Icons* were rated as most dramatic because they involve the actual showing of a person or event. When icons are unavailable, news directors generally use *indexes* to convey information that eludes direct observation. For example, pictures of the devastation wrought by a particular hurricane or typhoon can be used as an index of the ferocity of major tropical storms. Depending on the nature of the situation depicted in the index, its impact can be as dramatic as that produced by an icon. Many aspects of life can be expressed parsimoniously through the use of *symbols*. A picture of the president hugging a grandchild or playing with a puppy symbolizes a kind and caring leader. A national flag can stand for a particular nation. Symbols often carry drama, particularly when they evoke a lot of emotional memories in the audience. This explains why, for example, people have such strong feelings regarding behavior that appears to show disrespect for their national flag.

The coding scheme used for the actual news stories was also applied to the story descriptions provided by our interviewees. The major difference between the actual and hypothetical productions was the fact that the interviewees mentioned alternative ways in which the story might be handled and that they occasionally skipped traditional story features, such as lead-ins, which they took as givens. Therefore, we had to record an array of picture scene options and note the absence of selected story elements. Three coders participated in the content analyses, and 10 percent of the findings were double-coded. Reliability ratings averaged 87 percent, excluding simple identifications, where reliability was nearly perfect. None of the reliability scores dropped below 75 percent.

FREESTANDING CONTENT ANALYSIS

"Making Sense of Televised International News: Can Citizens Meet the Challenge?" (Graber 1996b) and "The Many Faces of News: From Mainstream Media to Cybermedia" (Graber and White 1999) are studies that illustrate freestanding content analyses, unaccompanied by audience-impact studies.

Content Analysis of International News

We analyzed ABC coverage of international news stories for a full year, based on the early evening national news. Coders noted the countries mentioned in each story as well as their region, the scope of topics discussed for each country, and, because repetitions are important for memorization, the numbers of returns to a particular country's affairs. The story length and number and the nature and content of audiovisuals were also recorded. We identified audiovisuals that contributed information beyond the verbal text. Coders also recorded whether individual stories provided an explicit link to U.S. concerns that might enhance the audience's eagerness to watch and remember the story. To check whether countries that had been covered more than seven times throughout the year were remembered by television audiences, these data were compared to several unrelated indexes of audience attention to stories about these countries.

Comparing News Offerings across Venues

"The Many Faces of News" represents an effort to construct a representative sample of the news available to average citizens about an important news event—the verdict in the impeachment proceedings against President Clinton. To capture a full spectrum of available news offerings, we sampled twenty-four hours of coverage in newspapers, television, news magazines, and the Internet. Resource constraints forced us to skip a number of venues from our original design, including radio broadcasts. The selections reflect news in the Chicago area market, which is fairly typical of other major metropolitan media markets.

We selected the *Chicago Tribune* as the in-state metropolitan newspaper of record, the *New York Times* as the national newspaper of record, and the *Springfield Journal-Star* as the regional in-state newspaper. We also analyzed issues of *Time, Newsweek,* and *U.S. News & World Report.*

For our television sample, we videotaped the broadcasts of the Chicago ABC affiliate and a local television station operated by the Tribune Company. Recording covered the broadcasts at noon and at 6:00, 9:00, and 10:00 P.M. We also videotaped and analyzed *ABC World News Tonight with Peter Jennings,* broadcast at 5:30 P.M., and *Nightline,* with Ted Koppel, broadcast at 10:30 P.M. From PBS, we chose *The NewsHour with Jim Lehrer,* which is broadcast at 6:00 P.M., and *Washington Week in Review,* then moderated by Ken Bode, which follows *The NewsHour* on Fridays. For cable programs, we examined the 8:00 P.M. broadcast of *The News with Brian Williams* on MSNBC as well as several hours of CNN's live coverage. For website analysis, we chose MSNBC and the *New York Times* on the web. Both sites mirrored their traditional media sisters, network news in one case and newspaper coverage in the other. Content and stories were similar to those available on NBC and in the *New York Times.* However, the web offered far more information than traditional media and provided unique opportunities for searching content. **Quantitative Variables.** We used a combination of quantitative and qualitative content analysis procedures to assess the depth, breadth, and quality of news coverage. Quantitatively, we wanted to know how much significance was accorded to the story, as judged by its prominence and the proportion of space or time allotted to it by the various media. We also wanted to know how much information was offered to average citizens when they used each of the different kinds of news sources at different times of the day. Finally, we wanted to know who the informants were whose perspectives were used to structure the stories. The main goal of coding throughout was to provide a foundation for making comparisons across media, including widely used web pages. Variables were counted paragraph by paragraph and minute by minute.

Significance Criteria. The significance of the story was evaluated in terms of its feature status within each modality and the proportion of the news devoted to the impeachment and related stories. Prominence was judged by whether the story was the lead story or the front-page top story or whether it ranked lower in the broadcast or publication. Proportion was gauged by the percentage of the news hole given to the impeachment coverage compared to all news, including sports, weather, and lifestyle on local television. Percentages were figured in terms of total space allocated, divided by total space available, expressed as pages or minutes.

Story Emphasis. The substance of stories was evaluated in terms of how much information was provided about the events of the day as well as about the background of the impeachment case and the implications for the future. Specifically, for event reporting, we estimated the proportion of coverage devoted to breaking events, such as roll call votes, press conferences, or atmospherics, versus other reporting, such as analysis, explanation, or background. Our estimates were based on comparing the themes in individual stories by paragraphs or minutes devoted to the theme. For background stories, we estimated the proportion of coverage devoted to the background of the impeachment, such as past votes, analysis of legal strategies or tactics, testimony, past significant events, or other information pertaining to happenings prior to the impeachment vote. The figures for consequences of the reported events were based on estimates of the proportion of coverage devoted to stories about the present and future impact of the events. All estimates reflected the combined findings of three coders.

Story Sources. In terms of story sources, we were most concerned with whose views were most frequently mentioned as well as which side they represented. We coded sources as White House, House Republicans, House Democrats, Senate Republicans, Senate Democrats, or Notables and Non-notables. For each source or set of sources, we noted the frequency of citation in relation to the number of sources cited in the story.

Qualitative Variables. Qualitatively, we judged how the story was framed. What were the most dominant and subordinate frames? What aspects of the case were emphasized most, and what overall judgments about the significance of the impeachment vote emerged in terms of politics and history? Finally, we wanted to speculate about the overall collective memory that coverage might inspire.

Dominant and subordinate frames were identified by reading or watching news stories, recording all frames, and then listing them in order of frequency for each medium. Frames were gathered from headlines and key phrases, language, and quotes. Most frames could be grouped into one of several categories. The first category, Interpreting the Vote, included stories that were framed in terms of the impeachment vote as rebuke, as predictable partisan politics, as closure, and as vindication. The second category, Impacts, included stories that were framed in terms of the short-term and long-term impacts of the impeachment vote on President Clinton's future and on the future of the Republican Party. The third category of frames discussed Impeachment as Historical Drama. In this category, we subsumed stories that framed the impeachment as a historical event, as a national ordeal, or as a major political drama. These stories tended to focus on the atmospherics of the events of the day, on the significance of the impeachment for history, and on the sense of relief among participants and public alike that the impeachment process had ended. The various categories made it possible to construct graphs to illustrate multiple aspects of news coverage.

REFERENCES

Altheide, David L. 1985. *Media power.* Beverly Hills, Calif.: Sage.

Anderson, Daniel R. 1998. Educational television is not an oxymoron. *Annals of the American Academy of Political and Social Science* 557 (May): 24–38.

Anderson, John R. 1983. *The architecture of cognition.* Cambridge: Harvard University Press.

Arterton, F. Christopher. 1978. The media politics of presidential campaigns. In *Race for the presidency: The media and the nominating process,* edited by James David Barber. Englewood Cliffs, N.J.: Prentice-Hall.

Barber, James David. 1979. Not the New York Times: What network news should be. *Washington Monthly,* September, 14–21.

Bargh, John A., Mark Chen, and Lara Burrows. 1996. Automaticity of social behavior: Direct effects of trait constructs and stereotype activation on action. *Journal of Personality and Social Psychology* 71:230–44.

Bargh, Jonathan. 1995. Paper read at a meeting of the American Psychological Association.

Barringer, Felicity. 1999. Leading media companies forming joint web venture. *New York Times,* 18 November.

Barry, Ann Marie Seward. 1997. *Visual intelligence: Perception, image, and manipulation in visual communication.* Albany: State University of New York Press.

Bartels, Larry M. 1996. Uninformed votes: Information effects in presidential elections. *American Journal of Political Science* 40:194–230.

Basil, Michael D. 1994. Multiple resource theory I: Application to television viewing. *Communication Research* 21:177–207.

Bendavid, Naftali. 2000. Sound political strategies. *Chicago Tribune,* 9 March.

Bennett, W. Lance. 1997. *News: The politics of illusion.* 3rd ed. New York: Longman.

Bennett, W. Lance, and David L. Paletz, eds. 1994. *Taken by storm: The media, public opinion, and U.S. foreign policy in the Gulf War.* Chicago: University of Chicago Press.

Berman, Laurence. 1993. *The musical image.* Westport, Conn.: Greenwood Press.

Berry, Charles, and Hans-Bernd Brosius. 1991. On the multiple effects of visual format on TV news learning. *Applied Cognitive Psychology* 5:519–28.

Bineham, Jeffery L. 1988. A historical account of the hypodermic model in mass communication. *Communication Monographs* 55:230–46.

Biocca, Frank. 1991. The role of communication codes in political ads. In *Television and political advertising: Signs, codes, and images,* edited by Frank Biocca. Vol. 2. Hillsdale, N.J.: Erlbaum.

Bird, S. Elizabeth, and Robert W. Dardenne. 1989. Myth, chronicle and story: Exploring the narrative qualities of news. In *Media, myths, and narratives: Television and the press,* edited by James W. Carey. Beverly Hills, Calif.: Sage.

Birdwhistell, Ray L. 1970. *Kinesics and context: Essays on body motion communication.* Philadelphia: University of Pennsylvania Press.

Blakeslee, Sandra. 1993. Seeing and imagining. *New York Times,* 31 August.

———. 1994a. Brain locates source of a sound with temporal, not spatial, cues. *New York Times,* 10 May.

———. 1994b. Tracing the brain's pathways for linking emotion and reason. *New York Times,* 6 December.

———. 1995a. The mystery of music: How it works in the brain. *New York Times,* 16 May.

———. 1995b. Traffic jams in brain networks may result in verbal stumbles. *New York Times,* 26 September.

———. 2000. A decade of discovery yields a shock about the brain. *New York Times,* 4 January.

Blank, Robert. 1999. *Brain policy: How the new neuroscience will change our lives and our politics.* Washington, D.C.: Georgetown University Press.

Brooke, James. 2000. Old traditions on new network: Igloos and seals. *New York Times,* 11 February.

Brosius, Hans-Bernd. 1993. The effects of emotional pictures in television news. *Communications Research* 20:105–24.

Budd, Malcolm. 1985. *Music and the emotions.* London: Routledge and Kegan Paul.

Bundesen, Claus. 1990. A theory of visual attention. *Psychological Review* 97:523–47.

Burgoon, Judee K. 1980. Nonverbal communication research in the 1970's: An overview. In *Communication Yearbook IV,* edited by Dan Nimmo. New Brunswick, N.J.: Transaction Books.

Buscemi, William I. 1997. Numbers? Borrinnnggg!!! *PS: Political Science & Politics* 30:737–42.

Caldwell, John Thornton. 1995. *Televisuality: Style, crisis, and authority in American television.* New Brunswick, N.J.: Rutgers University Press.

Calvin, William H. 1997. *How brains think.* London: Weidenfeld and Nicolson.

Cappella, Joseph N., and Kathleen Hall Jamieson. 1997. *The spiral of cynicism: The press and the public good.* New York: Oxford University Press.

Carlson, James, and Rebecca Trichtinger. 1997. Perspectives on entertainment television's portrayal of a racial incident: An intensive analysis. Unpublished manuscript.

Carr, Forrest. 1999. Six o'clock rocks: What happens to your local news between 6 and 11? Available at www.journalism.org/1999/html/sixrock.html.

Carter, Bill. 1996. Broadcasting: CBS counterattacks the cable networks, hoping to reclaim its old loyalists. *New York Times*, 16 September.

Carter, Rita. 1998. *Mapping the mind*. Berkeley: University of California Press.

Chase, William G., ed. 1973. *Visual information processing*. New York: Academic Press.

Chong, Dennis. 2000. *Rational lives: Norms and values in politics and society*. Chicago: University of Chicago Press.

Chubb, John E., Michael G. Hagen, and Paul M. Sniderman. 1991. Ideological reasoning. In *Reasoning and choice: Explorations in political psychology*, edited by Paul M. Sniderman, Richard A. Brody, and Philip E. Tetlock. Cambridge: Cambridge University Press.

Clarity, James F. 1999. In land of Joyce and Yeats, a struggle to read ABC's. *New York Times*, 24 July.

Clark v. ABC. 1982. 684 F.2d 1208 (6th Cir.).

Committee of Concerned Journalists. 1999a. Changing definition of news: Subject of news stories by medium. Available at www.journalism.org/lastudy2.htm.

———. 1999b. News as entertainment/entertainment as news. Available at www.journalism.org/USCreporta.htm.

Condry, John. 1989. *The psychology of television*. Hillsdale, N.J.: Erlbaum.

Conover, Pamela Johnston, and Stanley Feldman. 1984. How people organize the political world: A schematic model. *American Journal of Political Science* 28:95–126.

———. 1989. Candidate perception in an ambiguous world: Campaigns, cues, and inference processes. *American Journal of Political Science* 33:912–40.

Cook, Timothy E. 1998. *Governing with the news: The news media as a political institution*. Chicago: University of Chicago Press.

Crigler, Ann N., Marion R. Just, and Timothy E. Cook. 1993. Character, issues, and performance. Paper read at a meeting of the American Political Science Association.

Crigler, Ann N., Marion Just, and W. Russell Neuman. 1994. Interpreting visual versus audio messages in television news. *Journal of Communication* 44:132–49.

Curtice, John, Rüdiger Schmitt-Beck, and Peter Schrott. 1998. Do the media matter? Paper read at a meeting of the Midwest Political Science Association.

Dahlgren, Peter. 1987. Tuning in the news: TV journalism and the process of reality. In *The focused screen*, edited by Jose Vidal-Beneyto and Peter Dahlgren. Strasbourg, France: AMELA/Council of Europe.

Damasio, Antonio R. 1994. *Descartes' error: Emotion, reason, and the human brain*. New York: Grosset/Putnam.

———. 1999. *The feeling of what happens: Body and emotion in the making of consciousness*. New York: Harcourt.

Dayan, Daniel, and Elihu Katz. 1992. *Media events: The live broadcasting of history*. Cambridge: Harvard University Press.

Delli Carpini, Michael X., and Scott Keeter. 1991. Stability and change in the U.S. public's knowledge of politics. *Public Opinion Quarterly* 55:583–612.

———. 1993. Measuring political knowledge: Putting first things first. *American Journal of Political Science* 37:1179–1206.

———. 1996. *What Americans know about politics and why it matters*. New Haven, Conn.: Yale University Press.

———. 2000. Gender and political knowledge. In *Gender and American politics*, edited by Sue Tolleson-Rinehart and Jyl Josephson. Forthcoming.

Delli Carpini, Michael X., and Bruce A. Williams. 1994a. Fictional and "nonfictional" television celebrates Earth Day: Or politics is comedy plus pretense. *Cultural Studies* 8:74–98.

———. 1994b. Metaphors and media research: The uses of television in political conversation. *Communication Research* 6:782–812.

Dobkin, Bethami A. 1996. Video verité: Language and image in the interpretation of power. In *The theory and practice of political communication research*, edited by Mary E. Stuckey. Albany: State University of New York Press.

Donelan, Karen, Robert J. Blendon, and Craig A. Hill. 1995. What does the public know about entitlements? Paper read at a meeting of the American Association for Public Opinion Research.

Donsbach, Wolfgang, Hans-Bernd Brosius, and Axel Mattenklott. 1993. How unique is the perspective of television? A field experiment on the perception of a campaign event by participants and television viewers. *Political Communication* 10:37–53.

Downs, Anthony. 1957. *An economic theory of democracy*. New York: Harper & Row.

Eagly, Alice H., and Shelly Chaiken. 1993. *The psychology of attitudes*. Fort Worth, Tex.: Harcourt Brace Jovanovich.

Edelman, Murray. 1993. Contestable categories and public opinion. *Political Communication* 10:231–42.

———. 1995. *From art to politics*. Chicago: University of Chicago Press.

Elber, Lynn. 2000. Population group reaches out through soap operas to teach life lessons. *Chicago Tribune*, 30 June.

Entman, Robert M. 1989. *Democracy without citizens: Media and the decay of American politics*. New York: Oxford University Press.

———. 1993. Framing: Toward clarification of a fractured paradigm. *Journal of Communication* 43:51–58.

Fallows, James. 1995. *Breaking the news: How the media undermine American de-mocracy.* New York: Pantheon Books.

Feenan, Kelly, and Joan Gay Snodgrass. 1990. The effect of context on discrim-ination and bias in recognition memory for pictures and words. *Memory and Cognition* 18:515–27.

Fiske, Susan T., Richard R. Lau, and Richard R. Smith. 1990. On the varieties and utilities of political experience. *Social Cognition* 8:31–48.

Fiske, Susan T., and Shelley E. Taylor. 1991. *Social cognition.* New York: McGraw-Hill.

Flavell, John H., Eleanor R. Flavell, Frances L. Green, and Jon E. Korfmacher. 1990. Do young children think of television images as pictures or real objects? *Journal of Broadcasting and Electronic Media* 34:399–419.

Ford, Paul Leicester, ed. 1894. *Writings of Thomas Jefferson.* Vol. 5. New York: Putnam's.

Fowles, Jib. 1992. *Why viewers watch: A reappraisal of television's effects.* Rev. ed. Newbury Park, Calif.: Sage.

Frey, Kurt P., and Alice H. Eagly. 1993. Vividness can undermine the per-suasiveness of messages. *Journal of Personality and Social Psychology* 65:32–44.

Gamson, William A. 1992. *Talking politics.* Cambridge: Cambridge University Press.

Gazzaniga, Michael S. 1992. *Nature's mind: The biological roots of thinking, emotions, sexuality, language and intelligence.* Harmondsworth, England: Penguin.

———. 1998. *The mind's past.* Berkeley: University of California Press.

Geiger, Seth, and John Newhagen. 1993. Revealing the black box: Information processing and media effects. *Journal of Communication* 43:42–50.

Geiger, Seth, and Byron Reeves. 1991. The effects of visual structure and con-tent emphasis on the evaluation and memory for candidates. In *Television and political advertising,* edited by Frank Biocca. Hillsdale, N.J.: Erlbaum.

———. 1993a. The effects of scene changes and semantic relatedness on atten-tion to television. *Communication Research* 20:155–75.

———. 1993b. We interrupt this program . . . Attention for television se-quences. *Human Communication Research* 193:368–87.

Gerbner, George, Larry Gross, Michael Morgan, and Nancy Signorielli. 1982. Charting the mainstream: Television's contributions to political orienta-tions. *Journal of Communication* 32:100–127.

———. 1986. Living with television: The dynamics of the cultivation process. In *Perspectives on media effects,* edited by Jennings Bryant and Dolf Zillman. Hillsdale, N.J.: Erlbaum.

Gilens, Martin. 1999. *Why Americans hate welfare: Race, media, and the politics of antipoverty policy.* Chicago: University of Chicago Press.

———. 2000. Political ignorance and American democracy. Paper read at a meeting of the Midwest Political Science Association.

Glynn, Ian. 1999. *An anatomy of thought: The origin and machinery of the mind.* New York: Oxford University Press.

Goleman, Daniel. 1994. Miscoding is seen as the root of false memories. *New York Times,* 31 May.

———. 1995. *Emotional intelligence.* New York: Bantam Books.

Gollwitzer, Peter M., and John A. Bargh. 1996. *The psychology of action: Linking cognition and motivation to behavior.* New York: Guilford Press.

Goode, Erica. 2000. How culture molds habits of thought. *New York Times,* 8 August.

Goodman, Walter. 1992. TV images from Bosnia fire passion and politics. *New York Times,* 6 August.

Grabe, Maria Elizabeth, Annie Lang, Shuhua Zhou, and Paul David Bolls. 2000. Cognitive access to negatively arousing news: An experimental investigation of the knowledge gap. *Communication Research* 27:3–26.

Graber, Doris A. 1986. The picture language of television news: Boiler plate and baby talk. Paper read at a meeting of the Midwest Association for Public Opinion Research.

———. 1990. Seeing is remembering: How visuals contribute to learning from television news. *Journal of Communication* 40:134–55.

———. 1991. What you see is what you get. Paper read at a meeting of the American Political Science Association.

———. 1993. *Processing the news: How people tame the information tide.* Lanham, Md.: University Press of America.

———. 1994a. The infotainment quotient in routine television news: A directors' perspective. *Discourse and Society* 5:483–508.

———. 1994b. Why voters fail information tests: Can the hurdles be overcome? *Political Communication* 11:331–46.

———. 1996a. Say it with pictures. In The media and politics, Kathleen Hall Jamieson, special ed. *Annals of the American Academy of Political and Social Science* 546 (July): 85–96.

———. 1996b. Making sense of televised international news: Can citizens meet the challenge? Paper read at a meeting of the International Communication Association.

———. 1997. *Mass media and American politics.* 5th ed. Washington, D.C.: CQ Press.

———. 1998. Whither televised election news: Lessons from the 1996 campaign. *Harvard International Journal of Press/Politics* 3:112–20.

Graber, Doris, and Brian White. 1999. The many faces of news: From mainstream media to cybermedia. Paper read at a meeting of the American Political Science Association.

Granberg, Donald, and Thad A. Brown. 1989. On affect and cognition in politics. *Social Psychology Quarterly* 52:171–82.

Greenfield, Patricia Marks. 1984. *Mind and media: The effects of television, video games, and computers.* Cambridge: Harvard University Press.

Gregory, Richard L. 1997. *Eye and brain: The psychology of seeing.* 5th ed. Princeton, N.J.: Princeton University Press.

Griffin, Michael. 1992. Looking at TV news: Strategies for research. *Communication* 13:121–41.

Grimes, Tom. 1990. Encoding TV news messages into memory. *Journalism Quarterly* 67:757–66.

Gunnthorsdottir, Anna. 1995. Worth a thousand words? Affective processing of visual symbols in environmentalist and anti-environmentalist propaganda. Paper read at a meeting of the International Society of Political Psychology.

Gunter, Barrie. 1991. Responding to news and public affairs. In *Responding to the screen: Reception and reaction processes,* edited by Jennings Bryant and Dolf Zillman. Hillsdale, N.J.: Erlbaum.

Gutstadt, Lynn. 1993. Taking the pulse of the CNN audience: A case study of the Gulf War. *Political Communication* 10:389–409.

Gyselinck, Valérie, and Hubert Tardieu. 1999. The role of illustrations in text comprehension: What, when, for whom, and why? In *The construction of mental representations during reading,* edited by Herre van Oostendorp and Susan R. Goldman. Mahwah, N.J.: Erlbaum.

Habermas, Jürgen. 1989. The public sphere: An encyclopedia article. In *Critical theory and society: A reader,* edited by Stephen E. Bronner and Douglas M. Kellner. New York: Routledge.

Hacker, Kenneth L., Tara G. Coste, Daniel F. Kamm, and Carl R. Bybee. 1991. Oppositional readings of network television news: Viewer deconstruction. *Discourse and Society* 2:183–202.

Halberstam, David. 1979. *The powers that be.* New York: Knopf.

Hall, Stuart. 1980. Encoding/decoding. In *Culture, media, language,* edited by Stuart Hall, D. Hobson, A. Lowe, and P. Willis. London: Hutchinson.

Hallin, Daniel C. 1986. *The "uncensored war": The media and Vietnam.* New York: Oxford University Press.

———. 1992. Sound bite news: Television coverage of elections, 1968–1988. *Journal of Communication* 42:5–24.

Hart, Roderick P. 1987. *The sound of leadership: Presidential communication in the modern age.* Chicago: University of Chicago Press.

———. 1994. *Seducing America: How television charms the modern voter.* New York: Oxford University Press.

Hearold, Susan. 1986. A synthesis of 1043 effects of television on social behavior. In *Public communication and behavior,* edited by George A. Comstock. Vol. 1. New York: Academic Press.

Hilts, Philip J. 1995. Brain's memory system comes into focus. *New York Times,* 30 May.

Huesmann, L. Rowell, and Leonard D. Eron, eds. 1986. *Television and the aggressive child: A cross-national comparison.* Hillsdale, N.J.: Erlbaum.

Huston, Aletha C., and John C. Wright. 1998. Television and the informational and educational needs of children. *Annals of the American Academy of Political and Social Science* 557 (May): 9–23.

Iyengar, Shanto. 1991. *Is anyone responsible? How television frames political issues.* Chicago: University of Chicago Press.

Iyengar, Shanto, and Donald R. Kinder. 1987. *News that matters: Television and American opinion.* Chicago: University of Chicago Press.

Jamieson, Kathleen Hall. 1992. *Dirty politics: Deception, distraction, and democracy.* New York: Oxford University Press.

Jamieson, Kathleen Hall, and Karlyn Kohrs Campbell. 1992. *The interplay of influence: Mass media and their publics in news, advertising, politics.* 3rd ed. Belmont, Calif.: Wadsworth.

Jamieson, Kathleen Hall, and Joseph N. Cappella. 1998. The role of the press in the health care reform debate of 1993–1994. In *The politics of news: The news of politics,* edited by Doris Graber, Denis McQuail, and Pippa Norris. Washington, D.C.: CQ Press.

Jeffres, Leo W. 1997. *Mass media effects.* 2nd ed. Prospect Heights, Ill.: Waveland Press.

Jensen, Klaus Bruhn. 1986. *Making sense of the news: Towards a theory and an empirical model of reception for the study of mass communication.* Aarhus, Denmark: Aarhus University Press.

———. 1995. *The social semiotics of mass communication.* Thousand Oaks, Calif.: Sage.

Johnson, Steve. 1998a. First, the bad news. *Chicago Tribune,* 19 January.

———. 1998b. A newscast is a newscast is a newscast. . . . *Chicago Tribune,* 20 January.

———. 1999. Landslide of opportunity. *Chicago Tribune,* 26 November.

Jones, Tim. 1997. New media may excite, while old media attract. *Chicago Tribune,* 28 July.

———. 1999. Digital television. *Chicago Tribune,* 8 February.

Kaid, Lynda Lee. 1998. *The uses and abuses of technology in political advertising.* Norman: University of Oklahoma Political Communication Center. Videotape.

Kamalipour, Yahya. 1994. The brain drain: What television is doing to us. *Chicago Tribune,* 2 May.

Kepplinger, Hans Matthias. 1991. The impact of presentation techniques: Theoretical aspects and empirical findings. In *Television and political advertising: Psychological processes,* edited by Frank Biocca. Vol. 1. Hillsdale, N.J.: Erlbaum.

Key, V. O., Jr., with the assistance of Milton C. Cummings Jr. 1965. *The responsible electorate.* Cambridge: Harvard University Press.

Kingdon, John. 1981. *Congressmen's voting decisions.* 2nd ed. New York: Harper & Row.

Kinsbourne, Marcel. 1982. Hemispheric specialization and the growth of human understanding. *American Psychologist* 37:411–20.

Kirk, Jim. 1999. Morning news rises and shines. *Chicago Tribune,* 17 May.

Klapper, Joseph T. 1960. *The effects of mass communication.* New York: Free Press.

Kosslyn, Stephen. 1994. *Image and brain: The resolution of the imagery debate.* Cambridge, Mass.: MIT Press.

Kraus, Sidney, ed. 1979. *The great debates: Carter vs. Ford, 1976.* Bloomington: Indiana University Press.

Krosnick, Jon. 1990. Americans' perception of presidential candidates: A test of the projection hypothesis. *Journal of Social Issues* 46:159–82.

———. 1991. Government policy and citizen passion: A study of issue publics in contemporary America. *Political Behavior* 12:59–93.

Krosnick, Jon A., and Laura Brannon. 1993. The impact of the Gulf War on the ingredients of presidential evaluations: Multidimensional effects of political involvement. *American Political Science Review* 87:963–78.

Kubey, Robert, and Mihaly Csikszentmihalyi. 1990. *Television and the quality of life: How viewing shapes everyday experience.* Hillsdale, N.J.: Erlbaum.

Kuklinski, James H., Paul J. Quirk, Jennifer Jerit, David Schwieder, and Robert F. Rich. 2000. Misinformation and the currency of democratic citizenship. Paper read at a meeting of the Institute of Government and Public Affairs, University of Illinois at Urbana-Champaign.

Kuklinski, James H., Paul Quirk, David W. Schwieder, and Robert F. Rich. 1998. "Just the facts, ma'am" Political facts and public opinion. *Annals of the American Academy of Political and Social Science* 560 (November): 143–54.

Kuleshov, Lev. 1974. *Kuleshov on film: Writings of Lev Kuleshov,* translated and edited by R. Levaco. Berkeley: University of California Press.

Ladd, Everett. 1996. The data just don't show erosion of America's "social capital." *Public Perspective* 7:1, 5–6.

Lang, Annie, and Marian Friestad. 1993. Emotion, hemispheric specialization, and visual and verbal memory for television messages. *Communication Research* 20:647–70.

Lang, Gladys Engel, and Kurt Lang. 1953. The unique perspective of television and its effects: A pilot study. *American Sociological Review* 18:3–12.

———. 1983. *The battle for public opinion: The president, the press and the polls during Watergate.* New York: Columbia University Press.

Langston, Mark, and Tom Trabasso. 1999. Modeling causal integration and availability of information during comprehension of narrative texts. In *The construction of mental representations during reading,* edited by Herre van Oostendorp and Susan R. Goldman. Mahwah, N.J.: Erlbaum.

Lanzetta, John T., Denis G. Sullivan, Roger D. Masters, and Gregory J. McHugo. 1985. Emotional and cognitive responses to televised images of political leaders. In *Mass media and political thought,* edited by Sidney Kraus and Richard M. Perloff. Beverly Hills, Calif.: Sage.

Larson, Charles U. 1989. *Persuasion, reception and responsibility.* 5th ed. Belmont, Calif.: Wadsworth.

Larson, James F., and Heung-Soo Park. 1993. *Global television and the politics of the Seoul Olympics.* Boulder, Colo.: Westview Press.

LeDoux, Joseph E. 1996. *The emotional brain: The mysterious underpinnings of emotional life.* New York: Simon & Schuster.

Lewis, Carolyn D. 1984. *Reporting for television.* New York: Columbia University Press.

Liebes, Tamar. 1988. Cultural differences in retelling television fiction. *Critical Studies in Mass Communication* 5:277–92.

Lippmann, Walter. [1922] 1965. *Public opinion.* New York: Free Press.

Litwak, Mark. 1986. *Reel power: The struggle for influence and success in the new Hollywood.* New York: William Morrow.

Livingston, Steven, and Todd Eachus. 1995. Humanitarian crises and U.S. foreign policy: Somalia and the CNN effect reconsidered. *Political Communication* 12:413–29.

Livingstone, Sonia M. 1990. *Making sense of television: The psychology of audience interpretation.* Oxford: Pergamon Press.

Lodge, Milton, Kathleen McGraw, and Patrick Stroh. 1989. An impression-driven model of candidate evaluation. *American Political Science Review* 83:399–419.

Lodge, Milton, Marco R. Steenbergen, and Shawn Brau. 1995. The responsive voter: Campaign information and the dynamics of candidate evaluation. *American Political Science Review* 89:309–26.

Lodge, Milton, and Patrick Stroh. 1993. Inside the mental voting booth: An impression-driven process model of candidate evaluation. In *Explorations in political psychology,* edited by Shanto Iyengar and William J. McGuire. Durham, N.C.: Duke University Press.

Lodge, Milton, Patrick Stroh, and John Wahlke. 1990. Black box models of candidate evaluation. *Political Behavior* 12:5–27.

Loftus, Elizabeth. 1979. *Eyewitness testimony.* Cambridge: Harvard University Press.

Loftus, Elizabeth, and Katherine Ketcham. 1994. *The myth of repressed memory.* New York: St. Martin's Press.

Lupia, Arthur, and Mathew D. McCubbins. 1998. *The democratic dilemma: Can citizens learn what they need to know?* New York: Cambridge University Press.

Marcus, George E. 1988. The structure of emotional response: 1984 presidential candidates. *American Political Science Review* 82:735–61.

Marcus, George E., W. Russell Neuman, and Michael MacKuen. 2000. *Affective intelligence and political judgment.* Chicago: University of Chicago Press.

Masters, Roger D., and Denis G. Sullivan. 1993. Nonverbal behavior and leadership: Emotion and cognition in political attitudes. In *Explorations in political psychology,* edited by Shanto Iyengar and William McGuire. Durham, N.C.: Duke University Press.

McChesney, Robert W. 1996. The Internet and U.S. communication policy-making in historical and critical perspective. *Journal of Communication* 46:98–124.

McClain, Dylan Loeb. 1999. Where is today's child? Probably watching TV. *New York Times,* 6 December.

McGraw, Kathleen M., Milton Lodge, and Patrick Stroh. 1990. On-line processing in candidate evaluation: The effects of issue order, issue importance, and sophistication. *Political Behavior* 12:41–58.

McGraw, Kathleen, and Neil Pinney. 1990. The effects of general and domain-specific expertise on memory and judgment. *Social Cognition* 8:9–30.

McGraw, Kathleen M., Neil Pinney, and David S. Newmann. 1991. Memory for political actors: Contrasting the use of semantic and evaluative organizational strategies. *Political Behavior* 13:165–89.

McNulty, Timothy J., and Steve Daley. 1992. Audience participation restrains, focuses 2nd presidential debate. *Chicago Tribune,* 16 October.

Messaris, Paul. 1994. *Visual literacy: Image, mind and reality.* Boulder, Colo.: Westview Press.

———. 1998. Visual aspects of media literacy. *Journal of Communication* 48:70–80.

Metz, Christian. 1974. *Film language: A semiotics of the cinema.* New York: Oxford University Press.

Meyrowitz, Joshua. 1985. *No sense of place: The impact of electronic media on social behavior.* New York: Oxford University Press.

———. 1994. Medium theory. In *Communication theory today,* edited by David Crowley and David Mitchell. New York: Polity Press.

Mickiewicz, Ellen. 1996. *Changing channels.* New York: Oxford University Press.

———. 1998. Transition and democratization: The role of journalists in Eastern Europe and the former Soviet Union. In *The politics of news: The news of politics,* edited by Doris Graber, Denis McQuail, and Pippa Norris. Washington, D.C.: CQ Press.

Mifflin, Lawrie. 1998a. As band of channels grows, niche programs will boom. *New York Times,* 28 December.

———. 1998b. The countdown to "60 Minutes II." *New York Times,* 21 December.

Milburn, A. Michael, and Anne B. McGrail. 1992. The dramatic presentation of news and its effects on cognitive complexity. *Political Psychology* 13:613–32.

Millerson, Gerald. 1992. *Video production handbook.* 2nd ed. Oxford, England: Butterworth-Heinemann.

Mindak, William H., and Gerald D. Hursh. 1965. Television's functions on the assassination weekend. In *The Kennedy assassination and the American public,* edited by Bradley S. Greenberg and Edwin B. Parker. Palo Alto, Calif.: Stanford University Press.

Minow, Newton. 1964. *Equal time: The private broadcaster and the public interest,* edited by Lawrence Laurent. New York: Atheneum.

Minow, Newton N., and Craig L. LaMay. 1995. *Abandoned in the wasteland.* New York: Hill & Wang.

Minton, Steven. 1988. *Learning search control knowledge: An explanation-based approach.* Boston: Kluwer Academic Publishers.

Mondak, Jeffery J. 1994. Cognitive heuristics, heuristic processing, and efficiency in political decision making. In *Research in micropolitics,* edited by Michael Delli Carpini, Leonie Huddy, and Robert Y. Shapiro. Vol. 4. Greenwich, Conn.: JAI Press.

Mondak, Jeffery J., and Diana C. Mutz. 1997. What's so great about league bowling? Paper read at a meeting of the Midwest Political Science Association.

Morreale, Joanne. 1991. The political campaign film: Epideictic rhetoric in a documentary frame. In *Television and political advertising: Signs, codes, and images,* edited by Frank Biocca. Vol. 2. Hillsdale, N.J.: Erlbaum.

Morton, William H. 1996. *The cerebral code.* Cambridge, Mass.: MIT Press.

Myers, James H. 1996. *Segmentation and positioning for strategic marketing decisions.* Chicago: American Marketing Association.

National Institutes of Health. 1999. Multitasking behavior mapped to the prefrontal cortex. News release, National Institute of Neurological Disorders and Stroke, 12 May. Available at http://www.ninds.nih.gov.

Nelson, John S., and G. Robert Boynton. 1997. *Video rhetorics: Televised advertising in American politics.* Urbana: University of Illinois Press.

Neuman, Susan B. 1991. *Literacy in the television age: The myth of the TV effect.* Norwood, N.J.: Ablex.

Neuman, W. Russell, Marion P. Just, and Ann N. Crigler. 1992. *Common knowledge: News and the construction of political meaning.* Chicago: University of Chicago Press.

Neuman, W. Russell, Michael B. MacKuen, George E. Marcus, and Joanne Miller. 1997. Affective choice and rational choice. Paper read at a meeting of the American Political Science Association.

News in the Next Century: Profile of the American News Consumer. 1996. Sponsored by the Radio and Television News Directors Foundation. Duplicated.

Nimmo, Dan, and James Combs. 1985. *Nightly horrors: Crisis coverage by television network news.* Knoxville: University of Tennessee Press.

Nisbett, Richard E., and Lee Ross. 1980. *Human inference: Strategies and shortcomings of social judgment.* Englewood Cliffs, N.J.: Prentice-Hall.

Nørretranders, Tor. 1998. *The user illusion.* New York: Viking.

Norris, Pippa. 1996. Does television erode social capital? A reply to Putnam. *PS: Political Science and Politics* 29:474–80.

———. 2000. *A virtuous circle: Political communications in post-industrial democracies.* New York: Cambridge University Press.

Norris, Pippa, John Curtice, David Sanders, Margaret Scammell, and Holli Semetko. 1999. *On message: Communicating the campaign.* London: Sage Publications.

Ottati, Victor C. 1990. Determinants of political judgments: The joint influence of normative and heuristic rules of inference. *Political Behavior* 12:159–79.

Ottati, Victor C., and Robert S. Wyer Jr. 1990. The cognitive mediators of political choice: Toward a comprehensive model of political information processing. In *Information and democratic processes,* edited by John A. Ferejohn and James H. Kuklinski. Urbana: University of Illinois Press.

———. 1993. Affect and political judgment. In *Explorations in political psychology,* edited by Shanto Iyengar and William J. McGuire. Durham, N.C.: Duke University Press.

Page, Benjamin I., and Robert Y. Shapiro. 1992. *The rational public: Fifty years of trends in American policy preferences.* Chicago: University of Chicago Press.

Paine, Albert Bigelow. [1904] 1971. *Th. Nast: His period and his pictures.* New York: B. Blom.

Paivio, Allen. 1979. *Imagery and verbal processes.* Hillsdale, N.J.: Erlbaum.

Patterson, Thomas E. 1993. *Out of order.* New York: Knopf.

Perris, Arnold. 1986. *Music as propaganda.* Westport, Conn.: Greenwood Press.

Petty, Richard E., and John T. Cacioppo. 1986a. The elaboration likelihood model of persuasion. In *Advances in experimental and social psychology,* edited by Leonard Berkowitz. Vol. 19. Orlando, Fla.: Academic Press.

———. 1986b. *Communication and persuasion: Central and peripheral routes to attitude change.* New York: Springer.

Pew Research Center for the People and the Press. 1998a. 1998 media consumption: Section 3: American news habits. Available at http://www.people-press.org/med98rpt.htm.

———. 1998b. Public attentiveness to major news stories, 1986–1998. Available at http://www.people-press.org/database.html.

———. 1998c. Online newcomers more middle-brow, less work-oriented. Available at http://www.people-press.org/tech98sum.htm.

———. 1998d. 1998 media consumption questionnaire. Available at http://www.people-press.org/med98que.htm.

———. 1999. Gender gap analysis. Available at http://www.people-press.org/gap.htm.

———. 2000a. Data archive. Available at http://www.people-press.org/database.htm.

———. 2000b. Media report. Available at http://www.people-press.org/media00rpt.htm.

Philo, Greg. 1990. *Seeing and believing: The influence of television.* London: Routledge.

Popkin, Samuel L. 1994. *The reasoning voter: Communication and persuasion in presidential campaigns.* 2nd ed. Chicago: University of Chicago Press.

Popkin, Samuel, and Michael A. Dimock. 1999. Political knowledge and citizen competence. In *Citizen competence and democratic institutions,* edited by Stephen L. Elkin and Karol Edward Soltan. University Park: Pennsylvania State University Press.

Postman, Neil. 1984. *Amusing ourselves to death.* New York: Viking Penguin.

Project for Excellence in Journalism. 1997–99. Projects—1997/1999. Available at http://www.journalism.org.

Pryluck, Calvin. 1976. *Sources of meaning in motion pictures and television.* New York: Arno Press.

Public Perspective. 1995. Vol. 6, no. 5 (August/September).

Putnam, Robert D. 1995. Tuning in, tuning out: The strange disappearance of social capital in America. *PS: Political Science and Politics* 28:664–83.

Rahn, Wendy. 1993. The role of partisan stereotypes in information processing about political candidates. *American Journal of Political Science* 37:472–96.

Rahn, Wendy M., John Aldrich, and Eugene Borgida. 1994. Individual and contextual variations in political candidate appraisal. *American Political Science Review* 88:193–99.

Rahn, Wendy M., John H. Aldrich, Eugene Borgida, and John L. Sullivan. 1990. A social-cognitive model of candidate appraisal. In *Information and democratic processes,* edited by John A. Ferejohn and James H. Kuklinski. Urbana: University of Illinois Press.

Rahn, Wendy M., and Katherine Cramer. 1996. Activation and application of political party stereotypes: Specifying the effects of different communication media. *Political Communication* 13:195–212.

Rahn, Wendy M., Jon A. Krosnick, and Marijke Breuning. 1994. Rationalization and derivation processes in survey studies of political candidate evaluation. *American Journal of Political Science* 38:582–600.

Reeves, Byron, and Daniel R. Anderson. 1991. Media studies and psychology. *Communication Research* 18:597–600.

Regents of the University of California v. Bakke. 1978. 438 U.S. 265.

Rhee, June Woong, and Joseph Capella. 1997. The role of political sophistication in learning from news. *Communication Research* 24:197–233.

Robinson, John P., and Dennis K. Davis. 1990. Television news and the informed public: An information-processing approach. *Journal of Communication* 40:106–19.

Robinson, John P., and Mark R. Levy. 1986. *The main source.* Beverly Hills, Calif.: Sage.

Rosenberg, Shawn W. 1988. *Reason, ideology and politics.* Princeton, N.J.: Princeton University Press.

Rosenstiel, Tom, Carl Gottlieb, and Lee Ann Brady. 1999. Local TV: What works, what flops, and why. Available at http://www.journalism.org.

Rundquist, Barry, and Gerald Strom. 1995. The Illinois Voter Project: An experiment in enhancing issue information and citizen participation in the 1994 Illinois gubernatorial election. Paper read at a meeting of the American Political Science Association.

Salvaggio, Jerry Lee. 1980. *A theory of film language.* New York: Arno Press.

Samuelson, Robert. 1998. Public can't stomach abstract politics. *Chicago Tribune,* 4 December.

Schudson, Michael. 1995. *The power of news.* Cambridge: Harvard University Press.

———. 1998. The public journalism movement and its problems. In *The politics of news: The news of politics,* edited by Doris Graber, Denis McQuail, and Pippa Norris. Washington, D.C.: CQ Press.

Sears, David O. 1993. Symbolic politics: A socio-psychological theory. In *Explorations in political psychology,* edited by Shanto Iyengar and William J. McGuire. Durham, N.C.: Duke University Press.

Shanahan, James, and Michael Morgan. 1999. *Television and its viewers: Cultivation theory and research.* Cambridge: Cambridge University Press.

Shrum, L. J., and Thomas C. O'Guinn. 1993. Processes and effects in the construction of social reality: Construct accessibility as an explanatory variable. *Communication Research* 20:436–71.

Shulman, Robert G. 1993. Report on Yale University brain research. In *The Proceedings of the National Academy of Science,* 1 June. Quoted in Sandra Blakeslee, Seeing and imagining, *New York Times,* 31 August 1993.

Simon, Herbert A. 1967. Motivational and emotional controls of cognition. *Psychological Review* 74:29–39.

Smiley, Marion. 1999. Democratic citizenship: A question of competence. In *Citizen competence and democratic institutions,* edited by Stephen L. Elkin and Karol Edward Soltan. University Park: Pennsylvania State University Press.

Smith, Eric R. A. N. 1989. *The unchanging American voter.* Berkeley: University of California Press.

Smith, Ted J., III, S. Robert Lichter, and Louis Harris and Associates, Inc. 1997. *What the people want from the press.* Washington, D.C.: Center for Media and Public Affairs.

Sniderman, Paul M., Richard A. Brody, and Philip E. Tetlock, eds. 1991. *Reasoning and choice: Explorations in political psychology.* Cambridge: Cambridge University Press.

Somers, Paul P., Jr. 1998. *Editorial cartooning and caricature.* Westport, Conn.: Greenwood Press.

Somit, Albert, and Steven A. Peterson. 1999. Rational choice and biopolitics: A (Darwinian) tale of two theories. *PS: Political Science and Politics* 32:39–44.

Stanley, Harold W., and Richard G. Niemi. 1998. *Vital statistics on American politics 1997–1998.* Washington, D.C.: CQ Press.

Sterngold, James. 1998. A racial divide widens on network TV. *New York Times,* 29 December.

Stevens, Russell. 1992. Talk show democracy: How the new venue changed the 1992 campaign. Master's thesis. Kennedy School of Government, Harvard University.

Sullivan, Denis G., and Roger D. Masters. 1993. Nonverbal behavior, emotions, and democratic leadership. In *Reconsidering the democratic public,* edited by George Marcus and Russell Hanson. University Park: Pennsylvania State University Press.

Terkildsen, Nayda. 1993. When white voters evaluate black candidates: The processing implications of candidate skin color, prejudice, and self-monitoring. *American Journal of Political Science* 37:1032–53.

Tetlock, Philip E. 1983. Cognitive style and political ideology. *Journal of Personality and Social Psychology* 45:118–26.

———. 1993. Cognitive structural analysis of political rhetoric: Methodological and theoretical issues. In *Explorations in political psychology,* edited by Shanto Iyengar and William J. McGuire. Durham, N.C.: Duke University Press.

Tichenor, Philip, George A. Donohue, and Clarice N. Olien. 1980. *Community conflict and the press.* Beverly Hills, Calif.: Sage.

Tiemens, Robert K. 1978. Television's portrayal of the 1976 presidential debates: An analysis of visual content. *Communication Monographs* 45:362–70.

Times Mirror Center for the People and the Press. 1992a. The press and Campaign '92: A self assessment. Washington, D.C., 20 December.

———. 1992b. Voters say "thumbs up" to campaign, process & coverage. Washington, D.C., 15 November.

Tomlinson, Don E. 1993. *Computer manipulation and creation of images and sounds: Assessing the impact.* Washington, D.C.: Annenberg Washington Program.

Tuchman, Barbara. 1984. *The march of folly: From Troy to Vietnam.* New York: Knopf.

Tufte, Edward R. 1997. *Visual explanations: Images and quantities, evidence and narrative.* Cheshire, Conn.: Graphics Press.

Valkenburg, Patti M., Holli Semetko, and Claes H. de Vreese. 1999. The effects of news frames on readers' thoughts and recall. *Communication Research* 26:550–69.

Van den Broek, Paul, Michael Young, Yuhtsuen Tzeng, and Tracy Linderholm. 1999. The landscape model of reading: Inferences and the online construction of a memory representation. In *The construction of mental representations during reading,* edited by Herre van Oostendorp and Susan R. Goldman. Mahwah, N.J.: Erlbaum.

Vanderbilt Television News Abstracts. 1997, 1998. http://tvnews.vanderbilt.edu/eveningnews.html.

Van Der Molen, Walma, and Tom H. Van Der Voort. 2000. The impact of television, print, and audio on children's recall of the news. *Human Communication Research* 26:3–26.

van Dijk, Teun. 1988. *News as discourse*. Hillsdale, N.J.: Erlbaum.

———. 1999. Context models in discourse processing. In *The construction of
mental representations during reading,* edited by Herre van Oostendorp
and Susan R. Goldman. Mahwah, N.J.: Erlbaum.

van Oostendorp, Herre, and Christian Bonebakker. 1999. Difficulties in updat-
ing mental representations during reading news reports. In *The construction of mental representations during reading,* edited by Herre van Oostendorp and Susan R. Goldman. Mahwah, N.J.: Erlbaum.

van Oostendorp, Herre, and Susan R. Goldman, eds. 1999. *The construction of
mental representations during reading*. Mahwah, N.J.: Erlbaum.

Wagner-Pacifici, Robin Erica. 1986. *The Moro morality play: Terrorism as social
drama*. Chicago: University of Chicago Press.

Wells, William D. 1974. *Life style and psychographics*. Chicago: American Marketing Association.

Wilson, Timothy D., Dana S. Dunn, Dolores Kraft, and Douglas J. Lisle. 1989.
Introspection, attitude change, and attitude-behavior consistency: The
disruptive effects of explaining why we feel the way we do. *Advances in
Experimental Social Psychology* 22:287–341.

Winick, Charles. 1988. The function of television: Life without the big box.
In *Television as a social issue,* edited by Stuart Oskamp. Newbury Park,
Calif.: Sage.

Woodall, W. Gil. 1986. Information-processing theory and television news. In
The main source, edited by John P. Robinson and Mark R. Levy. Beverly
Hills, Calif.: Sage.

Wyer, Robert S., Thomas Lee Budesheim, Sharon Shavitt, Ellen D. Riggle,
R. Jeffrey Melton, and James H. Kuklinski. 1991. Image, issues, and ideol-
ogy: The processing of information about political candidates. *Journal of
Personality and Social Psychology* 61:533–45.

Zadny, Jerry, and Harold B. Gerard. 1974. Attributed intentions and information selectivity. *Journal of Experimental Social Psychology* 10:34–52.

Zaller, John. 1992. *Nature and origins of mass opinion*. Cambridge: Cambridge
University Press.

Zelizer, Barbie. 1998. *Remembering to forget: Holocaust memory through the camera's eye*. Chicago: University of Chicago Press.

Zukin, Cliff, and Robin Snyder. 1984. Passive learning: When the media environment is the message. *Public Opinion Quarterly* 48:629–38.

INDEX

academic critics. *See* scholars

altruism, 81

Americans. *See* public

audience: concern with, 103; preferences, 169; research methods,
164–65, 190–91; size of, 2, 160–
61, 167

audiovisuals: and bottom-up processing, 19; and collective memory,
67; content of, 19, 92–94, 157–
58; and content analysis methods,
196–202; as distraction, 118–20;
evaluations of, 8, 92–94; and
gestalt coding, 197–202; inherent
weaknesses of, 8, 98; and learning
ease, 30–31, 72, 95, 184; overload
of, 150; and picture/word coordi-
nation, 150; and reasoning, 32,
79; and recall accuracy, 20, 33–34;
and reputation problems, 8–9,
70–71, 93–94, 185; and schema
activation, 71–72; venues for display of, 12

auditory processing, 38

average people. *See* public

Avianca air crash broadcast analysis,
154–56

Barber, James David, 112

Birdwhistell, Ray, 23

body language: as behavior cue, 76;
and facial cues, 76

bottom-up processing, 17, 19

Boynton, G. Robert, 40

brain functions: in audiovisual processing, 14, 24, 30–31, 35–36; gender
differences in, 27; in speech pro-

cessing, 39. *See also* information
processing

brain research, 12

Brokaw, Tom, 155

cartoons, political impact of, 70

children: and audiovisuals, 31–32;
learning capacities of, 19, 30–31

citizens: duties of, 53; and information
needs, 53–54; and information
supply, 106–8; and political
knowledge, 62–64. *See also* public

civic IQ, 5, 43–45, 64

civic journalism. *See* public journalism

civic participation, 80, 118–19

Clark v. ABC (1982), 90, 151–52

CNN effect, 80, 124

cognitive complexity: existence of, 34–
35, 54–55; and focus group findings, 59–64; measurement of, 55

collective memory: and socialization
effects, 66–67, 96; as story supple-
ment, 102

connotation: determinants of, 23;
meaning of, 21–23; sources for, 22

content analysis: of audiovisuals, 93;
by Committee of Concerned
Journalists, 177–78

copycat crimes, 91–92, 117

cross-disciplinary research, 5

Csikszentmihalyi, Mihaly, 120

cultivation studies, 102

decision-making: heuristics of, 48;
shortcuts in, 48–49; steps in, 47–
48

Delli Carpini, Michael, 44–45